# WHAT DIPLOMATS DO

# WHAT DIPLOMATS DO

## *The Life and Work of Diplomats*

### Sir Brian Barder

ROWMAN & LITTLEFIELD
Lanham • Boulder • New York • London

Published by Rowman & Littlefield
A wholly owned subsidiary of The Rowman & Littlefield Publishing Group, Inc.
4501 Forbes Boulevard, Suite 200, Lanham, Maryland 20706
www.rowman.com

16 Carlisle Street, London W1D 3BT, United Kingdom

British Library Cataloguing in Publication Information Available

**Library of Congress Cataloging-in-Publication Data**

Barder, Brian.
What diplomats do : the life and work of diplomats / Brian Barder.
p. cm.
Includes bibliographical references and index.
ISBN 978-1-4422-2635-7 (cloth : alk. paper) -- ISBN 978-1-4422-2636-4 (electronic)
1. Diplomats. 2. Diplomacy. I. Title.
JZ1405.B35 2014
327.2--dc23

2014018106

∞™ The paper used in this publication meets the minimum requirements of
American National Standard for Information Sciences Permanence of Paper for
Printed Library Materials, ANSI/NISO Z39.48-1992.

Printed in the United States of America

For Lily and Florence

in case they ever wonder what kind of thing their

grandfather used to do

and

for Virginia, Louise, and Owen

who were such an important part of it

# CONTENTS

# FOREWORD

## By Ivor Roberts

Brian Barder knows of what he speaks. His book describing *What Diplomats Do* draws on his thirty years of experience in that funny old trade. He served in widely varying posts in four continents, ranging from New York and Canberra at one end of the comfort spectrum to Moscow, Warsaw, Addis Ababa, and Lagos at the other. For twelve years he represented Britain as an ambassador or high commissioner (the equivalent of an ambassador representing one Commonwealth country in another) to five countries—Ethiopia, during the great international famine relief operation of the 1980s, Poland, in the dying days of the communist régime, Nigeria and Bénin when the military government of the former seemed to be moving towards the restoration of democracy, and Australia during the years of debate over retaining the monarchy or moving to a republic. His varied experiences in these and other posts around the world, including the UK delegation to the United Nations, are reflected in the material skilfully used in this book to illustrate various facets of diplomatic life.

Brian and I only overlapped once, when I was a brand new entrant and he a relatively junior diplomat though with an overseas posting already behind him. I admired his work often from afar, my own diplomatic experience being largely in Europe (Paris, Luxembourg, Madrid, Belgrade, Dublin, and Rome) and also in Lebanon, Australia, and Vanuatu. Between us we have served in about 10 percent of the world's states and have well over twenty years of experience as heads of missions.

With that experience and as the editor of the new edition of the classic diplomatic textbook *Satow's Diplomatic Practice,* I hope that I can be considered capable of distinguishing a diplomatic hawk from a handsaw. So while books on diplomacy and diplomatic life are not a rarity, Brian's offering fills a real gap in the market. It is neither a manual, though it offers excellent practical advice, nor is it a memoir, though the text is interspersed with often entertaining and illuminating anecdotes. It does instead what it promises: it tells you exactly what it's like to be a diplomat and what sort of challenges you face on an every-day basis. It cleverly follows an imaginary young couple, a diplomat and his spouse, up the ladder from earliest days in the Diplomatic Service to stepping down from an ambassadorial role. It strips away much of the flim-flam surrounding the image of diplomacy in the more ignorant elements of the popular press and brings out how unglamorous and indeed downright dangerous much of the work is. Likewise it pulls no punches in laying into the British Treasury as one of the bastions of small mindedness and short-term thinking in the British establishment. There is, however, no sense of didacticism here: the narrative is written to be clear to absolute ingénus in the field of diplomacy and thoroughly enjoyable at the same time. Although written through a clearly British prism, it translates well into diplomacy generally. Thus anyone aspiring to join this most rewarding of professions would be well advised to read *What Diplomats Do* first. It will perhaps deter some from seeking to join diplomacy if they are put off by the way the glamour is overshadowed by the grind, but there will be no loss.

**Sir Ivor Roberts KCMG** has been President of Trinity College, Oxford University, since 2006. Before he retired from the British Diplomatic Service, he was British ambassador successively to Yugoslavia, Ireland, and Italy. He was the Editor of the international diplomatic handbook, *Satow's Diplomatic Practice*, 6th ed. (2009).

# ACKNOWLEDGMENTS

This book would never have been either written or published without the encouragement, sometimes in the form of productive nagging, of two academic experts in the field: Dr. Lorna Lloyd, Senior Research Fellow in International Relations at Keele University, who finally persuaded me that there was a book to be distilled from my years in the UK Diplomatic Service, and Emeritus Professor G. R. Berridge, formerly Professor of International Politics at Leicester University and author of (among many other classic works) the authoritative *Diplomacy: Theory and Practice*, who also spurred me on and who persuaded my publishers, Rowman & Littlefield, that the book would fill a gap and was worth publishing. Both of them also spent more time than the book deserves in writing detailed comments and suggestions on the text, nearly all of which I have gratefully accepted, much enhancing such value as the work might have.

Others who gallantly read the full text in draft and who provided equally insightful comments and encouragement included Professor Alan Henrikson, Lee E. Dirks Professor of Diplomatic History at The Fletcher School of Law and Diplomacy, Tufts University; my old diplomatic service colleague and friend Sir Ivor Roberts, a distinguished former ambassador and currently President of Trinity College, Oxford University, as well as Editor of the international diplomatic handbook, *Satow's Diplomatic Practice*, 6th edition; and my daughter, Louise Barder, now a longtime New Yorker, who supplied not only several constructive stylistic suggestions but also a list of words and phrases in the text that risked being unintelligible, embarrassing, or objectionable to American readers.

Another old friend and diplomatic service colleague, Sir Bryan Cartledge, former British ambassador in Budapest and later Moscow, former Principal (Master) of Linacre College, Oxford and author of what is now the classic history of Hungary, read the original proposal for the book and made generous comments on it which were immensely reassuring to me and persuasive to my publisher.

The whole manuscript was also read in draft by a current serving member of the British diplomatic service who provided enormously valuable advice on passages in the book about activities where procedures or terminologies have changed and where current practice needed to be acknowledged and described. The diplomat concerned was on temporary secondment to another country's diplomatic service at the time and was thus able to comment on the basis of first-hand experience of not one but two leading western diplomatic services, doubling the value of the advice. I have also had useful and encouraging comments from two other serving members of HM Diplomatic Service who read the manuscript in draft. A fourth, with his wife, Laurie and Fiona Bristow, gave me (and my wife) an extremely useful briefing on the many changes in the procedures, practices, technologies, and language that have taken place in UK diplomatic life in recent years.

Finally, I pay two heartfelt tributes to the two indispensable godmothers of *What Diplomats Do*: Marie-Claire Antoine, my editor at Rowman & Littlefield, whose patience with an ancient first-time author has thankfully been inexhaustible and whose comments and suggestions for improving my text have been expressed with more diplomatic finesse than any professional diplomat could have mustered; and my wife, Jane, who has gracefully put up with even more absent-mindedness and abstraction on my part than usual during the book's gestation—and (even more importantly) has contributed substantial elements of the text describing not only What Diplomats Do but also What Diplomatic Spouses Do, and what they have to put up with.

I am hugely grateful to all those mentioned, but I enter the obligatory caveat that while their comments have saved me from numerous errors, I alone am responsible for those that remain.

**Brian Barder**
*London*
*November 2013*

# I

# INTRODUCTION

An ambassador is not simply an agent; he is also a spectacle.
—*Walter Bagehot, "The English Constitution" (1867) chap. IV*

*What Diplomats Do*, among many other things, is make and carry out their countries' foreign policy—every day, in thousands of ways. I have found experienced teachers of diplomacy who assume that diplomats only ever act on the specific instructions of their governments. On the great international issues, of course, they do; but the day-to-day business of diplomacy, the routine conduct of relations between countries and their governments, is carried on by professional diplomats, officials who understand the policies of their own governments sufficiently to act without specific instructions from their capitals; and when they do need instructions, it is mostly other officials back home, usually diplomats themselves, who send them, not ministers or other politically appointed bosses.

Thus foreign policy is being made daily all round the world, in the tens of thousands of conversations, speeches, and symbolically pregnant actions of individual diplomats serving away from home. Often the smart diplomat in his country's embassy abroad writes his own instructions and simply invites the foreign ministry at home[1] to approve them—again, usually at official level. The Foreign Minister (Foreign Secretary in British parlance, Secretary of State in American) or one of his political deputies may need to be consulted if a new issue has arisen on which ministerial decisions have not been made previously, but most of the time officials at home know their political masters' minds well enough to send accurate guidance and instructions to their diplomats abroad.

Diplomats keep abreast of their governments' constantly evolving foreign policy objectives on a vast range of international issues, and a good professional diplomat is always conscious of his country's changing interests, which it is his main purpose to promote. He always speaks and acts within the constraints of those broadly agreed policy objectives and interests, or at any rate he should, although occasionally a diplomat, however senior, may succumb to the temptation to bend his government's views, even its instructions, to accommodate his own political or other personal prejudices. He may explain and defend his government's policies in a perfectly unexceptionable manner while indicating by body language or facial expression that he privately thinks it all a lot of misguided nonsense. Either kind of personal dissociation from the diplomat's government's policies and views amounts to a kind of disloyalty that is liable eventually to undermine his credibility as a trustworthy representative of his country. (In this book, I adopt the lawyers' convention of referring to diplomats in general as "he," "his," etc., where it's clear from the context that I mean "he or she," "his" or "her." Using three words where one will do just causes verbal clutter. But the reader needs to be as aware as I am that these days a high and growing number of most countries' top diplomats, and many of their political bosses, are women; and that the title of "ambassador" belongs equally to women as to men—an "ambassadress" is the wife of an ambassador, not a woman ambassador. We don't yet have a word for the husband of an ambassador, but that will come.)

The oversimplified picture of foreign policy made by ministers issuing orders, and diplomats obeying them, tends to overlook the role of diplomats, especially those doing a stint at home in the foreign ministry, in advising their ministerial bosses and official colleagues on policy questions in a never-ending stream of recommendations and arguments. Generally ministers accept their officials' recommendations; sometimes they do not. Either way, once the official has had a chance to express a view and make a recommendation or raise an objection, it's his job loyally to accept his government's decision and to do his best to make it work, whether he agrees with it or not. If he's a British or other European diplomat (but not an American),[2] his ministers have (mostly) been democratically elected to make policy; their officials, whether diplomats or civil servants, have not.

With some notable exceptions, such as in big European Union capitals where a European diplomat's own ministers are in frequent personal contact with their EU opposite numbers, diplomats generally have greater scope for individual initiative and personal contribution to policy-making than their civil servant cousins at home. This is partly because most of them are far from their capitals and from the constant scrutiny of their official and ministerial superiors, and partly because foreign policy, in contrast with domestic policy, is less the product of party politics and much more dictated by national interests whose fundamentals don't change with every change of government. No one government can change the course of international affairs by an exercise of will, in the way that ministers can often control and change domestic policy. There's less scope for cosmic, life-changing policy decisions in foreign affairs. Ministers and their diplomatic officials alike are constrained by the limits of the possible in a multi-polar world. When a British company acts in a way that is flagrantly antisocial and contrary to the public interest, the relevant minister can always take some action to restrain it—in the last resort by new legislation, although often a minatory telephone call from a senior minister will be enough. By contrast, when a foreign government takes some action that is inimical to, even destructive of, British interests, the Foreign Secretary may issue as many statements as he likes, deploring what has been done and calling on the foreign government concerned to desist; he may refer the matter to some international organ in the hope that international opinion will persuade the erring government to change course; he may even ask others to join his government in imposing sanctions on the offending régime as long as it persists in its wrong-doing, although others may well be disinclined to comply. But in the end, there is usually nothing that the British government and its Foreign Secretary can do about it, if the foreign government concerned chooses to ignore their threats and appeals. Unlike his ministerial colleagues in charge of domestic policy, our Foreign Secretary has very limited power to alter the course of international affairs. He must act mainly by persuasion; and persuasion is, among other things, What Diplomats Do. Even a superpower such as the United States possesses diminishing scope for controlling global events and the behaviour of other countries, however small, weak, and insignificant: with each deployment of the enormous military might of the United States, the threat of its use again in circumstances short of a direct physical threat to American national security becomes a little less credible.

It's commonly argued that modern technology, especially the phenomenal speed of communications made possible by electronics and the Internet, has made the job of diplomats redundant. The social media add a new dimension. The British Foreign & Commonwealth Office, for example, uses Facebook, Twitter, blogs, etc., to get its message across to various audiences. Those to whom they are sending their message can—and do—answer back, in a way that was not possible with conventional means of addressing the public. Many, perhaps most, British diplomatic missions are now encouraged by the FCO to publish their own regular blogs: some bland, others interesting and informative. It can be very resource intensive. Many [wo]man-hours go into writing these blog posts and keeping them up to date. The ease and immediacy of communications, including the ability to copy any message to an unlimited number of recipients, has also greatly increased the sheer volume of diplomatic work.

Instant communications also make diplomacy potentially more powerful by allowing diplomats overseas to report developments instantaneously to their capitals, and—in principle, anyway—also instantaneously to receive their governments' instructions on how to respond to them. The reality, though, is often different. A sour joke that used to go the rounds in the diplomatic service recalled:

> In the old days, an ambassador serving overseas and far from home used to inform his government of a revolution that has taken place in his host country by describing it in writing, using a quill on fine parchment, in a formal dispatch to the Secretary of State. His clerk rolled up the dispatch, secured it with a ribbon, wax-sealed it, and sent it by messenger to the host country's port to await the next sailing-ship to take it to Greenwich, the port near London. From there another messenger would take it by coach to Whitehall, where it would sit in the In Box of the Secretary of State's private secretary for a day or two until it was due to be opened and submitted to the great man. For a few days, the Secretary of State would discuss with his staff and colleagues, at leisure, the implications for British interests of the revolution that had occurred in the far-away country of which he probably knew nothing. Later still, the clerk drafted a reply to the ambassador

with instructions on the attitude that His Excellency was to adopt towards the new revolutionary régime. Once approved, this reply would be elegantly copied out onto parchment, signed with a flourish by the Secretary of State, rolled up and sealed, and sent by messenger to Greenwich. . . . By the time the minister's reply was delivered into the hands of the ambassador, three or four months might have elapsed since the revolution on which his instructions had now arrived.

Nowadays things are very different (or are they?). Within minutes of hearing the result of the revolution, the ambassador dictates or types a telegram (or email, or diptel) to the Secretary of State. It is automatically and instantly enciphered and dispatched electronically to the FCO in London. Just a few minutes after being written, it's deciphered and in the hands of the Secretary of State's private secretary, and a few minutes later again it's being read by the Secretary of State himself— who has anyway already learned of the revolution from the television set in his office. Now begins the process of interdepartmental consultation on the implications of the revolution for UK interests, meetings to discuss them, and eventually the drafting and submission to the minister of a reply to the ambassador with his instructions.

**Three months later** . . . the ambassador receives a reply to his report from the Secretary of State with his instructions on the attitude he is to adopt towards the new revolutionary régime.

Communications may have become virtually instantaneous; but the time required to devise, submit, and authorise a response and instructions in what has long been an overworked and seriously understaffed Foreign & Commonwealth Office in London has probably doubled or trebled. The ambassador often has plenty of time to make his own decisions on how to react to fast-changing situations without the luxury, or frustration, of having to wait for instructions from home. Surprisingly often, he has to speak and act first, and ask London (or whichever is his country's capital) for retrospective approval later.

Within obvious limits, it's the relative freedom of personal action and initiative, the feeling that along with hundreds of others you're helping to make foreign policy every day by what you do and what you say and who you say it to, that makes being a diplomat such a satisfying job. It's that, along with other rewards, which largely compensates for the drawbacks, discomforts, and sometimes the dangers of the diplomatic life.

The purpose of this book is to describe, through the daily doings of an imaginary but typical diplomat, "Adam," a kind of diplomatic Everyman, what diplomats actually do, the pains and penalties as well as the rewards and satisfactions, and how the sum of what diplomats do contributes substantially to the country's foreign policy. Since What Diplomats Do impacts on their spouses (increasingly often husbands) and on their children, as well as on themselves, Adam's wife—Eve, of course, prototypical man and woman—also figures in the purely fictitious narrative. To be clear, though, the choice of names for these avatars has no biblical, theological, or other significance.

My fictitious Adam is necessarily a British diplomat, because that's what I was for thirty years and it's the British Diplomatic Service that I know best, or used to know. But most of what Adam does and experiences is common to members of other national diplomatic services: diplomacy is an international activity largely governed by internationally agreed rules. Some differences are little more than semantic. In Adam's British Diplomatic Service, for example, there's a sharp distinction between "officials"—career diplomats—and their "ministers"—nearly all of them elected professional politicians. In the United States Foreign Service the distinction is less clear-cut, but essentially the same: between the career diplomats on the one hand, and on the other hand the party political appointees in the State Department in Washington who change when there's a change of party administration.

Adam's and Eve's adventures in their diplomatic wonderland are almost all fictitious, although always based on real life. To avoid causing a real diplomatic incident, some of the countries in which Adam serves are also fictionalised: the imaginary countries and their capitals are indicated when first mentioned by single quotation marks: thus 'Côte Noire,' 'Pazalia,' not to be found in any atlas. But I have repeatedly interrupted the Adam and Eve narrative with anecdotal examples drawn from my own experience as a British diplomat who served in a variety of countries and roles, eventually representing Britain as successively as an ambassador or high commissioner[3] in five countries across three continents. "**As an example** ..." in the pages that follow precedes fact, not fiction.

I have used "Adam" and "Eve" to illustrate some of the many activities of diplomats ancient and modern, and their spouses. No real-life Adam could pack into a single career all the postings and experiences that I have attributed to him. The chapters that follow deal with different aspects of the diplomat's career but they are not a chronicle of the career of any one person, whether fictitious (like Adam) or real (such as myself, or so I like to believe). Any attempt to piece together Adam's experiences into a realistic chronological account of a single career is doomed to fail. Similarly, the examples from my own career, used to illustrate different aspects of a diplomat's activities, can't be stitched together into a coherent history of that career; they are in no particular order, being introduced purely according to the subject under discussion. This is not a memoir. Adam is not me, but a device employed to demonstrate what diplomats do in various capacities and in the immensely varied circumstances that diplomats find themselves in as they are posted around the world.

My description of some of the things that Diplomats Do doesn't pretend to be comprehensive. A comprehensive account would run to many volumes. Diplomats get involved in almost every aspect of modern life and government. Diplomats in developing countries have to acquire some expertise in aid policy, development economics, aid transparency, and the international implications of poverty. In rich countries diplomats are dealing with commercial policies and practices, working with their countries' businessmen to promote their countries' exports—and inward investment in the opposite direction; learning the language of the balance of trade and trade deficits and surpluses; building up a database of local firms that can act as agents for small companies at home; collecting data for use in briefing visiting businessmen on export opportunities as well as on the host country's trade policies, its government's future prospects and the degree of stability that the businessman can expect as protection for his investment. Other diplomats are speaking and writing knowledgeably in the international jargons of climate change, environmental protection, biodiversity, and the conservation of species, the law of the sea, international cooperation on drugs and other kinds of crime, and the consequences of mass migration between countries and continents. Others again are immersed in the intricacies of the laws and politics of the European Union and its Commission and other organs, and of countless other multilateral organisations to which their country belongs or with which it conducts significant relations. Even Adam, my own creation, couldn't possibly have been involved in every one of these fields of activity. So I have had to be selective, choosing for different parts of Adam's career those which are closest to core diplomacy.

The practices and procedures of the various national diplomatic services are in a state of constant flux, buffeted by changes in technology, by new international challenges (security, climate change, recessions, development), and by fluctuating managerial fads and fashions. Britain's Diplomatic Service has been particularly disrupted, distracted, and dismayed by what Trotsky would have recognised as Permanent Revolution. It has been plagued by external consultants with little understanding of What Diplomats Do, by a traditionally parsimonious Treasury, and by managers, themselves mostly working diplomats, many of whom apparently couldn't grasp that neither the Diplomatic Service nor Britain is, or even resembles, a limited company or corporation with shareholders and a board of directors interested mainly in maximizing shareholder value. As a result, procedures and terminology, among other things, have constantly changed over the years. Some of what Adam did in the earlier years of his diplomatic career, as described in this account, may consequently need to be translated into the contemporary jargon of the Foreign & Commonwealth Office. The "telegrams" that he sent then would be "diptels" now, sent electronically like emails, not by wireless telegraphy. The letters that he wrote and signed in hard copy and sent in the diplomatic bag in those days are now mostly transmitted electronically, as attachments to emails. The names of the various grades and appointments have changed (as explained later). No matter: the substance of the job has remained much the same.

The roles and experiences of women, both women diplomats and the wives or partners of male diplomats, have changed especially radically over the years. Not long ago a British woman diplomat who got married was obliged to resign from the diplomatic service, regardless of her talents and perhaps starry career prospects. For many years the wives of British diplomats were forbidden to work for money when their spouses were posted overseas. Later "Eve" was allowed to work while overseas but only with the permission of her husband's ambassador or high commissioner. Later still, if Adam's head of mission refused to give permission for Eve to take a job, he was required to report his refusal, with reasons, to the Foreign & Commonwealth Office in London. Finally even that restriction lapsed. Nowadays it would take a bold ambassador to stop the wife of a member of his staff from finding local employment, unless it was an obviously unsuitable job liable to bring the embassy and its country into disrepute. But in many countries, especially those with high rates of indigenous unemployment, the government forbids diplomats' spouses to take jobs that could be done by local people—so in practice Eve may still be prevented from pursuing her career when accompanying Adam on an overseas posting, however much the UK system has been liberalised over the years. When Adam becomes an ambassador, Eve is probably too busy in her role as an (unpaid) ambassadress even to think about combining it with a separate local job, however lucrative, unless she's lucky enough to be a commercially successful novelist, artist, or poet—although in recent times some British ambassadors' spouses, mainly wives, have been able to take on the paid job of "Residence manager," a neat solution of sorts. More often it is difficult or impossible for the spouse of an ambassador or high commissioner to get or to do a paid local job, and this may have significantly adverse financial consequences for both of them, as we shall see later.

A potentially important recent development in the activities of diplomats has been the creation in December 2010 of what is generally called "the EEAS"—the "European External Action Service," i.e., the diplomatic service of the European Union (EU). Headed by the "High Representative for Common Foreign and Security Policy" or, colloquially, the EU Foreign Minister, these EU diplomats act on behalf of the EU as a whole and not as representatives of any single country or government. They promote only those aspects of foreign policy that have been agreed among all the EU's member states; but just as a Nicaraguan diplomat seeks to promote a favourable image of Nicaragua and its policies to the government and people of the country in which he is posted ("the host country"), so EU diplomats explain, defend, and justify the EU itself in their host countries, both in their dealings with their governments and also publicly. Many, perhaps most, of the activities described in this book will apply equally to EU diplomats; but to the extent that they represent a new, supra-national brand of diplomat, their activities are bound to differ somewhat from those of single-nationality diplomats.

Two other interesting and potentially important developments in diplomatic life deserve mention. One is the expansion in what has come to be called "public diplomacy," dismissed somewhat summarily in the recent *Dictionary of Diplomacy,*[4] as "a late-twentieth-century term for propaganda conducted by diplomats."[5] Another is a growing resort to "Track Two" diplomacy, where informal contacts between countries, aimed at playing down threats or resolving problems, are discreetly con-

ducted by non-official, non-governmental bodies and persons, not by diplomats or other representatives of governments.

None of this, though, affects the basic character of national diplomacy
as it has been practiced over centuries, and will continue to be practised
so long as the nation-state remains the main building-block of international relations.

I hope that this book will help students and teachers of diplomacy and
international affairs, whether amateur or professional, to understand the
role of working diplomats in the formation and execution of foreign
policy. Those who are considering embarking on a diplomatic career or
switching to one, and their spouses, may get from the book a clearer idea
of what they may be letting themselves in for—the pluses as well as the
inevitable minuses. Those already pursuing a career in diplomacy may
find it useful as a yardstick against which to compare what they are
already doing and hope to do. Those enviable people who have no particular connection with diplomacy but who are interested in contemporary
history and politics may gain some interesting insights into the workings
of the international diplomatic engine, usually discreetly hidden away
under the bonnet (hood, in American).

One final introductory point. Diplomacy is widely, but mistakenly,
regarded as possessing a special mystique, at any rate, in the eyes of those
who have never come into contact with its practitioners. It's often seen as
an exotic, even glamorous, profession. Anyone who has ever been an
ambassador has experienced the shocked reaction when a stranger at
some reception asks "What's your position at the embassy exactly?" and
receives the reply, "I'm the ambassador." The first response is invariably
a horrified apology (implicitly for having failed to treat the great man or
woman with the exaggerated respect assumed to be due to such a personage). Sooner or later the apology is followed by the question: "But what
do diplomats actually *do*?" This book aims to provide an answer.

## NOTES

1. In the diplomat's own Ministry of Foreign Affairs in his capital, variously
called the Foreign & Commonwealth Office or the Department of State, or other
variants.

2. In the British and other "Westminster" systems, almost all Ministers in the government are also members of parliament, generally of the House of Commons. In the United States Presidential system, members of the administration are appointed by the President from outside the Congress, under the doctrine of the separation of powers.

3. The diplomatic representative of one Commonwealth country in another Commonwealth country is called a high commissioner, not an ambassador, although his functions are to all intents and purposes the same as an ambassador's.

4. *A Dictionary of Diplomacy*, second edition, GR Berridge and Alan James, Palgrave Macmillan, 2003.

5. More on this in chapter 6.

# 2

# THE CANDIDATE FOR A DIPLOMATIC CAREER

Joining the Diplomatic Service, *the temperament, skills, and qualifications needed beforehand and those to be acquired later; surviving the application processes.*

Adam was thinking of applying to join the UK Diplomatic Service when he was still at university. He was reading Modern Languages and took an active interest in international affairs. He was advised by the University careers service to ask if he could visit the Foreign and Commonwealth Office, or FCO, to discuss what would be involved in a diplomatic career, and was able to arrange this without difficulty, although Adam was sorry to hear, many years later, that such individual visits were no longer possible, having been replaced by formal competitions for internships or work experience placements, both with an emphasis on the policy of the UK diplomatic service to encourage applications from members of ethnic or socio-economic minorities.

On his visit to the FCO, Basil, an earnest but enthusiastic young man, who himself had joined the diplomatic service only two years earlier, gave Adam a solemn warning.

"Every year there are nearly a hundred applications to join the diplomatic service for every one place to be filled. Don't get your hopes too high, Adam. The diplomatic service is one of the most sought-after careers for university graduates like yourself. The competition is really intense. The fact that you speak two modern languages could be a bonus, but knowing a foreign language is by no means a requirement for diplomatic service candidates. Those who get through all the stages of the selection process and join the service are tested for their ability to learn a language, and if they're found to be capable of it, they may be taught one of the most difficult languages, like Arabic or Mandarin. Anyone with an interest in international affairs and politics, who knows a bit about them, who has good analytical and reasoning powers, and good interpersonal and communicating skills, has a much bigger advantage than someone who already happens to speak a bit of French or Italian but doesn't have the personal skills that the selection process is looking for."

Adam was somewhat disappointed that his hard-won language skills would not necessarily get him off to a flying start as a candidate. He tried another tack.

"What about not having gone to Oxford or Cambridge or one of the other posh universities? Will that count against me?"

"That would be totally irrelevant to your chances," said Basil. "Indeed, the FCO, like the home civil service, is desperately keen to widen its net when it comes to recruitment. If anything, your comprehensive state school background plus a degree from one of the good newish universities will most likely be to your advantage. Why not chuck your cap in the ring and see what happens? The odds are against you, but they're against all the other candidates, too."

Adam was stung by Basil's reference to his "newish" university, although it was factually correct, if a snobbish way of putting it. He ventured to ask Basil about his own educational record.

"Oh, I'm afraid I was at Eton. But I honestly don't think that gave me an advantage. Probably counted against me, if anything."

"And university?" Adam asked.

"Well, King's College Cambridge, since you ask. Rather a lot to live down, obviously."

So Basil had been to the most élite school and the most élite college at one of the two most exclusive universities in Britain. What chance would a lad from a state school in the midlands have against candidates like this?

"Well, good luck if you do try for the Service," said Basil, shaking Adam's hand rather too vigorously as Adam prepared to leave.

"Thanks, Basil," Adam said. "I'll have to think about it. You've given me a lot to think about. I'm grateful."

In fact, Adam's mind was already made up. He knew in his bones that he was just as bright and energetic as anyone from Eton and King's, even if his years of effort at learning modern languages weren't going to help his pitch. He decided that there was nothing to lose but his self-respect and that he should give it a go. But he had only a hazy idea of what would be involved: and no idea at all about What Diplomats Do.

The selection procedure for applicants from university for both the diplomatic service and the home civil service was, and still is, in three parts, like Caesar's Gaul. At the time when Adam was a candidate for the British diplomatic service, the first part of the selection process was a series of written tests, some in Adam's university subject, some comprising general knowledge questions, and some standard intelligence tests. Adam had decided to apply only for the diplomatic service and not for the home civil service, lest applying for both might seem to cast doubt on his commitment to either, in the light of the FCO's insistence that only candidates who gave the diplomatic service as their first choice would be considered. He was gratified to find himself in the minority of candidates who were successful at this first stage, and accordingly went on to the second stage, the Civil Service Selection Board or CSSB, at that time often known as the house-party.

Two challenging but strangely exhilarating days at the CSSB in a six-person group were spent doing a number of demanding group exercises, each member of the group taking turns to chair the team's discussion of an imaginary but realistic task. These were based on a thick file containing enough information for the team to work out possible solutions to a series of problems. Adam noticed that the three assessors attended all the group exercises, almost never intervening but taking copious notes, even at the interviews that each assessor conducted with every candidate in his group. There were more written exams, in the form of tasks based on the situations described in the same file.

Adam had been genuinely surprised to have survived the first stage cull and to have gotten as far as the CSSB "house party." He had decided to apply for the diplomatic service mainly to experience the selection process, and because he knew he would regret it later if he had not even tried. He still thought it extremely unlikely that he would survive the second and third stages and find himself actually offered a career in diplomacy. He accordingly approached the CSSB tests and interviews in the spirit of having nothing to lose: he might as well enjoy himself, he reckoned, devising ingenious if sometimes fanciful solutions to the various problems set for him and his group, strenuously supporting the rest of the group even when their proposals were dull or impractical, allowing himself the occasional risky witticism—but never at the expense of a fellow candidate.

The selection process included a long interview with each of the three examiners: the chairperson, a retired senior civil servant or diplomat; a younger, still serving, civil servant or diplomat; and a civil service psychologist. Each interview, lasting between forty minutes and an hour, probed different aspects of Adam's character, knowledge, reasoning skill, ambition, and ability to remain calm and articulate under pressure. All three interviewers were friendly and civil, but none of them allowed him to get away with inadequate answers to their questions, or with attempts to fudge them. Adam found himself physically exhausted after each of these interviews. At his interview with the Selection Board Chair, he found himself quite intensively interrogated about his ability to subordinate his own political views to the policies of a government of a different hue—he had been active in one of his university's party political clubs in his second year. He thought he had convinced the Chair that he could, and would. He recognised that elected ministers were entitled to the loyalty of their unelected officials, regardless of their personal views, and that officials, once ministers had decided on a policy, had an obligation to do their best to make it work, to overcome any obstacles to its success, and to do everything possible to put it in the most favourable possible light. But he had the impression that very few candidates arrived at stage two of the selection process with a record of active participation in party politics at their universities.

### As an example . . .

*Soon after I reached diplomatic service retirement age (then 60) I spent a year or two chairing Civil Service Selection Boards (CSSB) responsible for choosing which candidates for both the home civil service and the diplomatic service would pass the second stage of the entrance exams and thus to go forward to the final interview.*

*I was greatly impressed by several aspects of this experience. First, all those applying to serve on CSSB Boards, whether as Chairs like myself or as members or psychologists, were rigorously trained, not only in how to conduct the various tests and examinations and assess their results, but also in how to conduct a carefully structured interview with strictly designed and weighted objectives.*

*Secondly, it was impressed on us all that our judgements were invariably to be based only on evidence, not on gut feelings, and least of all on a mistaken faith in our instinctive ability to judge people on sight. In the sessions of the three examiners on the third day, each in turn would describe his or her assessments of the six candidates and recommend the marks to be awarded to each of them under a series of pre-determined headings. Each examiner would be repeatedly challenged by the other two to provide evidence from his detailed notes of the interviews and tests in support of his proposed marking, especially if it differed significantly from those of the other two. Any such difference would be exhaustively discussed and the reasons for the discrepancy analysed until a consensus was reached on a fair and accurate marking.*

*Thirdly, it was encouraging to find that the results of the CSSB had a strikingly high predictive value. Those who passed with the highest marks were those most likely to go on to occupy the highest positions in their chosen service; those with borderline marks who just scraped through the selection process tended to go on to only average or below-average careers. This was the result of many years of constantly refining and improving the selection process so as to eliminate or correct those tests which had a relatively poor predictive value, and devising new techniques further to improve it.*

*I was only once the subject of a complaint by a failed candidate, who wrote to the head of the CSSB to complain that I had been unfairly hard on him at his interview, pressing him to hurry up with his replies and constantly challenging his expressions of opinion. Fortunately the other two examiners agreed with my assessment of the candidate and both had also found him flustered when subjected to limited stress—one of the objectives of the interview being to judge the candidate's behaviour under reasonable, but not excessive, pressure. But the complaint was useful in forcing me to consider whether I might tend to be unduly aggressive in my interviewing and if so to be careful to curb any such tendency. Still, a hint of aggression might be a useful weapon in the selection board examiner's armoury . . .*

Adam, contrary to his expectation, was once again successful in the second stage of the selection process, the two-day CSSB, and was thus among the (by now very small) minority of the original candidates who went forward to the third and last stage, the final interview. The inter-

viewing panel comprised an assortment of the great and the good: the
statutory businessman, trade unionist, woman, politician, and journalist,
and one senior diplomat as Chair. Adam remembers little of what he was
asked on that fateful day, and even less of what he had said in reply. Few
of the questions presented any particular challenge, as far as he could
remember. He answered them as frankly as he could, introducing a note
of humour now and then without, he hoped, making himself appear a
clown. He had the impression that the interview was not rigorously structured or determined by pre-arranged objectives. Most of the panel seemed
content with no more than a general impression of Adam's personality
and manner; Adam secretly doubted whether in consequence its results
would have any real objective value. At any rate, a few weeks later, he
received a letter from the FCO congratulating him on having passed,
telling him that he had been in the top 25 percent of the candidates for the
FCO, and suggesting a date on which he might usefully report to the
Foreign & Commonwealth Office in King Charles Street for his first day
as a fully-fledged member of HM Diplomatic Service. Adam celebrated
his success with a bottle of rosé with his parents and a friend, went to bed
slightly tipsy, and slept the sleep of the just.

A few years after Adam's successful navigation of the selection process, the first of its three stages, formerly a series of written examinations,
was changed to a succession of computerised tests and exercises which
candidates were (and still are) required to take online, each test or task
given a demanding deadline for completion. The whole process, for those
who survived to the end, was spread over several weeks. A substantial
number of candidates would be failed at each point in the process. Those
who had successfully jumped each of the hurdles would then be invited to
take an invigilated exam in two parts, an "e-Tray exercise" or "In box
Task" to determine which candidates would be selected to go on to the
second stage of the selection procedure, while the other part (the "Written
Task") would be assessed only at the second stage. Adam, a seasoned
diplomat by the time these changes were made, wondered to what extent
the new online process measured a candidate's computer skills rather
than any of the competences needed for a successful career in diplomacy;
but then he realised that by this time computer skills were, and are,
among those essential competences anyway.

Adam was not greatly surprised when the second stage of the selection process, the Civil Service Selection Board (CSSB) tests and interviews, was also radically changed at around the same time. The CSSB was privatised; the two days of tests, exercises, and interviews were compressed into a single day, each candidate interviewed by only one of the three assessors and not, as in Adam's day, by each in turn. Not surprisingly, there was increased emphasis on the need for each test, exercise, and interview to be completed punctually, increasing the pressure on the candidates. Another radical change was that the three assessors started the day with no knowledge of the five or six candidates' backgrounds, experience, or performances in the first stage. Looking back on his own earlier experience of the two-day CSSB, Adam wondered whether it was really possible for the assessors, at what was now called the Fast Stream Assessment Centre, to form as thorough and reliable an impression of their candidates' abilities and prospects in just half the time available to the old CSSB. He wondered whether privatisation had really been in the public interest. The firm managing the procedures must, he thought, be exposed to the temptation to steer promising candidates into applying for more immediately lucrative jobs in the private sector whose selection procedures were managed by the same firm. He wondered whether the changes to the procedure he had himself undergone a few years earlier might have been driven more by the need to save money than by any wish to improve the effectiveness of the system in picking winners. Whatever the motivation and side effects of the change, it was clearly now irreversible, so there was probably little point in regretting it.

Adam never discovered whether in later years the Final Interview process had been tightened up, with each of the interview panel tasked to pose questions tailor-made to reveal specific competences. He knew that there was plenty of evidence that unstructured, spontaneous interviews of the kind he had experienced produced results that were no better as indicators of future success than listing the successful candidates and the failures completely randomly. No doubt the whole thing had by now been reformed along scientific lines. If so, Adam reflected that a once welcome hint of comedy would have been lost.

### As an example . . .

*At my own final interview, the statutory trade unionist was also the statutory woman, two birds thriftily killed with one stone. Earlier in the interview, this genial lady had picked up the not very interesting fact that I had done most of my compulsory national service in the army in Hong Kong, still then a British colony. When it came to her turn to question me, she looked shrewdly at me and asked: "Tell me, Mr. Barder, after your time in Hong Kong, do you still feel the lure of the Orient?" I replied that I had indeed been fascinated by Hong Kong, and would like one day to return to that part of the world. "Yes, yes, but what I'm trying to get at, Mr. Barder, is whether you ever feel the lure of the Orient?"*

*This was becoming embarrassing. I tried again.*

*"Well, it depends on what you mean by 'the lure of the Orient.' If you mean a feeling about the special attractions of the East, its interest and unique character, probably I do feel that."*

*"But I don't think you're answering my question, Mr. Barder. I was asking specifically about the lure of the Orient, you see."*

*I began to feel my chances of becoming a diplomat slipping away.*

*"Um, I'm awfully sorry if I don't seem to be answering the question, I thought I had given you a rather conditional Yes, but—"*

*At this point the Chair, looking almost as embarrassed as I felt, intervened.*

*"Lady Buncombe, thank you very much, I think we have covered this area quite thoroughly. Sir Neville, do you have any questions for, er, Mr. Barber?"*

Currently there are different routes to entry into the Foreign & Commonwealth Office and the UK diplomatic service. Just because someone went to university, it doesn't any longer mean they apply only for the fast stream route, which, in Adam's younger days, the great majority of university graduates took, almost automatically. Since Adam's time in the diplomatic service, nearly all entrants by all available routes and at all different levels have been graduates. Only a minority now come in through the fast stream, as Adam did; others enter at "operational" level (a grade below); and others as Administrative Assistants (lower still). There are also occasional ad hoc recruitment campaigns to attract people at higher levels (first secretary and above). Theoretically the level of entry is less significant now that Assessment and Development Centres have been introduced and individuals can (in principle at least) advance as quickly as their brilliance allows. Moreover, promotion is now in principle never automatic: it is said to be based purely on merit. To proceed from one grade to the next, a British diplomatic service officer has to "pass" an Assessment and Development Centre (ADC). It would be theoretically possible to stay at the same grade for an entire career if you can't (or won't) pass an ADC. Whether in practice, a below-average competent officer would be left in peace to bump along year after year in the same grade, either failing every ADC or never applying to one, is, of course, another matter.

After receiving the news of his success in the competition for an appointment in the diplomatic service, and before the time came for him to report for duty to the Foreign & Commonwealth Office, Adam received two offers of other jobs for which he had applied during his last term at university. One of these was from a well-known advertising agency with a reputation for recruiting talented and creative men and women straight from university at attractive starting salaries and with reportedly good prospects of early promotion. The other was from a multinational group of companies with interests in several fields including metal-bashing manufacturing, high-tech construction companies, and electronics. The group offered Adam a place on a management training course targeted at a subsequent job in the construction company that was part of the group.

He had applied for both these private sector jobs as well as to the diplomatic service because he had never really expected to get through all the stages of the public service selection process against what was likely to be pretty formidable competition. He had thought that the selection procedures would be a useful and interesting experience even though he would probably be weeded out at an early stage. Success in the application for a job in the construction group of companies seemed likelier than failure, and it would be a reasonably acceptable fall-back if all else failed. Advertising would be more fun, probably, but applying for it would be a riskier option: a lot of bright students at universities all over the country fancied themselves as creative directors in advertising. Both these offers were tempting. Either would start Adam on a salary scale more than 50 percent higher than what the Foreign & Commonwealth Office would pay him. The higher salaries on offer were not to be despised.

In the end, Adam turned down both the advertising and the construction industry offers, although he was not entirely clear in his own mind why he did so. Partly it was a generalised distaste for the private sector with its fixation on profit and maximizing shareholder value. It wasn't that he regarded sound practical private sector work as beneath him. He knew most people in both the private and public sectors worked hard and honestly for the benefit of society as well as for themselves. He just doubted his own ability to summon up enough interest, enthusiasm, or commitment to enable him to do a decent job of work.

Adam's other motivation for choosing life as a diplomat, despite the financial sacrifice it would obviously entail, was a nagging feeling that it would feel like hubris to jump through all the narrow hoops of the selection process, finally winning a place for which hundreds of other equally bright young men and women would gladly have given their right arms, only to turn it down and go off to write advertising jingles or build tower blocks of flats instead. Although Adam's conception of What Diplomats Do was extremely vague, a diplomatic career would surely be concerned with such questions as the preservation of peace, the defence of the national interest, and the encouragement of amicable relations among the peoples and nations of the world. These were things that must, he reasoned, be worth working for, however modest his own personal contribution to these grand causes might turn out to be.

Adam wrote grateful and regretful letters to the advertising agency and the construction group explaining that he had decided that his ambitions lay elsewhere. He took out a subscription to *The Economist* in order to educate himself in the mysteries of international affairs, before the day came for him to set off for King Charles Street, London SW1, just behind Whitehall and a stone's throw from Parliament, for his first day as a professional diplomat.

# 3

# ARRIVAL AT A NEW POST

*How the new arrival spends his working day, first as a new entrant in his foreign ministry and later in his first overseas post: tasks and challenges; big posts and small. Training policy, or lack of it.*

Arrival at a new post, whether at an embassy overseas or in the Foreign Ministry at home, is always a daunting experience, as the newcomer soon discovers. The most daunting of all is the first day in the Office—the term used for the Foreign and Commonwealth Office by those who work in or for it. Adam arrived punctually at 11 a.m., as instructed in his letter of appointment, and reported to a member of the Personnel Department (nowadays predictably called Human Resources), a friendly youth barely older than Adam himself. He told Adam to call him Rufus: "We all use first names here, except of course when you're talking to the Permanent Secretary, the most senior official in the FCO and Head of the Diplomatic Service, whom you address as 'P.U.S.,' standing for Permanent Under-Secretary, or to the Secretary of State, whom you call 'Secretary of State,' or one of the other FCO ministers—you call them 'Minister.' Then after that 'Sir' will do for all of them. But I'm just Rufus."

Adam learned his fate.

"You'll be spending two years here in the Office before you get your first overseas posting. You'll normally spend one year doing policy work in a department dealing with a specific region of the world, or with a particular aspect of foreign policy, and your second year doing what we call 'delivering services' (for example, helping to support British citizens forced into marriage overseas) or in a 'corporate' role (such as working on recruitment to the FCO). Or you might have the option of spending your second year studying a difficult language such as Mandarin or Arabic."

"In fact, we've decided that you're going to start off in the Cyprus section of the Mediterranean Department," Rufus continued.

Adam was struggling to cope with such a mass of vital information.

"You'll find it interesting—a Commonwealth country partly occupied by the Turks, relations with Greece, question of membership of the EU, that sort of thing. You'll be taking over from John Dove, another new entrant who arrived a few months ago. Luckily for you, we've managed to arrange a short overlap so that he can show you the ropes before you start flying solo, if you'll forgive the mixed metaphor. Unless you have any questions, I'll take you along to meet John, and also Dick who's his section head and will be your line manager. One of them will take you around and introduce you to the other people in the department."

Adam said: "Before we go, could I ask about training? Will I be doing some kind of introductory course to learn what the job's all about, the mechanics of it, and so forth?"

"Not really," the Personnel Department youth said cheerfully. "We reckon the best thing is to learn on the job. You'll soon pick it up. Dick will be an excellent mentor for you. You'll probably do plenty of training courses later, depending on the needs of your future posts here in the Office and overseas—there are masses of them, naturally, courses on commercial work, the European Union, duties of an accounting officer, personal and post security, etc. I think there's even one on international law, although we have our own Office Legal Advisers who advise on legal matters for us."

Long after his initial introduction to the mysteries of "the Service," after Adam had had several promotions and had been appointed head of a busy FCO department, he found himself responsible for the welcome and initial training of two new entrants to the diplomatic service allocated to his department each year. By then a short induction course was provided for new entrants during their first few weeks in the FCO. Adam used to ask them how helpful these induction courses had been. Most of the bright young women, and occasionally equally bright young men, committed to his care were decidedly sceptical. They had found the induction course mostly superficial and unduly concerned with minor procedural matters, so of limited utility. But later still, initial induction courses were beefed up and made more substantial, comprising a two-week introductory training course for new "policy" entrants—one week of talks, etc., in London, and one week shadowing the new entrant's predecessor.

Rufus had more information to impart about training.

"Then, of course, there's language training. For example, if you're posted to Turkey—the embassy in Ankara, probably, or it could be to the Consulate-General in Istanbul—we'll aim to get you on a Turkish language course before you go, if time permits. If they're in a great hurry for you to get there—it happens!—you may have to do Turkish lessons en poste, which can be a bit of a bore in a very busy post. You'll shortly be sitting the language aptitude test to find out whether you would be able to learn a hard language, like Mandarin or Amharic—which would tend to point you in the direction of being a specialist in the area where your particular language is spoken. You will need to be a bit careful about that, when the time comes: say you learn Amharic, which is only spoken by the governing class in Ethiopia, you'll obviously only be able to use it on an Ethiopian posting, but that will restrict your postings options, because the embassy in Addis Ababa is fairly small, so if you're coming up for a head of mission posting at a later stage, and the post of ambassador at Addis Ababa isn't due to fall vacant for two or three years, you're liable to be out of luck. Whereas if you learn Arabic and do the standard Arabic course, there'll always be lots of opportunities for postings all round the Middle East, or dealing with Middle Eastern affairs in a big post such as Washington. But it's early days, and I don't think you need to start worrying about such matters yet."

Adam was not entirely clear about the significance of the policy of teaching a diplomat the language of the country to which he's being posted before he leaves to take up his duties in the embassy only "if time permits."

"Well," Rufus admitted, "obviously that's the ideal thing, but sometimes an officer may have to get to his post before he's had time to do a language course before he leaves. When that happens, we encourage him to take language lessons from one of the local people, and study it as intensively as—"

"As time permits?" Adam suggested.

"Exactly," Rufus agreed.

"One other thing," said Adam. "You said that Dick would be my line manager. What exactly does that mean?"

"It means that he's your immediate boss. He's the one who will write your annual confidential report when the time comes—you'll see all of it and be able to discuss it with him before it comes up to us. Also your line manager keeps an eye on how you're doing, sets you straight if you're going off the rails, and generally shows you how to do the job. If you draft a letter or a telegram or a submission for someone more senior to sign, you'll need to look and see how Dick changes your draft or if necessary rewrites it in the house style so that you'll do better the next time. When you've done six months or so dealing with Cyprus we'll need to have a conference with you to decide the best trajectory for your career, in the light of your performance so far. Obviously we'll get Dick's advice on that—he'll have seen more of your work than anyone else—and also the head of your department, Ronnie Small, who you'll be meeting later; he is away on a trip with the Secretary of State at the moment, so the most senior of the desk officers is in charge of the Department until Ronnie gets back."

"The desk officers?" Adam asked.

"The heads of the various sections of the department—which are sometimes called 'desks,' for some reason," Rufus said. "The head of department is generally a Counsellor, and the 'desk officers' heading each section are first secretaries. You'll be starting off as a third secretary, almost but not quite the lowest of the low. But you'll go up to first secretary after a few years in the ranks."

**As an example:**

*Before I transferred from the home civil service to the diplomatic service, I had occupied the civil service grade of Principal, having been an Assistant Principal on first joining. My father, who had no prior knowledge of these arcane matters, felt that it was very satisfactory to be able to tell his friends, equally unlettered in the ways of Whitehall, that his son was a Principal in the civil service. After my transformation into a diplomat, my rank was First Secretary, the diplomatic service equivalent of a Principal in the home civil service. My father, however, was aghast. How could he tell his friends that his son was some kind of secretary? His solution was to express his pride that his son was now a Diplomat. After a decent interval, and some diplomatic experience in a variety of posts both in London and overseas, I was duly promoted from First Secretary to Counsellor. My father was unsure what to make of this. I told him that a diplomatic service Counsellor was the equivalent of an Assistant Secretary in the home civil service.*

*My father's face went pale.*

*"But—you're not an Assistant Secretary, for heaven's sake? Even First Secretary was better than that!"*

*"No, no. Don't worry. I'm the equivalent of an Assistant Secretary . . ."*

*"Dear God," muttered my father.*

*". . . but I'm actually a Counsellor. The lowest diplomatic grade is Attaché, the next grade up is Third Secretary, then Second and then First Secretary, and then Counsellor, which is what I am now."*

*"All right. I suppose you can't expect ever to be promoted to Ambassador, after you started from such a lowly beginning."*

*"Dad, ambassador is not a grade, or a rank, in the diplomatic service hierarchy."*

*"What on earth is it, then?"*

*"Well, basically it's a job. It's an appointment. A person may be appointed an ambassador when he's a Minister, which is the next grade up from Counsellor—"*

*"A Minister?" exclaimed my father, increasingly bewildered. "You mean to say that when you get your next promotion you're going to join the government?"*

*"No, no, not at all. This is another meaning of minister. Not a member of the government, not a Church of Scotland clergyperson, but a diplomat of the grade above Counsellor."*

*My father relaxed a little.*

*"I was trying to explain, Dad," I said. "In the British system a person in the grade of Minister, which generally means an Assistant-Under-Secretary or AUS or occasionally a Counsellor, may be appointed an ambassador; or a Counsellor may do a stint as an ambassador, or even as a Minister, and these days even some First Secretaries are given an opportunity to serve as an ambassador—obviously not to an important country—to get some experience of what that involves in case they get a more senior ambassadorship later in their careers."*

*"So if you're made an ambassador, you don't necessarily keep that grade for the rest of your career?"*

*"It's not a grade, Dad," I reminded him. I thanked my lucky stars that I hadn't attempted a career as a teacher. "It's a job. You can be*

*an ambassador as a first secretary and after that you might get an-
other posting still as a first secretary working for a Counsellor who
works for a Minister who works for an even more senior ambassador.
Ambassador or Minister isn't a grade like Counsellor or First Secretary, it's just a job. Like being, say, an actor or an underwear sales-
man."*

*"Not many of them get to be called His Excellency," my father
pointed out.*

*For once I had no answer to that.*

*When, a good many years later, Assistant Under-Secretaries were
re-named "Directors" and Deputy Under-Secretaries were re-named
"Directors-General," in implausible imitation of commercial companies, I was glad not to have had to explain that further complication to
my father on top of everything else.*

*It was of course my mongrel origins, emerging from one Service
and being accommodated in another after only a few years as a public
servant, that caused these baffling confusions of rank, grade, and their
equivalences. No wonder my father found the whole thing impossible
to follow. For the great majority of diplomats moving systematically
up through the system, even their elderly parents should have no difficulty in keeping track of what they're called at each stage.*

As Adam and Rufus walked across the FCO courtyard to the entrance of
the wing housing Mediterranean Department, Adam asked if the managers of the Service such as Rufus were professional administrators.

"Not at all," Rufus replied. "We're ordinary working diplomats like
yourself and everyone else, just doing a stint in one of the management
departments for two or three years before returning to the diplomatic
treadmill. We try to combine common sense with a superficial knowledge
of current management practice—not always successfully, some might
say. But I think most members of the Service would prefer to be managed
by their own kind, who know from first-hand experience what it's like
working in an overseas post or here in the Office, rather than by special-
ists with little or no understanding of our special needs."

So Adam began his career suggesting solutions to the various prob-
lems involved in Britain's relations with Cyprus. John Dove, whom
Adam was to succeed, dumped an armful of files in Adam's In Tray.
"The best thing is just to start reading the files and deciding what needs to
be done about the top item in each one—it might be a telegram from our
High Commissioner in Nicosia reporting some query he's had from the

Cypriot Foreign Ministry and asking for instructions on how to reply to it, or reporting on his latest meeting with the other Commonwealth High Commissioners in Nicosia about various current issues, in case we have any comments or guidance to give him about any of them; or there could be a request from the Private Office (that means the Secretary of State's private secretaries) for a brief on Cyprus in case it comes up in a debate next week in the House of Commons. I'll need to tell you how to draft a brief when you need to do one.

"The great thing," observed young Mr. Dove, "is to keep an eye on all the files in your In Tray and to try to deal with most urgent ones first, which may not be the same thing as the most important ones. When I first met Ronnie, our head of department, he gave me a useful tip: he said I shouldn't let a difficult but non-urgent problem fester in my In Tray for too long before I dealt with it; its difficulty would grow and grow in my mind, the longer I left it, until eventually I would be too scared to tackle it at all. Pretty good advice, I thought. I suspect that one of the files I've given you is in exactly that category. It's not that urgent, compared with some of the others, but it needs careful handling and a lot of thought. I'm quite glad that it's you who'll be wrestling with it and not me!"

Adam was privately somewhat crestfallen after listening to this. Evidently the job consisted mainly of shunting papers to and fro, just the same as in any dusty office in the city or some declining industrial town in the rustbelt. Was this what he had passed all those exams and tests and interviews to do? It sounded rather different from the kind of elegant activity he had associated with being a diplomat—skilfully negotiating with foreigners, shrewdly picking up valuable information from earnest discussions at cocktail parties, attending meetings with a placard on the table in front of him identifying him with the UNITED KINGDOM. Meanwhile an intimidating pile of files awaited him, and he had virtually no idea what to do with any of them.

**As an example:**

*My own experience was quite different from Adam's. In my last year at university I had applied for a place in the home civil service, not the diplomatic service, having had no interest in spending a large part of my working life in foreign countries, and suspecting—wrongly, for the most part—that the social life of a British diplomat would be out of my own league, as well as probably uncongenial. I was lucky to get my first choice of home department, the Colonial Office, then in the early stages of the great enterprise of decolonisation. The Colonial Office was a purely London-based department, staffed by home civil servants who had no obligation to serve overseas. It was not to be confused with the Colonial Service, comprising the adventurous men in khaki shorts who served the colonial governments, alongside suitably qualified local inhabitants. It became increasingly clear that with each colonial territory that became independent the Colonial Office was working itself out of a job, and accordingly the prudent course was to transfer to a different home department before all the most interesting ones were filled up with other refugees from administering a shrinking colonial empire.*

*I had found what looked like a promising bolt-hole elsewhere in Whitehall and was just waiting for agreement on a date for the transfer, when I received a summons to go and see the Colonial Office's Administration Officer. Congenitally non-committal, this gentleman intimated, with countless hedgings, that if, instead of transferring to another Whitehall department, I were to apply for a four-year posting to the United Kingdom Mission to the United Nations in New York, dealing with decolonisation issues as a first secretary on secondment to the Foreign & Commonwealth Office, my application might well be successful, although naturally he couldn't promise. . . . I expressed an immediate interest in the idea of four years in New York, but said I'd need to consult my wife and consider the implications for our two small daughters. As I was leaving the room, the Administration Officer called me back, and as an unconvincing afterthought mentioned that if I were to be accepted for the New York posting, I would naturally be expected to transfer permanently to the diplomatic service, since it would be a waste of four years' experience of diplomatic work if I were then to return to the home civil service. This greatly complicated the situation. If I applied and signed up for the four years at the United Nations now apparently on offer, I would be making a decision that would mean a complete change for my wife and myself for the rest of our lives, not just for the next four years.*

*On my arrival in New York as First Secretary (Colonial Affairs) at the UK delegation to the UN, I was chagrined to find that my new diplomatic service colleagues automatically assumed that (1) I had originally applied to join the diplomatic service but had failed the selection process, (2) I had gone into the home civil service as the next best thing, and (3) my transfer to the diplomatic service was a sneaky way of achieving what I had wanted all along, without passing the necessary exams and tests as they had had to do. None of these three*

*assumptions was correct, but I don't think I ever succeeded in convinc-*
*ing my fellow-diplomats in New York that this was the case. So I*
*became a diplomat by accident, not by design.*

*In those days visiting New York as a tourist was impossibly expen-*
*sive for a struggling civil servant and his family, and my wife and I*
*knew that if we turned down the chance of a four-year posting there,*
*we would regret it for the rest of our lives, even if the price we were*
*going to pay was henceforth spending the bulk of our working lives in*
*foreign parts. But I'm still not entirely sure that we made the right*
*choice!*

Later in the following week Adam spotted Ronnie Small, his head of
department, just back from his trip with the Secretary of State, having
lunch in the Office canteen. Adam asked if Small would mind if he took
the seat next to him.

"Of course," Ronnie Small said. "Be my guest—or should I say my
paying guest? I'm assuming you'll pay for your own lunch. Anyway, how
are you getting on? Things beginning to fall into place yet?"

"Look," Adam said, afraid of sounding hopelessly naive, "it sounds
like a silly question, but I'm not entirely clear what all this is about. I
mean, if we were working in a company that made widgets, I'd understand that the job would be to make widgets and sell them at a profit for
the benefit of the company's shareholders. But what's the Foreign Office
for, exactly? Of course it's obvious what we're doing from day to day,
but what are we doing it for?"

"Not a silly question at all," Ronnie admitted. "Perhaps we don't ask it
often enough. Well: we're here to promote and protect Britain's domestic
and international interests in its relations with other countries. It's up to
our elected ministers to define those interests and to lay down the guide-
lines for how they want us to promote them. As their diplomatic officials,
we act as a two-way communication system. We inform the overseas
country that we're serving in, the host country, about Britain: our policies
and how they affect the host country, what we're trying to do in the world
and the ways in which our interests coincide with theirs or maybe conflict
with theirs. We try to explain to them what kind of country we are and
why it's in their interests to collaborate with us. At the same time, we
make ourselves familiar with every aspect of the country we're in, what
makes it tick, who really runs it, who influences its policies, what kind of
arguments and approach will ring a bell and persuade them to act in ways

we would find helpful, how strong or weak it is economically and militarily and politically, and how things will develop in future. And we keep London—our ministers, the FCO, other government departments—informed from day to day of what kind of country we're dealing with and what problems are liable to crop up that might affect us and if so how best to deal with them. We interpret Britain to the host country and the host country to Britain, so that each side understands the other better. Preventing misunderstandings between countries is an important part of what we do. We may get to understand the country we're serving in so well that we begin to sympathise with it in any dispute with the UK. But we never forget that we're representing Britain and no-one else. We try to put ourselves in the other guy's shoes so that we can understand the reasons for what he does and says, and try to predict how he's going to react to some new initiative that we may be instructed to present to him, so that we can advise our masters at home on how best to dress it up and the arguments for it that are likeliest to persuade him. But we're working for Britain and not any other government. You'd be surprised how often even quite senior people in our service lose sight of that. They start to go native—and from that moment on, they're no use to us."

"That all makes good sense," Adam said, "when you put it like that. But what do you mean by saying that we inform the overseas country concerned about Britain? And when you say we represent Britain overseas, do you mean just the British government? Or just the FCO?"

Ronnie dismissed the idea that our diplomats represented only their government. "British ambassadors represent their head of state, the Queen, as well as her government—that's why it's technically wrong to talk about 'our ambassador' in Paris or sending instructions to 'our ambassador' in Timbuctoo, even though in practice of course almost everyone does, these days. Strictly speaking, he's Her Majesty's ambassador, not ours, although that's just a technicality nowadays. So as the Queen's representative, the ambassador (and by extension his diplomatic staff) represents the whole country. If the leader of the opposition or other opposition MPs pay an official visit to a country, its embassy or high commission looks after them just as conscientiously as it would a member of the government or a governing party MP. And if it's justified by our formal 'post objectives,' revised each year and approved by London, we help to organise visits by UK cricket or football teams and artists and orchestras and bishops and businessmen and bankers in the same way, ensuring that they meet the right people and have a rewarding programme and that the visit goes smoothly—or anyway as smoothly as we can make it."

"As for informing the host country about Britain, of course a major duty is to keep the host government informed and to explain to its ministers (and often to its head of state) and their officials what the UK is doing and why. But we also have a public relations role, to try to encourage local public opinion to take a favourable view of Britain and British policies and values. We try to get to know the local movers and shakers, whether they're television commentators or newspaper editors or trade union leaders or whoever, so that they know us well enough to get in touch with us when they have a problem with us, and so that we get put straight through to them when we telephone them or make an appointment to see them with a request or a message. We take every opportunity to give interviews to the press and television and radio, nationally and locally, to explain our policies and what Britain is doing that's of benefit to that country."

"We also need to keep in touch with local opposition elements, even if they're banned in some countries, so that if and when they come to power they're already well disposed to Britain, and so that when they're the government, we already have lines open to them. We're legally forbidden to interfere in the host country's internal affairs, but there's a pretty fuzzy line between interference and maintaining contact with people the host government doesn't like—so long as we don't actively encourage them to overthrow the government and string up the deposed president from the nearest lamp-post. Wherever we're posted around the world we try to publicise and promote Britain's commitment to human rights and free speech and the rule of law, even when this implies criticism of local practices and the behaviour of the host government. In some cases we openly condemn the local authorities when their treatment of their own people falls short of what we regard as minimum ethical standards. This doesn't always go down terribly well locally. If we overdo the holier-than-thou strictures on local shortcomings, our embassy is liable to find itself virtually frozen out and cold-shouldered by the local government, which can be a high price to pay, for example, when we suddenly need some vital piece of information from them, or when we want their crucial vote in the UN, or when we suddenly need their cooperation in dealing with a consular emergency involving British citizens. Some of our hyper-virtuous and more priggish media at home don't often realise that it's not always the principal job of our diplomacy to pass public judgement on less fortunate foreign countries, and indeed that people in glass houses— well, you know the rest of that."

"Yes," Adam said, "that's fairly clear about what we do when we're posted abroad, although it all sounds to me a pretty tall order. But here in the FCO we can't do any of those things."

"True," Ronnie agreed. "Here in London it's a different kind of job. We still have the major task of keeping our ministers informed about the countries we're dealing with. Of course with 24-hour-a-day radio and television, news of a natural disaster or a revolution usually arrives in ministers' offices before the first report from the embassy in the country concerned, but here in the Office in London it's our job to advise ministers urgently on the implications of new developments for British interests, whether a British government response is required and if so what we should say and do, and provide an analysis of the wider implications— mainly using the information and interpretations that flow in all the time from our embassies—"

"Our embassies?" Adam queried satirically.

"Sorry, HM embassies—but also by analysing and assessing all the other kinds of information that are available, intelligence reports, expert analyses in the media, talking to academic experts in the relevant field, keeping in touch with the diplomats in the London embassies of the countries we're dealing with, and our personal impressions from occasionally visiting the countries ourselves (at any rate when you have a little more seniority under your belt, Adam, my friend). But then we're also the channel of communication between our ministers and their most senior officials in the Office at this end, and the British embassies and high commissions and other posts at the other end. They send us their advice and their recommendations, as well as information, and we send back their instructions."

"Instructions from ministers?"

"Always instructions are based on our knowledge of what ministers want—and they're always sent in the name of ministers and with their authority, even if they haven't been consulted about the specific matter in question. These instructions, and sometimes just guidance, they're going out all the time, to posts all over the globe. We couldn't possibly refer every single one of them to ministers for approval. Their private secretaries and senior officials keep an eye on virtually everything that goes out and if they spot something that looks questionable, they will warn ministers and take it up with the head of department concerned to make sure that nothing goes off the rails. But I should guess that 90 percent or more of the messages that wing their way to and fro between overseas posts and the Office here in London are between officials, and that ministers haven't had to be personally consulted about them."

"And what if we don't think that our ministers' policies are right, that they won't work? Can we advise them to change them?"

"Basically we're like lawyers advising a client. The client gives us his instructions and those are binding on us. Ministers are entitled to the best advice we can give them on how to make their policies work, whatever we might think of them privately. Of course we can often—usually—take part in the process of formulating policy, and at that stage we can offer advice based on our own judgement and values, but always in the context of the overall policies and aims of the government. It's up to ministers, at the end of the day, to accept or reject our advice: they have been elected (unless they're ministers in the House of Lords!) and we haven't, so we have no right to try to superimpose our opinions on those of ministers. Once they have made their decision, it's up to us to implement it as effectively as we can, just as a defence barrister makes the most convincing case he can for his client if his client insists on pleading Not Guilty, even if privately his defence counsel thinks he's as guilty as hell. But counsel must never knowingly lie to the court, just as diplomats must never tell lies in expounding or defending their country's policies."

"And if we think we're being asked to carry out policies that are dishonest or immoral or even illegal?"

"Luckily that's pretty rare, in my experience. If it's really illegal or indisputably immoral, you can report your objections to your line manager and if necessary all the way up to the Permanent Under-Secretary and Head of the Diplomatic Service, who in principle will then take it up with ministers, probably in consultation with the Cabinet Secretary. If it's not clear-cut and partly just a matter of your opinion and your conscience against those of ministers, you can ask to be moved to other work where you won't be asked to do anything that violates your conscience. What you can't do, however strongly you might feel, is go to the media about what you think is government wrong-doing, or tell your friends and hope that they will pass it on to the media, or leak incriminating documents anonymously to the media. Whistle-blowing is made to sound heroic by the media, for obvious reasons—juicy leaks sell newspapers and advertising space, and the hacks love to see themselves as the guardians of the country's conscience—but it's only really ever justified if you've tried every other legal way of dealing with the problem and failed all along the line. Even then it's still a very dodgy thing to do. It's a betrayal of your loyalty to the ministers that you work for and who are entitled to that loyalty: the system wouldn't work, government couldn't function, if every piddling little official spent his time salving his tender conscience by sending government secrets to the newspapers."

"I suppose one could resign from the Service, and then spill the beans to the media," Adam suggested.

"Yes, you could," Ronnie nodded, "so long as you're prepared to spend the next ten or twenty years behind bars for a flagrant breach of the Official Secrets Act—which is binding on you for the rest of your life, remember, whether or not you're still taking the Queen's shilling. Often all you can properly do, if you've exhausted all the other options, is quietly resign from the service, leave those beans unspilled, and try to get a job as the bridge correspondent on your local newspaper."

"Ah," Adam said thoughtfully. "Good point. I'd better learn to play bridge, just in case. Do you mind if I go and get some dessert?"

Adam learned from several chats with the officer in Personnel Department (now Human Resources or HR) responsible for the management of new entrants and others in their first three or four years in the Service that he could expect to be promoted from third to second to first secretary after a few years spent both in the Office in London and at one or more overseas posts. In those far-off days this would be semi-automatic, unless the judgment of his line manager and other senior officers familiar with his work was either that he was exceptionally brilliant and an obvious high flier, in which case he might be promoted a little earlier so that he could show what he could do in the higher grade; or that he seemed to be a below average performer, in which case he might be left somewhat longer in the starting grade and given a more extended opportunity to resolve any doubts about his capacity for doing the job. Long after Adam had been promoted through this semi-automatic system to first secretary grade, all promotions were made subject to success in an Assessment and

Development Centre (ADC), and even semi-automaticity disappeared, anyway in principle, from the entire promotion game, at all levels.

"We realise that not everyone can be above average," Adam was told. "There are lots of jobs for the loyal plodders without much sparkle. But plodders can't assume that it's safe to go on plodding indefinitely. Allowances will always be made for slow starters, but later in your career promotion will be purely on merit; no more sitting back and waiting for your name to float up to the top of the list for promotion—'Buggin's Turn,' we used to call it. A lot will depend on the assessment in your annual report by your line manager. You'll need to take that seriously. Your line manager will go through the whole 22-page report with you, line by line, your shortcomings and mistakes as well as your talents and successes. It's up to you to challenge anything in your report that you think is unfair or unduly critical and thrash out any disagreements with your reporting officer. You'll have an opportunity to comment in writing on how you see the report and even to say how you feel you have been managed by your line manager during the preceding year. Not only the timing of your promotions[1] but also decisions about your future postings and the direction that your career ought to take will depend heavily on the assessments and advice in your annual report. Of course you'll have every opportunity to discuss all these matters in confidence with us in the Personnel Department and to express an interest in some postings and an aversion to others, all of which we'll take into account, although obviously we can't guarantee that you'll get exactly what you want."

Adam decided that since he had no set ideas about where he particularly wanted to go, and in the hope that showing himself willing to go anywhere and do any job that the Personnel Department wanted him to do would earn him useful credits, he would adopt a fatalistic view and go wherever he was sent. Probably even jobs and posts that sounded uninteresting and unchallenging to begin with would turn out to provide plenty of job satisfaction and interest once you arrived and started doing the job. He appreciated the value of experience in all the main areas of diplomatic activity, including commercial work (encouraging and helping British exporters and encouraging foreign inward investment), and economic work (collecting and analysing information and opinions on the performance of the host country's economy and finances, so as to be able to advise both the FCO and the economic departments in Whitehall and also British businessmen needing to make key trade and investment decisions). But he knew his main interest would be in straight political work—analysing and reporting on the host country's politics, election prospects, leading politicians, trade union leaders, media influence, financiers and of course government ministers, and advising London on the implications of all this for British interests; and the regular task of explaining British policies to the host government and to the host country's business leaders and other influential decision-makers and opinion-formers, pinpointing opportunities for the two countries to support each other, strengthen their mutual ties, and work together in international forums to promote agreed common aims. Some of this work would fall to specialised diplomatic information officers, but "straight" political officers would be expected not just to provide information about Britain and British policies, but also to get involved in policy-making at home on the basis of experience in dealing with overseas governments.

Compared with that first anxious day in the diplomatic service, Adam's first day in his first overseas post was reasonably pain-free, although meeting those with whom he would be working in the embassy for the next three years was initially stressful. This is not like the first day in some office at home in Britain: most of Adam's social as well as working life will revolve around the embassy and his colleagues in it, and if they don't get on reasonably well together, it can be a difficult time. It's a small embassy in 'Côte Noire,' a big but thinly-populated French-speaking country in West Africa, with fairly limited scope for making friends with local people. Most of the small British embassy staff build their social lives out of working hours around each other and the (equally small) diplomatic corps, comprising the Americans and the larger countries of the EU, including predominantly the French with their large and imposing embassy—this is a former French colony and it still depends mostly on French largesse to remain more or less solvent. The Chinese and Indians are there, the Egyptians and a handful of other Africans, including Nigeria and Ghana. Apart from a few British businessmen and many more French, plus some French aid people and a couple of NGOs, the expatriate community in the country's capital is very limited, and outside it is almost non-existent.

Adam is met on arrival at the airport by the first secretary, who is to be Adam's immediate boss, and his young French wife. Both tell him at once, almost before they have had a chance to introduce themselves, that they are about to go home on their annual leave. Adam will be standing in for the first secretary while he's away, as well as learning and holding down his own job—quite a challenge for a new entrant on his first posting. There will be only ten days for a handover. The French wife has had a job as a secretary (in the ordinary civilian sense of secretary) in the French embassy so she has not been much involved in the life of her husband's embassy. But both of them are enthusiastic about the country and about the scope for using the small allocation of British aid to contribute modestly to its development. They urge Adam to get out and about as soon and as extensively as possible, touring the countryside and meeting ordinary people outside the capital. But they admit that with Adam more or less on his own for the next few weeks, the pressure of routine paper-work and other commitments in the capital won't make it easy for him to go out on tour.

Adam is suddenly aware of a sharp feeling of loneliness. There isn't a soul whom he knows within hundreds of miles. Those whom he has met so far seem amiable enough, but they're strangers. At the end of the day's work, he won't have any friends to ask round for a drink, or tell his worries to in a long telephone conversation. He won't be getting the occasional solicitous telephone call from his mother anymore: sometimes she annoyed him, ringing up for no particular reason, but just now he'd have loved the phone to ring and to hear her familiar voice on the other end asking if everything was all right. He envied his diplomatic service colleagues who were married and who always had a wife or husband nearby to share worries and hilarity and the occasional glooms with. Adam goes to bed in his small flat above the first secretary's slightly larger flat, worried, for perhaps the first time in his life, about whether he'll be able to cope.

Next morning Adam meets his ambassador for the first time, and is surprised to find a man younger and more informal than he had expected an ambassador to be. The ambassador greets him warmly and hopes he'll be free to come round to "the Residence" to meet his wife and have a cup of tea at the weekend so that they can get to know each other. He also, to Adam's barely disguised dismay, invites him to a small dinner party that he and his wife are giving the following evening ("nothing fancy, just lounge suits"), partly to help out with entertaining the foreign guests and partly to take the opportunity of meeting some local dignitaries expected to attend.

"The foreign minister and his wife have accepted the invitation but in this place you never know whether anyone will actually turn up, even if they do accept. Anyway, if he does turn up, you'll find him interesting—he's nearer your age than mine. How's your French, by the way? Hardly anyone around here speaks English."

Adam is glad to have studied French and German at university. His French is fluent but rather academic. Idiomatic or heavily accented French can leave him floundering.

"Oh, you'll be fine, then. 7:30 at the Residence. Look forward to seeing you then. I shan't be around in the office much for the next couple of days, I'm afraid: I've got the AUS Africa [*the Assistant Under-Secretary for Africa from the FCO in London, nowadays called the Director*] staying with us all this week and I'm spending every waking hour taking him round for calls on our local ministers, some of the *chers collègues* [*other ambassadors*] and the editor of the local rag [*newspaper*] among others. The dinner's for the visiting AUS of course. He's rather hard work, actually. Hasn't got much to say for himself and his French is terrible. By the way, we've got a small swimming pool in the Residence garden, such as it is. Feel free to use it any time—except of course when we're using it ourselves to entertain local people for a swim and a meal."

Adam feels that the Residence swimming pool is a good metaphor for being thrown in at the deep end. But it's obviously going to be more varied and more exciting, as well as more challenging, than sitting in London trying to draft diptels and letters and briefs about Cyprus. It just seems a pity that his laboriously won expertise about Cyprus, acquired in his first few months in the Office, is evidently going to be quite irrelevant here in West Africa. There isn't even a Cyprus embassy here—nor a Greek nor a Turkish one. Back to the bottom of the learning curve! But it's a bit more like what he'd expected and hoped for, so he can't complain.

## NOTE

1. NB—this was before the introduction of Assessment and Development Centres (ADCs) on success in which promotions entirely depended (and depend).

# 4

# LIFE IN THE EMBASSY

*Relations with colleagues and the head of post; dealings with the host government; decisions on future postings.*

Adam got somewhat above-average reports in his first two years in the Office and his first overseas posting, as he knew from his lengthy interviews with the writers of the reports. There was general agreement that political work was his forte, and that even if he was not in the top 5 percent of star performers, he could reasonably expect a good career, moderately early promotions and at least one—probably more than one—appointment as a head of mission (ambassador or high commissioner) before he retired.

By the time Adam had experienced life and work in his third overseas post, and had been promoted from third to second to first secretary, he had formed a clear pattern of behaviour and purpose. Peace of mind, the ability to remain cheerful, preservation of his sense of humour, and job satisfaction, all depended first and foremost on maintaining good relations with his embassy colleagues. This was true whether his closest colleagues were amiable or sullen, frivolous or solemn, idle or conscientious. It was no good waiting for them to adapt to Adam; he simply had to adapt to them, or his life would become a misery. Adam had forgotten who had told him that maintaining civil and fruitful relations with foreigners was the easiest part of the job: it was often maintaining decent relations with one's own colleagues that required the subtlest diplomatic skills.

It was not only, or mainly, his diplomatic service colleagues who were sometimes the problem: in the bigger posts—Washington, Bonn (later Berlin), Paris, the delegations to the EEC (EU), the UN, NATO, and a few others—it was often the wide array of sections of the embassy staffed from other Whitehall departments, whether the military, comprising army, navy, and air force, and often including generals, admirals, and air chief marshals; senior and junior officials from the home office, the treasury, the department of trade; departments dealing with food and agriculture, customs and taxation agreements, the environment, fisheries, and just about every other subject dealt with somewhere in Whitehall,[1] if it has any kind of international dimension. Some of these exiles from home departments in London took to the diplomatic dimension of their subjects like bees to honey; others floundered piteously, and had to be shepherded and encouraged through the diplomatic minefields by their diplomatic service colleagues. Some of these Whitehall warriors from other departments were suspicious of diplomatic protocol, and expected to be despised by the regular diplomats for their own supposed lack of social graces.

Adam learned to encounter thin skins in unexpected places. Diplomats were supposed to be acutely aware of their places in the order of precedence, quick to take offence at a supposed snub if their entitlement to respect had not been adequately observed, but Adam found that the military of all three armed forces could be even more hierarchy-conscious than the diplomats, and even more likely to take offence at any apparent failure to give them their ranking's due. It was never any good arguing about these sometimes dubious claims to X's seniority compared with Y's; the only thing to do was to humour them, and to apologise with exaggerated humility for any supposed breach. This could well lead to an enduring and fruitful friendship that would last the length of the posting.

**As an example:**

*I was an originally unknowing participant in one barely believable crisis of protocol and precedence that shook a British high commission (equivalent of an embassy but in another Commonwealth country) almost to its foundations. I was unexpectedly posted, on promotion from first secretary to counsellor, as head of chancery (head of the political section and coordinator of all the post's sections) at the high commission in question, replacing the previous head of chancery who had been moved, only half-way through his four-year tour of duty, to a post in another country.*

*Piecing together clues in an angry letter from the officer whom I was to replace and from an embarrassed account of the situation given to me after I arrived by the high commissioner in charge of my new post, I deduced that there had been a bitter quarrel between my predecessor as head of chancery on the one hand and the senior Defence Adviser (as the Defence Attaché in another Commonwealth country was then called) and the Air, Naval and Military Advisers on the other, over the relative precedence to be enjoyed by the civilian diplomatic counsellors of the high commission versus the defence advisers. The leader of the latter group, the Defence Adviser (or DA), had complained to my predecessor as head of chancery that because the high commission's four or five counsellors appeared in the host country's official Diplomatic List above the names of the DA and his military and naval colleagues, the latter were not receiving as many invitations to diplomatic functions as their seniority and importance entitled them to. This, they asserted, hampered them in their vital task of making contacts among the host country's key figures from whom they would hope to extract important defence intelligence to send home to the Ministry of Defence in Whitehall. A savage dispute had ensued over the relative seniority of a Major-General and a Counsellor in the UK order of precedence, with conflicting extracts from various works of reference flying to and fro, sent to each party by the FCO and the Ministry of Defence, respectively. Neither side would yield. Eventually matters were at such a pitch that the DA, the NA, the AA, and the MA refused to attend the daily morning meeting held by the high commissioner, or indeed any other high commission meeting, if the head of chancery was present (which he invariably was). Neither side had the courage or sense to refer the dispute to the high commissioner for resolution—he was a shy but immensely reasonable man—until it was far too late. Relationships had broken down irreparably; both sides eventually told their stories to the high commissioner, who judged the head of chancery to have been marginally more at fault for having allowed the quarrel to escalate so disastrously; and the high commissioner duly sent his head of chancery home half-way through his posting and asked the Office for a new one—who turned out to be me. I was told by Personnel not to worry about being consigned to what sounded like a can of worms: "He can get away with sacking one head of chancery, but he can't keep on doing it. You're fireproof."*

> *Needless to say (I hope), it took barely ten minutes, a week after my arrival in post, to resolve the dispute by means of unconditional surrender to the DA and his military colleagues. I had taken the precaution of consulting the other counsellors beforehand, and found that, like me, they didn't mind where they appeared in the Diplomatic List, whether above or below our military colleagues; and if a rearrangement resulted in us counsellors receiving fewer invitations to tedious diplomatic functions, and the military more, so much the better—or, as the old-school Foreign Service types used to say, "tant mieux." Common sense triumphed over strict adherence to protocol, and the DA and I got on extremely well for the duration of our postings, to the mutual benefit of our respective jobs and peace of mind.*

If his relations with his embassy or high commission colleagues loomed large in Adam's scheme of things, his relations with his head of mission, whether ambassador or high commissioner, were almost equally important to his peace of mind and his professional effectiveness. Such relations became increasingly substantial as Adam rose steadily through the ranks. Almost all heads of mission (ambassadors and high commissioners) hold a daily morning meeting with their diplomatic staff (or, in the biggest posts, a selection of them), at which each participant gives a summary of his or her current preoccupations, sometimes appealing for any information that might be gleaned by others round the table that could help to achieve a current objective. In some posts, the morning meeting is also used for a round-up of the morning's local press, each participant reporting on news items relating to his or her specialised field. During his posting in Turkish-speaking 'Pazalia,' a small, fictitious, independent, Turkish-speaking republic sandwiched between Turkey and Georgia, in the first year or so his command of Turkish was still far from perfect despite his having completed a Turkish for Beginners course in London as soon as his posting to Pazalia was confirmed and before he left London for Pazalia. His earlier experience as a new entrant of dealing with the affairs of Cyprus had whetted his interest in Pazalia and had been responsible for his expressing an interest in the Pazalia job in a discussion with the Personnel Department. However, not being confident about his facility with the language, Adam found it seriously burdensome to have to plough through the Pazalia newspapers each morning, Turkish dictionary at his elbow, in search of reports or commentaries on the national and international political scene, deciding in each case whether it was sufficiently momentous to require summarizing at the ambassador's 9 a.m. morning meeting. What was worse, a zealous colleague would never fail to score a Brownie point with the ambassador at Adam's expense by pointing out some significant snippet that Adam had missed.

It was at these meetings that Adam was able to take stock of his ambassador's personality, his likes, dislikes, and foibles, his willingness or otherwise to listen to occasionally off-message views from junior members of the embassy without necessarily putting them down, his attitude to the sometimes risible instructions and guidances coming out of the FCO in London, his tendency or lack of it to pomposity or equanimity, vanity or self-deprecation. Adam's assessment of these characteristics of his boss was an essential tool in fine-tuning his own dealings with the great man. He recognised, at the same time, that by the same token, his own behaviour at the morning meetings was his ambassador's principal opportunity for assessing Adam's own performance, including the apparent reliability of his judgment, whether he tended to be shy or to hog the limelight, and the nature of his relations with his own colleagues round the table, whether he seemed mainly supportive or competitive. Since in some posts one of Adam's frequent tasks was to draft speeches, letters, and telegrams (diptels) for his ambassador's signature, the ability to write in the style of the boss and to adapt the substance to what he knew of the ambassador's views and preoccupations was essential.

Adam knew that much of this is common to work in any reasonably big organisation, not unique to diplomatic life and work. But the special circumstances of an embassy tended, he found, to magnify what might otherwise have been quite trivial aspects of life and work. Partly this was because members of an embassy abroad, often far from home, are in some ways an isolated little community, surrounded by foreigners (however personally congenial), away from their families and often separated for months at a time from their own children at boarding-school in England, their own working colleagues the only available sources of help and support when needed, apart from their spouses. The distinction between work and private life normally experienced by those who live and work at home hardly exists for diplomats serving abroad. Working hours tend to be highly elastic: Adam might leave his office in the chancery (the central building of the embassy, housing the offices of the political section as well as the ambassador and his deputy) by 7 or 7:30 p.m. if he was lucky, but on perhaps four nights of every week he and his wife would have to go on to some diplomatic function, or host one themselves, at either of which he would be seeking out potentially useful contacts, exchanging information with local people or fellow diplomats from other embassies or whoever else he might come across, in the hope of filling in some of the gaps in his jigsaw representing the political and economic map of the country he was serving in, or trying, often unsuccessfully, to escape from an unprofitable exchange of courtesies and gossip with some uninteresting fellow guest without causing such deep offence that he would be in danger of making an enemy for the rest of his posting. In other words, still working, even though with a glass of execrable locally produced wine in one hand and a shrimp precariously perched on a fragment of stale bread in the other.

Relations within the embassy were potentially more fraught than they might be in an ordinary office at home, partly because of the unique role of the ambassador, not only enjoying the almost mystical prestige attached to his role and title, but also wielder of virtually unaccountable power over every member of his staff and their wives or husbands. Nominally accountable to his masters in London for his management of the mission and its staff, in practice his underlings, however senior, had little possibility of redress against petty injustice, excessive work demands or wounding discrimination. Only the most gross case of blatant mismanagement could be held to justify an appeal over the ambassador's head to the Personnel Department in London. Any such appeal would effectively wreck any chance of a repair to the victim's relations with his head of mission, whatever the merits of the case; so it would probably spell the premature end of that posting. Adam had the impression that very few ambassadors or high commissioners seriously abused their position in relation to their staff, but the possibility was always there, hanging in the air.

A diplomat working in an embassy abroad is never really off duty. He never sheds his diplomatic role and responsibilities when he takes off his suit and shiny black leather shoes in the evening (even supposing that he is free to do so). He is not granted the office worker's privilege of shedding his office personality in the evenings and at weekends, becoming again a husband or partner and parent within his own family, and forgetting about the challenges and problems of the office at 5 or 6 p.m. on Friday until the following Monday morning.

**As an example:**

*As a first secretary at the UK Mission to the UN in New York, dealing with decolonisation issues, I had especially frequent contact with the UK Permanent Representative and Ambassador to the UN, Lord Caradon, formerly Sir Hugh Foot, whose background was as a senior and sometimes controversial member of the Colonial Service. He had served in a number of colonial territories as Governor, including famously Governor of Cyprus during the Enosis emergency. As a result he naturally took a special personal interest in colonial issues at the United Nations. Like all the Foot family (he was an older brother, and admirer, of the better known Michael)[2] he not only occupied a political position somewhat to the left of centre, he also had a distinctive style of oratory when delivering major speeches, in his case in the UN. This style reflected a childhood in which the Foots had listened every evening to lengthy readings from the Authorised Version of the Bible. The cadences and verbal tricks of that great literary masterpiece entered into the souls of the Foots, and were often reflected in the way they spoke, anyway on formal occasions, and the way they wrote.*

*Lord Caradon often liked to make the speeches himself at UN meetings on colonial problems, rather than delegating the task to one of his deputies or to an even more junior officer, and it often fell to me to provide the first draft of what I thought he might say. On at least one occasion, reading through my draft shortly before submitting it through my immediate superior to Hugh Caradon, I suddenly became aware that my effort to draft in the Caradon (or Foot) semi-biblical style had run away with me, and the result read like an unmistakeably malicious parody. There was no time to re-write it, so I put it up and kept my fingers crossed that it would not earn me a disappointed rebuke and a demand for a straight draft in which I would be admonished to keep my sneering sense of humour under control. No feedback, admonitory or laudatory, reached me, and the next day I sat at the back of the UK delegation's block of seats while Lord Caradon strode to the speaker's rostrum—and delivered the speech word for word as I had drafted it, verbal tics and scriptural rhythms all intact. At the end of it, Hugh Caradon returned to his seat, and, turning round to me, thanked me profusely for "an excellent draft" which, he said, he could well have written himself.*

*Nevertheless, I took care never to do it again.*

As a middling-senior political officer at the British embassy in Pazalia, Adam was often visiting the Europe division of the Pazalian foreign ministry, either in obedience to a summons from the ministry, or else to deliver a message to the Pazalian government in accordance with instructions from London. Earlier in his career he had often accompanied his ambassador or another senior embassy colleague on such calls, mainly to take a note of the conversation for transformation later into a reporting telegram, but also so that there would be a reliable witness on the UK side in case of any subsequent dispute over what had been said. This had been an invaluable form of training for Adam.

Calls on the foreign ministry, especially if on touchy or controversial subjects such as the Turkish occupation of part of Cyprus, required a delicate balance between formality and informality. The interlocutor on the Pazalian side, frequently the UK desk officer or his head of department, would be well known to members of the British embassy both socially and officially, a very frequent contact, often to be seen at the drinks parties, lunches, and dinners given by British embassy officers from the ambassador down. The degree of formality to be adopted at an official conversation in the ministry would be marked by the use of surnames rather than first names in initial greetings, as well as by the seating arrangements in the desk officer's office. For a friendly discussion of the arrangements for the visit of a Pazalian minister or official to London, or of a British minister's or official's visit to Pazalia, the desk officer and his British embassy visitor would sit in comfortable armchairs at a table on which there would be coffee and soft drinks. To receive an official rebuke, or to deliver an official protest, over some event or behaviour that had given offence to the other party, the British embassy visitor would be invited to sit in an upright chair across the desk from the Pazalian official. In such cases there would probably be no coffee, and no lapse into friendly chat after the formal business had been completed.

On this occasion, Adam was under FCO instructions to deliver to the Pazalia foreign ministry "at an appropriate level" a complaint about the action of a Pazalian soldier serving with the Turkish military contingent in Cyprus who had crossed the informal boundary of the Turkish-occupied area into the Greek-Cypriot part of the island, where he had fired several shots at some Greek-Cypriot sailors playing netball on the beach. All the shots had missed, no one had been hurt, the Pazalian soldier had rapidly retreated back into the Turkish-occupied zone, and the Turkish military commander had sent a message to his opposite number in the Cyprus army assuring him that the straying Pazalian soldier had been severely disciplined—without, however, explicitly apologising for the incident. Adam's instructions were to "complain" (but not "protest," a much stronger term) about the undisciplined behaviour of the Pazalian soldier, and to note that if anyone had been killed or injured by the Pazalian soldier, the consequences would have been serious. He was to remind the Pazalian authorities that "Her Britannic Majesty's government" did not recognise the right of Pazalia to station its soldiers in any part of Cyprus, whether or not on secondment to the Turkish army, without the consent of the Cyprus government. He was instructed to make it clear that such a situation should not be allowed to continue indefinitely. The persistence of this situation constituted "a regrettable obstacle to the close and friendly relations between Pazalia and Britain which 'HBM Government' earnestly desired." (All the governments of the then EEC had agreed on this response to the incident and all had sent similar or identical instructions to their missions in Pazalia, having agreed in Brussels that on this occasion each should act separately rather than one acting on behalf of the whole of the EEC.)

Adam's ambassador had decided, in accordance with Adam's own recommendation and after telephoning round the most senior of his EEC diplomatic colleagues, that he, Adam, should deliver this message at the level of the head of the Europe department of the Pazalian foreign ministry, rather than the ambassador himself delivering it to the Pazalian foreign minister or any of his ministerial deputies: to have done it at ambassadorial and ministerial level would have risked raising the British reaction to the incident to disproportionate heights. The ambassador had also decided that Adam should deliver the message orally, but that he should leave behind an Aide Mémoire in writing that would reproduce the exact words of the instructions from London. This would be a less formal way of expressing the complaint than delivering a Note Verbale, a written document with more official status than an Aide Mémoire, which was usually just a reminder of what had been contained in an oral message. A Note Verbale, for example, could contain a formal message as important as a declaration of war, or merely a routine notification that the ambassador had left the country on leave and that his deputy was acting as Chargé d'Affaires in his absence. The use of "complain" rather than "protest" also signalled Britain's desire not to allow the matter to escalate into a more serious dispute than the incident warranted.

Experience had gradually convinced Adam that such apparently petti-fogging, finely nuanced distinctions between the more and the less serious kinds of communication to a foreign government were actually useful tools of the diplomatic trade. They sent signals that were universally understood around the foreign ministries of the world, because they conformed to universal practice and also to rule books which virtually all governments had accepted—the various Vienna Conventions, the latest edition of *Satow's Guide to Diplomatic Practice*, and other sacred texts. Because these rules and conventions were so widely understood and accepted, observance of them minimised the risks of misunderstandings in relations between governments—and Adam knew that when governments misunderstood one another's intentions on matters such as the occupation of territory, the treatment by a foreign country of one's own country's nationals, or questions of peace and war, the consequences could sometimes include unnecessary deaths of innocent civilians.

Another cause of possible misunderstanding arose from the lack of a common language between the deliverer and the recipient of a formal message between governments. In the case of the Pazalian soldier in Cyprus, Adam had chosen to deliver his oral message in English, waiting after each couple of sentences for the Pazalian foreign ministry's English interpreter to translate them orally to the Pazalian head of the Europe department. The latter in fact spoke excellent English, and by this time Adam's command of the local language would have enabled him to deliver his message in reasonably adequate Turkish. But to minimise the risk of misunderstanding, it was mutually if tacitly agreed that this was the safest way to proceed. Similarly, Adam handed over an Aide Mémoire of the message in both English and Turkish, the Turkish version having been prepared beforehand by a member of the British embassy's locally engaged Pazalian staff.

Adam reflected that the need for his message to be delivered in two languages, both orally and in writing, was a small symbol of the cultural as well as the linguistic gulf that separated the two countries, Britain and Pazalia. Examples of major cultural differences and their implications for the behaviour in Pazalia of British diplomats had been included both in Adam's briefing for this Pazalia posting and also in the Pazalia Post Report, the essential guidebook to life in the post concerned, written and kept up to date by every embassy and high commission. These had helped Adam to avoid the worst of the potential pitfalls during his first few weeks in Pazalia. As he saw more of Pazalian life going on around him and began to get to know a growing number of Pazalian contacts and friends, especially some of around his own age, he became more instinctively acculturated with a better understanding of the mindset of an ordinary youngish Pazalian male Muslim compared with a youngish male agnostic Englishman brought up in the mainly Christian-oriented but strongly multi-racial and multi-cultural environment that was twenty-first-century England.

Adam came to realise that bridging the cultural gulf, to the limited extent possible, was a necessary condition for interpreting Pazalia and Pazalian policies and actions to his government in London, and thus an important ingredient in the practice of diplomacy itself. A non-judgmental openness to cultural differences was of course important to anyone living outside his or her own country, whether a foreign correspondent for a London newspaper, a businessman working for a foreign firm or an oil company executive doing a stint in an oil-producing country in the middle east or Africa. It was not a challenge unique to diplomats. But Adam recognised that diplomats had a special need to understand and even in a sense to accept the alien culture of the country where he worked if he was to understand the mainsprings of its government's policies and explain them in unambiguous language to his masters at home.

At a much earlier stage of his career, on his first overseas posting, Adam had queried the use of the term "Her Britannic Majesty's Government" instead of the more familiar "Her Majesty's Government" or "HMG." He had kicked himself for not having worked out the explanation for himself. The Queen of the UK is also the head of state, i.e., the Queen, of fifteen other independent countries around the world, from Canada and Australia to the Bahamas and St. Kitts. Each of these governments has as much right to be called "Her Majesty's Government" as the British government at Westminster (although in practice none of them ever uses that formulation, partly because it might be thought by foreigners to imply a degree of continuing dependence on Britain, and partly for fear of confusion with HM United Kingdom government, which uses it all the time). To distinguish Adam's government from Her Majesty's other governments and realms in communications with the governments of third countries of the Commonwealth, therefore, the practice is to identify which of the Queen's national identities is being referred to: hence Her "Britannic" Majesty's government, as distinct from the government of Her Canadian Majesty or Her New Zealand Majesty. Adam had discovered from painful experience that some of his Commonwealth cousins whose head of state was shared with his own were liable to take offence at the typically British, or English, appropriation of the term "Her Majesty's Government" as if everyone would know which government was being referred to. But he found that in non-Commonwealth countries, this was now generally a non-issue: everyone nowadays took it that HMG referred to the UK government and the Majesty concerned was the Queen of the UK.

Until the Good Friday Agreement of April 10, 1998 took much of the sting out of relations between the British and Irish governments, Adam had had to be cautious when talking to his colleagues in the Irish embassy about the use of the term "Britain" and "British" to refer to the whole of the United Kingdom, since strictly speaking Great Britain does not include Northern Ireland (the formal name of the UK being "the United Kingdom of Great Britain and Northern Ireland"). Irish diplomats had been rather ambiguous about this, Adam discovered; they had tended to object to "the United Kingdom" because it explicitly included a part of their island, and to object equally strongly to "Britain" because it didn't. All this changed, to Adam's and others' relief, with the Good Friday Agreement: Ireland recognised UK sovereignty over the North even though its government and people still retain a wish to see a united Ireland subject to the majority wish of the populations in both north and south—"recognising that a united Ireland shall be brought about only by peaceful means with the consent of a majority of the people, democratically expressed, in both jurisdictions in the island."

Sometimes Adam felt that when serving his country overseas, he was walking on egg-shells. But the challenges, the rewards, and the varieties of experience of the practice of diplomacy abroad were undeniably exhilarating.

**As an example:**
*I had been doing a busy, often hectically busy, job as a first secretary and assistant head of department in the FCO for three years and began to feel that it was time for a change, although I knew that it was too early to start thinking about promotion to counsellor. I hadn't*

*heard anything from the Personnel Department for some time so I arranged to pop down and see "my" career manager. The latter agreed at once that I was in the time zone where I might expect an overseas posting before too long. As soon as there was anything at all definite, he would let me know.*

*So I took to ringing up every couple of weeks or so to ask if there was any news. At last the reply was that it might be useful if I could find the time to look in whenever it was convenient to hear about a possible posting that was likely to come up soon, and for which my name had been mentioned.*

*"I can't tell you in much detail what the job is because we haven't yet consulted the ambassador concerned and the present incumbent doesn't know that he's likely to be moved soon. But I can tell you that it's a country in Latin America, and that you would be in charge of its commercial section, still I'm afraid as a first secretary. Actually you ought to be able to work out where it is to within a range of about three possible countries: you can rule out the bigger ones where the head of commercial section is a counsellor, not a first secretary, or where the first secretary in charge of commercial work has only been in post for a couple of years."*

*"I'm not sure that I'm cut out for commercial work," I said, "and I've never had anything to do with Latin America—Africa and Europe are more my scene."*

*"We reckon that unless you've got some commercial work experi-ence under your belt, Brian, you won't in future be in line for the really exciting top jobs. Trade's top of the pops these days—balance of payments problem, budget deficit, trade gap, all that. Commercial work is really a* sine qua non *from now on. You'll find it's every bit as challenging and rewarding as political work. And I'll tell you a secret: Latin America is the up and coming area. Ministers have begun to realise that we've neglected it for far too long. Commercial work in Latin America—just exactly where the action's going to be. You won't regret it—assuming of course that you get it. A couple of other names have been mentioned but I think it's fair to say that you're the front runner. Sorry I can't tell you any more at this stage. Timing? Oh, in about six months' time, I'd guess. We'll keep you posted."*

*I borrowed some Parlophone Elementary Spanish Lessons records from the FCO Language Centre and promised myself a couple of hours a week listening to them, although the next few weeks turned out to be exceptionally busy and I was working most evenings and at weekends either in the Office or at home and didn't have time to start playing the Spanish records. But I kept on ringing up personnel to ask for any news of the mysterious Latin American country where the British embassy would shortly need a new commercial officer.*

*Eventually my impatience was rewarded. "Ah, good. Glad you called. I was on the point of asking you to look in at your convenience. We have some good news for you."*

*I hurried down to the Personnel Department and sat down facing the arbiter of my fate across his enormous desk.*

*"We have finally got a definite decision on your posting, Brian. Sorry it's taken so long, but, um, operational delays, you know . . ."*

*"Well?"*

*"We want you to go to Moscow as first secretary (political) and press attaché. Very good job, actually. Key position. Unfortunately they want you as soon as possible, so there won't be a lot of time for briefing and shopping. You'll need lots of warm clothes, of course."*

*"Moscow? First secretary political? I thought you said a commercial job in Latin America?"*

*"Oh, yes, I remember. No, no, we think the Moscow job is much more up your particular street. Much more."*

*"And you said I'd never be a candidate for a top job without experience of commercial work under my belt!"*

*"Oh, my dear chap, you needn't worry about that. We see you as a political animal, first and foremost. Anyway this obsession with commercial work and trade and all that—it's just a passing fad. A successful performance in Moscow will set you up nicely for a terrific next posting. And because of the pressures of Moscow, cold war, intense security, bit of harassment by the KGB, bloody cold winters, all that sort of thing, it's only a two-year posting. Home leave after one year. Professionally very rewarding. You'll enjoy it. Very good people in the embassy, too. We don't take any risks with Moscow. No passengers there. All potential stars. High grade of officer. You'll feel at home."*

*"What about a Russian language course before I go? I'm not one of the people who learned Russian for their national military service. I don't speak a word of it except Tsar and KGB."*

*"Well, that's a start. Afraid there won't be time for a beginner's Russian language course before you go. You'll just have to take Russian lessons after you get there. It won't really matter, you not speaking the language: you'll find all your embassy colleagues speak good Russian and they'll take care of all the work that requires Russian."*

*I was inwardly highly sceptical about this assurance. My scepticism soon proved to be fully justified. For my first six or seven months in Moscow the ambassador's morning meetings and round-ups of the latest issues of* Pravda *and* Izvestiya *and other Soviet journals and newspapers were a nightmare. I would be up at 5 or 6 in the morning every day to collect my batch of the morning's press and to plough through it with a big Russian-English dictionary at my elbow. Eventually I picked up enough Russian to pass the FCO's Intermediate Russian exam. The allowance that this brought with it, along with the Moscow Difficult Post allowance, were a real help in a post where one had to buy and pay in advance for a six-months supply of virtually every domestic item and all the food and drink required for entertaining, from toilet paper to gin (vodka was the one thing that could be bought locally). Everything else had to be imported twice a year and paid for up front from Stockmanns in Helsinki.*

*It was indeed fascinating to spend two busy years working in the headquarters of international communism, especially after four equally busy years in New York, the headquarters of international capitalism. But I still regret having been denied the opportunity to do a proper Russian language course before I went.*

In later years, Adam looked back with a certain nostalgia on the times when the Personnel Department arranged one's postings first, and only then thought up more or less plausible justifications for them. It was largely a lottery, in which one's own preferences played a minimal part, so if a posting turned out to be a bad career move, no blame attached to the officer concerned. In Adam's later years in the Service, when he was beginning to look forward to his first head of mission appointment, the system had changed out of all recognition. A list of postings, grade by grade, was (and is) published regularly, showing timings when a change was due. You could apply for any of them but you were wasting everyone's time if you hadn't checked with Human Resources (formerly Personnel Operations Department) that you would be a credible candidate and whether it would be agreed that the time had come for you to have a move. HR would also tell you whether you faced stiff or negligible competition and whether your CV and record of good annual reports gave you a sporting chance against likely rival applicants. For a posting that involved the crucial promotion from first secretary to counsellor, there was the even more unpredictable and capricious factor: one's performance at the two-day Assessment and Development Centre, the effect of which was to devalue good annual reports sustained over a long period. Adam had been far happier with his old policy of fatalism, letting the Personnel

Department send him wherever they wanted and relying on his lucky star to ensure that even a post which seemed at first glance distinctly unappetizing would turn out on further acquaintance to offer its own rewards, opportunities for job satisfaction, and worthwhile new life experiences.

As Adam's ascent of the diplomatic greasy pole continued, his friends in the Office and later his wife, Eve, began to urge him to think about a future head of mission appointment and to decide where he would like to serve for the first time as an ambassador or high commissioner. He should put in a firm bid with the Administration, they told him, once he had decided what he wanted, before others bolder and more confident than himself attached their SOLD labels to all the plum posts. So Adam, feeling that it was somehow undignified and ran the risk of tempting fate, after anxious hours poring over an atlas with Eve, went to see the Chief Clerk, the then title of the head of the whole administration of the diplomatic service, and pronounced himself actively interested, when the time came, in the post of high commissioner to 'St. Monica,' a pleasant Caribbean island, a member of the Commonwealth, where, to the best of everybody's knowledge, nothing much had happened since the territory's peaceful and uneventful accession to independence a few years earlier.

"You'd die of boredom in St. Monica," the Chief Clerk told him. "Even if you found something going on there to report to London, no one at this end would bother to read it. Very few people, even in the Office, have ever heard of it, frankly. You'd have nothing to do except some sunbathing and snorkelling in daylight hours and a lot of solid drinking in the evenings."

"I can think of worse ways to pass the time," Adam said.

"Even that would pall after the first month, my dear Adam," said the Chief Clerk. "Still, if that's really what you want, we'll pencil you in on the grid—our vast chart of who's going where—for St. Monica. I fancy there'll be quite a list of our colleagues who've already put in bids for the place—mostly dead-beats who only want a quiet life and a nice beach instead of even a hint of professional challenge, quite unlike yourself, I would have thought."

"Well, Eve and I thought that it might be a nice quiet interlude between the hectic crisis-ridden postings I seem to get the rest of the time. Anyway, stick my name down and we'll see what happens. Most grateful, Rufus," said Adam, for it was his old mentor Rufus who had by now risen to the heights of the Office's chief of staff. Soon after this conversation took place, Adam and many of his colleagues in the Service grieved when the historic job name of Chief Clerk was abolished, to be replaced by "Chief Operating Officer," widely seen as a sadly inappropriate title copied from medium-sized business.

In due course, Adam was posted elsewhere, to a job deemed more appropriate to his skills than St. Monica, regarded by the Administration as a kind of safe pre-retirement home for elderly and burned-out diplomats.

However, about the time when the title of Chief Clerk fell victim to the latest crop of historically insensitive management consultants, a bloody rebellion erupted in the hitherto somnolent island of St. Monica in the Caribbean. A group of disaffected local police officers captured and held hostage a number of VIPs attending a meeting in the offices of the Governor-General. Those taken included the island's prime minister, several other ministers, the Governor-General, the chief of police and General Officer Commanding the local defence force, and—not least—the then British high commissioner. When the rebels' ludicrous initial demands were not instantly met, they murdered the prime minister and threatened to murder each of the other hostages, one a day, until they received satisfaction.

In collaboration with the British government and after consultation with the Queen in her capacity as Head of the Commonwealth, a small party of United States marines crossed from Key West in Florida in rubber dinghies, landed on the island at dead of night, broke into the Government House, killed all but two of the rebels and released the remaining hostages, including the British high commissioner. The deputy prime minister, who had escaped his senior colleague's fate by absenting himself from the meeting in order to spend the day on the beach with his mistress, declared himself prime minister and president for life, issued a decree abolishing the St. Monica monarchy and declared the governor-general, as the Queen's representative, *persona non grata*, with an order that he should immediately leave the island. In response, the governor-general declared a state of emergency, announced that the former prime minister's powers would be vested in himself, called on the new "president" to give himself up to such loyal elements in the defence force as he could find, and ordered him to stand trial for high treason. The former Interior Minister, meanwhile, with a small band of supporters, succeeded in gaining control of the island's only broadcasting station from which he issued a number of appeals for calm, appointing a group of non-political and mostly aged local citizens as a caretaker government, and—much to the irritation of the young American ambassador, himself of West Indian descent—invited the British high commissioner to act as a mediator between the various rival groups.

Adam, who but for the grace of God and the Chief Clerk might have been the British high commissioner in St. Monica when this bedlam had erupted, followed these dramatic events with avid interest. He rang up the former Chief Clerk, now "Chief Operating Officer" of the Diplomatic Service, to enquire whether their colleague, the dead-beat sent to St. Monica as high commissioner to enjoy a quiet life until retirement, was managing to get in any snorkelling.

"Oh," said Rufus cheerfully, "he's risen splendidly to the challenge, much to everyone's surprise. He's taken complete charge, everyone's doing exactly what he tells them to, the violence has ended, and he's drawing up a new democratic constitution with himself as temporary constitution monitor with full powers. For a while we were sending him a lot of complicated instructions on what he should do, but either he never received them or else he's ignoring them, so we're letting him get on with it."

"So he didn't die of boredom, then."

"Ha!" barked Rufus. "I'll say he didn't. Amazing *what diplomats do* these days, don't you think?"

"Amazing," Adam agreed.

## NOTES

1. Whitehall is shorthand for government departments in London and the civil servants who work in them. It used to be said that the civil servants played from 10 to 5, like the fountains in Trafalgar Square (at the top of Whitehall itself). Nowadays most civil servants, and certainly diplomats, work a much longer day than that.

2. Michael Foot was leader of the Labour party from 1980 to 1983.

# 5

# LIFE OVERSEAS

*Getting to know the host country outside the capital; pleasures, risks and pains; recording and reporting. Big posts and small, well-known countries and the more obscure.*

Adam was well placed to recognise the enormous differences between diplomatic life in a big post in a rich developed country on the one hand, and life in a much smaller embassy in a poor, developing country on the other. He had served as a senior political officer in the vast embassy in Washington, D.C., capital of a country of absorbing interest to every part of his government at home in Britain; and he had served in the tiny British embassy in 'Côte Noire' in French-speaking west Africa, normally a place of negligible relevance to British interests and one of which the great majority of Adam's fellow citizens had never heard—until events in 2012–2013, long after the end of Adam's posting there, propelled its neighbouring country Mali onto the front pages of the western world.

In great, famous, and rich countries as in obscure, poor, and little known countries, it's the job of diplomats in the capital to familiarise themselves with the country as a whole, often radically different outside the capital city from the city itself. Adam, serving in 'Cameko,' the capital of Côte Noire, did several tours up-country, meeting local chiefs and other dignitaries, discovering what economic activity there was beyond Cameko, listening to local opinion of the Côte Noire government and its ruling party, hearing the often caustic views of local people about the situation across the border in Mali, getting a first-hand impression of the prevalence of Islam in the north as distinct from the Christian and animist sects to which most southerners belonged, and assessing the likely implications of this divide—which Adam discovered was common to many west African countries, including huge and influential Nigeria along the coast. Some of the tour reports he sent home to the FCO during this time proved invaluable a few years later when Islamist fundamentalist rebels, including al-Qaeda elements driven out of Libya after the fall of the Gaddafi régime, seized control of much of the north of neighbouring Mali, which closely resembled "Côte Noire" both ethnically and geographically. The rebellion threatened the rest of Mali, including the capital, Bamako, with anti-western Islamization, in a development that could easily have spread to Côte Noire and the rest of west Africa, and precipitating a significant military intervention in Mali by the French Socialist Party government with considerable logistic support from Britain.

All this was in the future when Adam was touring northern Côte Noire in an unreliable embassy Land Rover with a young Côte Noirien driver and an even younger third secretary, newly arrived at the embassy, in the back seat. The Land Rover's roof-rack carried eight jerry-cans full of petrol or drinking water lashed to it, along with a tent, tow-rope, spare tires, a machete, and cooking utensils. Inside the vehicle were a comprehensive first aid kit and a primitive radio set with a headset and microphone. This permitted sporadic contact at pre-arranged times with the embassy in Cameko.

Adam had not yet gone home on his mid-tour leave from Côte Noire and it had never occurred to him that when he did, he would meet the woman of his dreams, providentially named Eve, marry her in what his friends at home insisted on describing as "a whirlwind romance," and bring her back with him to Cameko for what had to count as their honeymoon, to live together as man and wife till death did them part, but not immediately, they hoped. Even if Adam had already married Eve when he set off on his tour, however, she would not have been able to accompany him up-country at public expense: that privilege, he was to learn later, was generally reserved for heads of mission, i.e., ambassadors and high commissioners.

Once Adam and his party were outside Cameko the roads rapidly deteriorated into rough tracks, sometimes flooded in muddy water after recent rains, the Land Rover bumping unsteadily over rocks and tree roots protruding from the surface. One area that the little expedition had to pass through was notorious for armed robbers preying on cars, buses, and trucks carrying supplies to the north or bringing peasants south in search of work in the city. Adam was frequently stopped at police road-blocks whose piratical gendarmes, fingers on revolver or tommy-gun triggers, would try to search the Land Rover, until the driver explained in the local dialect that his passengers were important British diplomats and that there would be serious trouble for the police if they violated the immunity from search which a diplomatic vehicle enjoyed. Sometimes it was impossible to distinguish between police road-blocks and bases for armed robbers (who were often indeed the same people, armed with the same weapons).

Before long the tropical vegetation along the track began to get more brown and less green, with patches of sand replacing earth and grasses. This was the beginning of the Sahara desert.

Adam and his two companions usually managed to find a local "hotel" in which to spend the night, even if the hotel comprised no more than a central shed and a few shacks dotted about nearby, each containing a primitive bed, a lantern, and not much more. Once Adam had to drive a camel from inside his shack before he could get out his "pyjamas" (a tracksuit), mosquito net, insect repellent, and water bottle containing warm drinking water from Cameko. They ate stews produced by the hotel cook, made from probably unmentionable ingredients, and supplemented them with bananas and mangoes. If they were lucky, they were able to buy small bottles of locally produced Orangina or fizzy lemonade. If all else failed, they could always fall back on tins of corned beef and sardines which they had brought from Cameko. Local bread was usually plentiful and palatable. They stocked up again whenever they passed through a small local market, often sporting old-fashioned television sets and even washing machines alongside the stacks of yams, cassava, melons, oranges, pawpaw, and bananas. Further north the food markets thinned out and they began to see desert-style bazaars offering a strange variety of goods. Once they came across a small group of Bedouin coming south out of the desert, leading their haughty camels, and the group's leaders, straight out of Lawrence of Arabia, offered Adam and his two companions a drink of camel's milk out of gaily decorated wineskins. Adam had no plans for venturing far into the northern Côte Noire desert but he was on the lookout for evidence of desertification relentlessly encroaching on more fertile mid-Côte Noire.

Adam's courtesy calls on local dignitaries were curiously formal affairs. The great local chief, surrounded by his counsellors and other attendants, would receive Adam, the third secretary, and the Côte Noirien driver from a kind of throne at the end of a long wicker hut. The visitors would be told to sit down in red velvet-covered opera house chairs at right angles to their host. Adam would introduce himself and the other two as representatives of the great Queen of England beyond the seas, claiming to bring Her Majesty's fraternal greetings to the chief. The latter would deliver a long and mostly unintelligible speech in reply, parts of which the Côte Noirien driver would translate into French for Adam. Bottles of warm Orangina would then be pressed on the three guests, and the chief and his attendants would then rise from their seats and shake Adam warmly by the hand, indicating that the audience was over. Further north there was no tradition of local chiefs and rulers among the mainly nomadic desert population.

Often Adam, with the help of his driver, would at this point identify one of the chief's advisers who spoke either English or, more often, French, and with whom Adam would be able to have a sometimes informative and revealing conversation about local problems and preoccupations, potential grist for his eventual tour report, before the three travellers returned to the Land Rover (which had been guarded by heavily armed village police during the audience with the chief). They stowed away in the Land Rover the ceremonial gifts bestowed on them by their host—primitive wood carvings of strange distorted human figures, a bronze or brass medallion, a ceremonial spear, occasionally a CD of songs by a once-famous French *chansonnier* (Mouloudji, French of Algerian origin, a special favourite). In return Adam would have presented his host with a small framed portrait of The Queen or of Diana, Princess of Wales, at the time venerated throughout west Africa as a kind of secular saint with supernatural powers.

**As an example:**

*As British high commissioner in Nigeria I saw it as essential to visit all parts of this vast and disparate country, usually with my wife, if I was to have a grasp of the interrelationship between the major tribes, and between the major tribes and the local minority groups; between the traditional rulers, mostly instinctively conservative, anxious to preserve their prestige and influence, and the often radical, modern, elected politicians who wielded real power in local government councils and provincial and state parliaments. Visits to local Big Men, wealthy businessmen who liked to be able to boast of having* entertained the British high commissioner, were also de rigueur. We were entertained to lunch by one of these in one of the Mid-Western States, who had no problem about impressing us with his wealth (and, just as importantly, his honorary title of Chief). He owned a medium-sized airline and a raft of other profitable enterprises, many of them indirectly connected with Nigeria's immense oil industry, most of whose profits leaked invisibly and untraceably away into the dense undergrowth of bribery, corruption, venality, and nepotism, although we had no evidence that our generous host, the Chief, was involved with any such illegality.

Our first obligation, on visits such as this, was to ensure that our excellent Nigerian driver, with whom we spent so many profitable hours on the road all over southern Nigeria as well as in Lagos (still at that time the federal capital), had somewhere comfortable to have a rest from driving while we were being entertained by "the Chief," and above all that he, too, was given some lunch and something to drink. The Chief and his acolytes were reluctant to do anything for this fellow countryman of theirs, arguing that he would be quite all right sitting in our high commission armoured Land Rover on his own, unfed and unwatered, until we were ready to leave. My wife had to threaten to refuse to enter the Chief's palatial house until she was satisfied that our driver was properly looked after. She wasn't bluffing, either.

Once we were inside, the Chief explained apologetically that he and his staff were preparing for the imminent wedding of one of his sons. This would be a very grand occasion, to be spread over a whole week and attended by three or four thousand guests. Part of the jollifi-cations would take place in the huge garage where the family's seven cars—a Rolls, a Mercedes, an Aston Martin, a Range Rover, etc.— were normally kept. All the cars had been found alternative temporary homes, but the only place they could find for the smallest, some kind of racy soft-topped sports car, was inside the spacious main dining-room where we would be having our lunch. The Chief hoped we would excuse this discourtesy. We assured him that eating lunch alongside a parked car would cause us no discomfiture at all. After several glasses of French vintage champagne (at that time a prohibited import in Nigeria) in the principal drawing-room, served with enough fancy canapés to feed half the Nigerian army for a week, we were led into the dining-room for lunch, and there, parked inconspicuously in a corner at the back of the room, was a full-size silver-painted sports car. Alongside it was parked a half-sized, fully functional miniature car which, it transpired, the 12-year-old youngest son of the Chief drove, *unaccompanied, to get around the family estate and to go into the village down the road for shopping and to meet his friends.*

*Nearly all the food served at the lunch had been flown in that morning from Harrods Food Hall in London, not specially in our honour—such flights bearing delicacies for the Chief's table took place, we learned, three times a week. The Harrods food was washed down, needless to say, by vintage French wines, also flown in by a well-known, long established London wine merchant. The Chief owned a house in Mayfair which he used on his frequent visits to Britain, and which was also used as a London* pied-à-terre *by one of the Chief's sons who was at Oxford and by another who was still at school at Harrow. The Chief himself was to all intents and purposes illiterate. We knew he had several daughters but they were never mentioned. We never met his wife.*

*We learned something about Nigeria from this visit, but gained no insights into local political or economic affairs. Our questions on such matters were politely fended off, and the conversation was steered smoothly back to the ways in which the Chief had devised to spend his fortune.*

Expeditions outside the capital during Adam's posting in Washington, D.C. were, not surprisingly, very different from going on tour in Côte Noire. There was no need for familiarisation visits to surrounding states such as Virginia or Maryland: one only had to read the local newspapers, watch television, or simply ask one's American friends what was going on in those areas, or indeed in any other part of the huge United States. In any case, in all the major cities of the United States away from Washington, D.C. there were experienced, senior British diplomats serving as Consuls-General, some with sizeable staffs, mainly involved in promoting British exports and American inward investment into Britain and also sending fortnightly reports on the political situations in their enormous areas to the British embassy in Washington, where one of Adam's duties was to collate them, clear up any queries in correspondence with their authors, and send a digest of them to the FCO in London. Moreover, Adam found it much easier to pick up political gossip containing occasional nuggets of valuable information inside the Beltway than on any visit to Charleston, South Carolina, or some small town in Delaware. Instead, visits outside Washington would generally be for a specific purpose: to deliver an after-dinner speech about U.S.-UK relations to a group of Elks in Baltimore who had sent a pressing invitation to the ambassa-

dor, or to visit a prominent local person of British origin who was dying
in a local hospital, or to present some award to another local celebrity, or
to visit the editor of an influential local newspaper or television or radio
station for an interview. Adam found from experience that prudence required him to prepare himself very fully for these interviews: some of the
interviewers could be as aggressive as any Paxman or Humphrys,[1] evidently keen to impress their local readers or listeners by humiliating the
no doubt pompous and patronizing visiting Briton from the embassy.
Sometimes Adam would arrive with his briefcase stuffed with briefs on
any political issue that could possibly be raised with him, only to find that
the interviewer was solely interested in teasing him about the respective
merits of the local baseball team and the Washington Nationals (of whom
any visitor from D.C. was assumed to be an ardent supporter—in fact,
Adam had been to only one baseball game in his life).

Any visit of this kind provided useful insights into American provincial life and attitudes, but none of them was as valuable and informative
as shadowing a Presidential or Senatorial candidate during an election
campaign—one or other of which occurred every two years. Adam
learned that the embassy's practice was to assign a member of the political staff to each of the main candidates at election time. This meant
accompanying them on their battle-buses and chartered aeroplanes and
special trains, mingling with the press pack also shadowing the candidate,
getting to know him or her personally and also making a point of establishing a relationship with the candidate's chief of staff, press secretary,
and other influential advisers as they flew or rode around their states and
Congressional districts campaigning for votes. The purpose of this ar-
rangement was not, or not mainly, to enable the embassy to forecast
accurately and in advance the result of the election and its implication for
British interests: such crystal-gazing was rarely successful and even more
rarely useful for policy-makers at home. The intention rather was to ensure that whoever won each major election would already have a personal
(and hopefully friendly) relationship with at least one senior member of
the British embassy, who would also be able to pick up his telephone at
any time and be sure of getting straight through to the successful politician's senior staffers. It was, in other words, an investment.

For the election that took place during Adam's time in Washington,
Adam was assigned to a Maryland Senator of many years' standing who
was running once again for re-election. This Senator had been allocated

to Adam because Adam already knew him as an occasional contact. He had first met him when they were both guests at a lunch given by the Dutch ambassador in honour of a visiting Dutch minister, and they had had a conversation in which the Senator, trusting the discretion of a British diplomat, had spoken with appalling frankness of some of his Senatorial colleagues and their often imaginative extramural activities. They had met again at the French National Day reception on the 14th of July, and this time the Senator had talked extraordinarily openly about the political situation in the Republican party, the role of religion in the right wing of the party, and the emerging presidential ambitions of two or three Republican leaders (admitting that he himself harboured such hopes if he was re-elected to the Senate in the elections taking place later in the year).

Accompanying his Senator and his entourage as they toured Maryland in search of re-election was for Adam a fascinating and in some ways a disillusioning experience. Senior Senators such as this were rightly treated with a respect verging on reverence; they acquired a gravitas and authority which seemed to make them more statesmen than politicians. Yet as he talked to the Senator, his chief of staff and his press secretary, and to the newspaper and television reporters covering the campaign, Adam became increasingly aware of the often grubby horse-trading and dealing in favours that were clearly the price of support for the Senator's candidature for re-election from influential local figures—mayors of the main cities, radio shock jocks, and grave commentators on current affairs, the Chairman of the local Republican party and the state's Congressmen. Even some of these who might have been expected automatically to support their party's candidate for one of the state's two Senate seats would turn out to have discreetly demanded a price for their support in promised favours from the Senator, then or after he had been safely returned to office.

Many of these secret deals, and gossip with the Senator and his staffers on the campaign bus, plane, or train after a public meeting and press conference, provided Adam with extraordinary insights into the internal disputes and personality feuds within the GOP, together with indications of the likely direction of policy development depending on whose political star was rising and whose was declining, all useful material to be reported in summary to London and then stored in the embassy archives for re-use at the time of the next presidential election.

Adam had heard it said that there was no role for diplomats in reporting American politics because ministers at home could get all the information and expert comment they could possibly need by reading the *New York Times* and the *Washington Post* with their detailed factual reporting and commentary columns by distinguished and well-connected analysts, compared with whom the embassy's diplomats could be regarded with some justice as amateurs and outsiders. Adam knew, though, from personal experience that American politicians and their staffers would talk much more openly to British (and a few other) diplomats whom they trusted not to speak or write publicly of what they had been told, and who might later prove useful contacts leading to invitations to the British ambassador's dining table.

Fascinated by politics from an early age, Adam loved the entrée into the U.S. political scene provided by his diplomatic embassy status, rejoicing that he was actually being paid for what in a different world he would gladly have spent good money to be allowed to do. To talk on notionally equal terms with national and international leaders who were household names to anyone with even the most superficial interest in international affairs was a rare and special privilege. Adam felt the same about the opportunity for adventurous touring in northern Mali, far from Bamako and even further away from sophisticated Washington, D.C. He reflected that variety was indeed the spice of diplomatic life, and that versatility was one of the job skills which that life demanded. Now that he was married to Eve (since halfway through his posting in Côte Noire) and shared his life with her in Washington, his one regret was that she couldn't be with him as he travelled up and down the length and breadth of Maryland, and sometimes beyond, shadowing the candidate on whose campaign he had been commissioned to report. Each night when he was on the road with the Senator's travelling circus he would telephone Eve, imagining her relaxing in front of the television or reading a book in their comfortable home in D.C., to give her a racy account of the scandals, revelations, farces, and adventures of the day. "I wish I could be there, too," Eve would say wistfully each night, before they swapped exhortations to sleep well, and reluctantly hung up.

**As an example:**

*As British high commissioner in Australia, representing a Conservative government in Britain in its dealings with an Australian Labor Party (ALP) federal government of Australia in Canberra, I was invar-*

*iably and necessarily careful not to betray any hint of my own left-of-centre leanings. Even when defending UK government policies with which I privately disagreed or even occasionally deplored, I was at pains to conceal my personal opinions when talking to senior Australian ministers and officials, putting the best possible spin on my government's policies, opinions, and objectives. But I never had to assert that these policies and views were my own; to be trusted by the government to which he's accredited, a diplomat must as far as humanly possible avoid ever telling a deliberate lie, contrary to the common perception of What Diplomats Do. The success or failure of every diplomat, especially of the ambassador or high commissioner, depends to a perhaps surprising degree on his—or in particular her—ability to establish personal relations of trust and confidence with ministers and officials of the host government as well as with other opinion-formers and decision-makers in every local walk of life. An ambassador who can never bring himself to say anything definite and clear, or who avoids commenting on anything until he has referred it back to his government for instructions, will soon acquire a reputation as someone not worth talking to or confiding in. An ambassador suspected of gossiping indiscreetly about official matters and personalities will not be entrusted with the private confidences that are essential to his ability to report with insight to his government on the affairs of the country where he is serving. Above all, an ambassador or any other diplomat who is caught out telling deliberate untruths to his host government, or to the local media or to other figures of authority and power, will not be trusted thereafter to tell the truth, however embarrassing. His relationship with those whose trust and confidence in him are essential if he's to do his job effectively will have been irreparably undermined. The popular image of a diplomat as someone who is a suave professional deceiver and manipulator of the truth is far wide of the mark. The diplomat speaks frankly and accurately on his government's behalf; his private opinions are irrelevant and he has no need to air them.*

*So I was gratified to find, shortly before the end of my tour of duty in Australia and my retirement from the diplomatic service, that my professional loyalty to my own government had been successful in keeping my own private political prejudices out of sight. At a lunch given in my wife's and my honour before we left Australia for the last time, I allowed the mask to slip a little by mentioning casually to our host, Gareth Evans,[2] the fiery left-wing Australian foreign minister at the time (whom I had got to know pretty well during my three years as high commissioner) that many years ago when an undergraduate I had been the elected Chairman—at a time when a Chair was still an inanimate object—of the University Labour Club. The foreign minister was astounded.*

*"You mean you were a Labour supporter, Brian?"*

*I said I thought that Evans, himself a graduate of Oxford University, knew that the chair of the Oxford or Cambridge Labour Club could safely be assumed to support the Labour party, and indeed that party membership was a required qualification for candidates seeking election to the club's chairmanship.*

*"Good God," exclaimed Gareth Evans. "I always assumed that senior British diplomats were dyed-in-the-wool reactionary Tories. How on earth did they let you in to the public service when you were a bleeding heart socialist?"*

*I explained that I had convinced the selection boards and interviewers that I recognised the obligation of public servants to subordinate their personal political views to those of the elected ministers for whom they worked, and that I had expressed confidence that I would be able to do this.*

*"Well, well. So all this time you were One of Us, and we never knew it," Evans said, a trifle ruefully.*

*I told him, truthfully, that I took this as a compliment whose memory I would treasure.*

Adam and his new bride returned to London for six weeks of well-earned home leave at the end of their posting to Côte Noire. Peter and Nora, two of their oldest friends (Eve had been at both school and university with Nora, and Adam had known Peter from university), asked them round to supper soon after they got home, along with three or four other mutual friends and a couple whom Adam and Eve had not met before.

"Are we allowed to ask you two distinguished people what life was like in—what's the place called?" asked Nora as they sat down to supper.

"Côte Noire," Eve said. "I must admit I'd never heard of it either until I met Adam. But why should you need permission to ask us about it?"

"Well," Nora said, "I assume it was all hush-hush. You know, Official Secrets Act. You probably aren't allowed to tell us what you were really up to out there."

"Why should you think that?" Adam laughed. "There was nothing remotely secret about what we were doing there. I was an ordinary British diplomat in a small embassy in a quite interesting country in west Africa, that's all. As for what Eve may have got up to, you'll have to ask her. But I'm sure it wasn't secret."

"You realise, Adam," said Peter, "that we're all unshakeably convinced that you're some kind of spy and just using this diplomat business as cover."

"Why on earth would you think that? If I was a spy, or more accurately an intelligence officer, which I take it is what you mean, they'd hardly send me to Côte Noire, now would they? Why would we want to spy on Côte Noire? If for some unfathomable reason we wanted to know the deepest secrets of the Côte Noire government, we'd just ask the French."

"Well, obviously if you were a spy—sorry, an intelligence officer—you wouldn't be allowed to tell us, would you? The more you deny it, the more you confirm our suspicions."

"You can believe what you like," Adam said, beginning to be irritated. "I've nothing to do with collecting that kind of secret intelligence. It's not something I want to talk about, but strictly between ourselves, secret intelligence can be an invaluable tool for avoiding misunderstandings, and misunderstandings can easily lead to bad and dangerous decisions. Don't knock it. It's basically no different from any other kind of 'intelligence'—which only really means information. "

"Don't worry, Adam, we won't give you away."

Adam studied his plate, lips pursed. This conversation was going nowhere.

"But do tell us all about this country that no one's ever heard of," Nora pleaded. "Now we know it's not secret after all. Eve, what's it really like, being in an embassy? What was the ambassador like? Did you have to suck up to him the whole time? Or was it a her?"

Eve tried to explain that it was probably no different from being in any other embassy. You had to treat the ambassador and his wife with proper respect, just as you would treat the President of the company you worked for with proper respect. "And the ambassador is the personal representative of the Queen, don't forget," she added. "You respect the person who's there representing your head of state, don't you?"

The man whom they hadn't met before gave a sceptical snort. "I wouldn't respect him if he turned out to be a stupid old git."

Eve said, a little too pompously, "You respect his office as an ambassador, whatever you think of him as a person. Actually our ambassador in Côte Noire is rather a sweetie. We all got on quite well, luckily for us."

"But you're still not telling us about your lives in Côte What's-its-name, Adam," Nora complained. "Come on, sing for your supper! Why do you think we asked you both to supper?"

"All right," Adam said. He began to describe Cameko: the damp heat, the lush vegetation, the mosquitoes, the little children with bare feet playing in the dust on the edge of the market; the stacks of tropical fruit in front of the market stalls with the shrewd market women shrilly but good-humouredly urging them to buy; the rocky earth tracks that served as roads, their pot-holes hard to pick out from the front of the Land Rover when the holes were full of brown muddy water during the rains; the gaudy costumes of the priests as they slowly walked in procession to the church; the even gaudier tropical birds, uttering angry squawks . . .

Adam realised that he had lost his audience. Their eyes had begun to glaze over as he tried to describe this exotic, unimaginable place, so far from the experience of anyone else in the room. He stopped in mid-sentence.

There was an embarrassed silence. After a while, Peter said: "Thanks, Adam, I think we get the general picture. We've all read our Graham Greene. I think we're more interested in what you and Eve used to do, rather than hearing a lecture about the fauna and flora."

Adam could see that he and Eve were being invited to talk about their experiences in Africa out of politeness. No one was really that much interested. They would be mightily relieved when the conversation was allowed to go back to London property prices, how the Labour party was doing in the latest opinion polls, and the new Alan Bennett play at the National Theatre, subjects on which all of them could—and certainly would—have an opinion.

"We did what diplomats do, I suppose," Adam said, as a way of putting an end to this particular conversation.

"The trouble is," said Nora, "none of us has the foggiest idea what diplomats do, apart from sipping cocktails at interminable drinks parties and smoking Russian cigarettes in long black cigarette holders."

"And passing round the Ferrero Rocher chocolates," Peter added. "Come on, drink up, everyone; there's plenty more of this Australian plonk in the kitchen. All must go."

With almost tangible relief, they started talking with intense serious-ness about the rival merits and defects of Chilean wine as compared with the Australian red that they were drinking. Côte Noire was never mentioned again, and no one asked Adam to describe what diplomats do.

## NOTES

1.  Jeremy Paxman and John Humphrys are British television and radio presenters respectively for prominent current affairs programs, famous for their aggressive and sceptical interviewing techniques.

2.  After leaving office as Australian Foreign Minister, Gareth Evans was Co-chair with Mohamed Sahnoun of the International Commission on Intervention and State Sovereignty which produced the report, *Responsibility to Protect,* in 2001. It was commissioned by the Canadian government and represented a development of international law of great potential importance.

# 6

# MULTILATERAL DIPLOMACY

"The question is," said Alice, "whether you can make words mean so many different things."

"The question is," said Humpty Dumpty, "which is to be master, that's all."

—Lewis Carroll, *Through the Looking-Glass* (1872) ch. 6

*Diplomats in Conference. Dealing with other diplomats and the Secretariat, as distinct from a host government; learning the interrelatedness of issues; drafting and negotiating resolutions and documents.*

Adam was always grateful to have had a short spell, early in his career, in a multilateral post—the United Kingdom Mission (delegation) to the United Nations in New York. A multilateral post is neither an embassy nor a high commission but a national delegation to a permanent conference, dealing with all the subjects with which the conference is concerned but not accredited to any specific foreign country or government. Adam was working in the United States but not tasked to report on U.S. affairs. He was a member of the section of the UK Mission dealing with Security Council matters, which invariably kept the British delegation to the UN busy, Britain being one of the five permanent members of the Council, together with the United States, France, China, and Russia, and thus one of the five with the power of veto under the United Nations Charter.

Adam was struck, very soon after his arrival in the mission, by two things which he suspected distinguished this multilateral diplomacy post from the majority of ordinary embassies and high commissions accredited to a single country: first, that the pace of the work was constantly hectic, with new problems blowing up in everyone's faces all the time; and secondly, that the calibre of his mission colleagues seemed to be universally and strikingly high. A slow learner, one who prized lengthy consideration above spontaneity, reluctant to say anything publicly without a carefully prepared script, would simply get left behind, overtaken by the remorseless rush of events.

Another feature of life and work at the UN was the need to familiarise yourself early on with the main tribal links and fissures between the member states: why Country X was always at loggerheads with Country Y, while Country A could almost always be relied on to support Country B. The reasons could be historical, cultural, linguistic, or even sometimes a matter of personalities. But in judging one's ability to gather support for a proposed new initiative in a UN Committee, or to put together a large enough alliance to defeat some harmful move by an adversary, it was vital to know which was the most influential African country to bring on board—because that delegation would bring a dozen other African votes with it; and which Latin American country would never agree to support you because its Latin American enemy was already on your side. These factors, Adam soon realised, tended to apply regardless of the specific issue at stake. The majority of UN member states had no particular national interest in most of the problems and crises that came before the Security Council or other UN bodies: they would either automatically follow the rest of their geographical group in deciding how to vote, or else make it clear that they were open to some quiet horse-trading: "I'll support you on this if you'll promise to support me next week in the vote on the border between Ruritania and Ozymandia." Many delegations were left on a very loose rein by their governments in their national capitals. Except on really major global issues, many could be persuaded to vote one way or the other by a friendly conversation in the Delegates' Dining Room or over a drink at a big boisterous buffet supper given by a second secretary in the delegation of a country of the utmost obscurity.

Adam's arrival at the Mission coincided with one of many crises in the middle east, marked by fighting between Israeli and Syrian forces and a partial occupation of the Gaza area of Palestine by the Israelis. Reading up on the FCO briefs for the Mission, Adam found confirmation of a situation familiar to anyone who had read the newspapers over the past two or three decades: each side, Israelis as well as the Arabs and the Iranians, had genuine grievances against the other, the Israelis because of low-level but relentless rocket attacks against Israeli territory from Gaza, as well as periodic infiltration into Israel of suicide bombers from Syria and Lebanon; the Arabs because of what they claimed was disproportionately savage military retaliation by the Israelis, and the steadily expanding Israeli settlements on the Palestinians' side of Israel's unofficial border with the West Bank.

The Mission's briefs had been broadly agreed beforehand in capitals with the United States and French governments, both also Permanent Members, and with the Germans who were at the time elected, nonpermanent members of the Council. Britain's objectives in the sudden flare-up of violence were to bring about an immediate and unconditional cease-fire; to be followed by a resumption of Arab-Israeli talks designed to work out concessions by both sides that could lead to a long-term settlement. Among the ingredients of the settlement envisaged in the briefs from London, Israel would be recognised by the Arabs as a permanent state within secure borders, in exchange for Israeli recognition of a Palestinian state and Israeli withdrawal from the illegal West Bank settlements, subject to any mutually agreed land swaps—the Arabs acquiring areas of Israeli territory in exchange for Israel retaining an equivalent area of the West Bank.

Soon after settling into a spacious apartment on the upper east side of Manhattan, rented for Mission officers by the UK Mission administration department, Adam, by now a first secretary, accompanied one of the Mission's senior counsellors, Rob Fellowes, on a series of calls on Arab Missions to discuss possible ways to end the fighting. This, Adam was told, was better done below the level of the respective Permanent Representatives (the Ambassadors who headed their Missions) since in lower-level talks the participants would be better able to explore options and fly trial balloons without initially committing their governments to anything. Adam was accompanying Rob principally to keep a record of what was said, but he was also encouraged by Rob to chip in with any thoughts or suggestions of his own, provided that any such contributions to the discussions didn't depart too far from the UK objectives as laid down in the briefs from London.

Rob and Adam went first to the offices near the UN of the UN Mission of the rich and influential Muslim Arab country 'Abudhara,' where they were received by the Abudharan number two, himself accompanied by a more junior Abudharan officer introduced as Mohammed. As the four men settled down round the table in the Abudharan Mission conference room, and Mohammed produced and distributed small cups of strong sweet black coffee to each of them, Mohammed murmured to Adam that he was delighted to meet him as he had himself been to Leicester University in Britain reading for a Master's degree in Diplomatic Studies with his professor, the leading academic expert on the subject, who had remained one of his many good British friends. The discussions between the two principals went along generally predictable lines, both sides agreeing on the need for an immediate cease-fire but neither having much idea about how the Israeli and Arab combatants could be persuaded either to observe a cease-fire which they feared would give their adversary an advantage, or to resume talks on a long-term settlement.

The Abudharan number two was pessimistic. There were, he confessed, extremist elements especially in Syria, Iraq, and Iran, as well as other Muslim countries, who would never agree to accept the permanent existence of a Jewish state on what they regarded "with some justification" as land forcibly stolen from the Arab Palestinian people with the active encouragement of the British and some other western powers. Such people would never agree to a two-state solution, whatever they might say now. The only hope was to persuade their governments to be more conciliatory and more ready to accept mutual compromise in the cause of peace, and to exercise strict control over dissident activity in their own populations. This, the Abudharan argued, would inevitably mean the suspension for a considerable time of progress to democracy in the countries concerned. Opponents of recognition of Israel as part of any conceivable settlement could not be allowed the freedom of expression and political organisation that Britain and the west would no doubt demand for them. Otherwise they would end up by undermining any settlement. Would Britain be willing to accept that any peace settlement would necessarily entail the continuation of authoritarian regimes across the middle east (including Abudhara, no doubt, Adam guessed)? Adam concentrated on taking notes of the conversation between the two principals and made no comments of his own.

As the discussion ended and Rob and Adam got up to leave for their next appointment (at the Jordanian Mission), Mohammed asked, shaking hands with Adam, whether Adam would be free for lunch in the UN building with him and a couple of his friends from other Missions the following day. Adam accepted the invitation enthusiastically: he was anxious to make potentially useful contacts without delay. In multilateral diplomacy there was little or no point in making contacts among the local indigenous (i.e., American) population, other than for purely social and personal reasons. The main contacts of professional value would be with the members of other missions, with the UN secretariat (who exercised considerable influence on UN decisions and processes) and to a limited extent with the international press corps covering UN affairs.

The following day, Adam found Mohammed already installed at a table for four in the Delegates' Dining Room at the UN. They were soon joined by first secretaries from the U.S. and Lebanese Missions, both also at Mohammed's invitation. In deference to the two Muslims' practices, the four drank only iced water, but all of them ate heartily and with relish. Their conversation was animated and at times emotional, but inevitably inconclusive. It became clear at the end that by unwritten UN convention the four lunchers would "go Dutch," each paying an equal share of the total cost of the lunches. And they agreed that in principle they would meet again at least once a month for strictly informal, off-the-record discussions of current Security Council issues.

Adam was happy to find that the conversation over lunch was more relaxed and informal than that at the Abudharan Mission the previous day. Mohammed had spoken even more openly than his senior colleague in his discussion with Rob about the obstacles to concessions, including unwillingness in some powerful quarters to accept the permanent existence of a Jewish state "in Palestine": if ever this resistance was to be overcome, the Arabs would need strong support and help from their western friends. The Americans especially, he argued, would have to move into a much more neutral position, moderating their current virtually unconditional support for Israel, which merely encouraged Israeli obstinacy and belligerence. It was clear to Adam that Mohammed was delivering an official prepared message from the Abudharans to the American first secretary and to himself, although Mohammed repeatedly claimed to be speaking "entirely personally."

In reply, the first secretary from the United States Mission pointed out that public opinion in the United States, by no means exclusively among Jewish Americans, was strongly committed to the defence of Israel and its survival as a Jewish state and that this was unlikely to change in the foreseeable future. Nevertheless the U.S. government was equally strongly committed to an eventual peaceful settlement between Israel and its Arab and other Muslim neighbours under which each side, including a new Palestine state, would recognise the other's right to exist within secure borders. The Americans, he stressed, would continue to work for such a settlement which would be as much in the interests of the Arab states as in Israel's. A U.S. guarantee of that settlement was generally recognised, if only tacitly, to be essential to international confidence in it.

Adam had discussed with Rob before leaving the UK Mission for the UN the line he might take at the lunch and Rob had agreed, without much enthusiasm, that Adam might speculate "on a purely personal basis" about the possible abandonment of the "two-state solution" encapsulated in the celebrated Security Council Resolution 242 of 1967,[1] long regarded as the bottom line of any eventual settlement. Adam accordingly suggested to his three lunch companions that if and when a two-state solution came to be generally recognised as beyond reach, it would become necessary to consider instead a single loose federation of Israel and Palestine under a single sovereignty, with internationally backed guarantees for the rights and security of the Jewish and Arab sections of the population and a single power-sharing federal government of the whole country. Adam pointed out that a solution on these lines was already being discussed in academic circles and in the think-tanks.

This proved to be a bridge too far for the other three, who all expressed scepticism about the chances of any such international U-turn, anyway in the foreseeable future. Adam stressed that he had merely been thinking aloud, as a newcomer to the UN scene, and that his government had absolutely no current intention of embarking on such a radical change of policy. Nevertheless he said he personally believed that events in the future might eventually force the governments concerned to recognise that the obstacles to a two-state solution, including Israeli demographics and the inveterate hostility of wide sections of Muslim opinion to the existence of a Jewish state on Arab soil, were simply insuperable, and that if the Israeli Jews were to have any chance of living in their current homeland on a permanent basis, some sort of federal alternative would eventually have to be devised. He was met by more raised eye-brows and no more comments. But he had the feeling that what he had said would be reported back by the other three to their Permanent Representatives and perhaps by them to their capitals, if only as an indication that the new

British first secretary was a bit of a loose cannon, but also, probably, with some speculation that he might have been testing the temperature of the water on instructions from London. Anyway, it might have planted a seed. . . . He would discuss with Rob later how much, if any, of the lunch-time discussion and Adam's contribution to it he should report to London.

### As an example:

*It was at the United Nations in the 1960s. Spain was still under a fascist régime led by the infamous Generalissimo Franco. Britain was locked in an interminable quarrel with Spain over the status of Gibraltar, then as now a British colony. Spain's claim to sovereignty over the Rock was based on—*

- *the commitment of the United Nations to universal decolonisation,*
- *the provision in the Treaty of Utrecht (1713) under which, if ever Britain gave up sovereignty over Gibraltar, Spain would have the option of resuming its sovereignty over the Rock (Spain claimed this would come into effect the moment that Gibraltar was "decolon-ised" as required by the UN), and*
- *the argument that Britain could not legally seize a piece of Spanish sovereign land, plant on it a group of British settlers, and grant them the right to self-determination.*

*Britain pointed out that—*

- *it had acquired permanent sovereignty over Gibraltar under a treaty that was still valid,*
- *Britain had not "planted" its own citizens as settlers on the Rock— they were of diverse national origins and many had been there for several generations.*
- *In numerous referendums over the years the vast majority of the Gibraltar inhabitants had repeatedly expressed their democratic desire to remain under British sovereignty. They had made it clear that they had no wish to be handed over against their will to Spain, whatever the character of its government.*
- *The population of Gibraltar were entitled to respect for their* **wishes** *concerning their future status, under the principle of self-determination, and not merely their* **interests** *, as Spain argued.*
- *No one, least of all its inhabitants, either wanted or proposed that Gibraltar should ever become independent, so the question of re-version to Spain under the treaty did not arise.*

*The impasse seemed immutable. Neither side was willing to move an inch. Spain continued its petty harassment of the Gibraltarians, who in turn continued to proclaim their Britishness.*

*Much of the argument over Gibraltar took place in the UN General Assembly (UNGA), the conference of all the UN members, each with one vote, whose resolutions are not binding on member states but are not to be lightly dismissed, especially if passed by a big majority, since they may be said to represent the views of most of mankind.*

*Soon after I had joined the UK Mission in New York, Spain tabled a draft General Assembly resolution on Gibraltar. The draft resolution didn't go as far as to demand the return of the Rock to Spain—the UN membership would not have countenanced anything as crude as that, not least because it would have been widely seen as substituting one colonial situation for another. But some of its provisions were clearly unacceptable to the UK while looking as if they might attract quite widespread support in the UNGA. Spain's draft resolution would have the UN recognise the Gibraltar issue as a "dispute," implicitly requiring a settlement (whereas Britain said there was no dispute, only a baseless claim by Spain), declared that in accordance with numerous previous General Assembly resolutions all non-self-governing territories must be decolonised, and called on Britain to hold immediate talks with Spain in order to resolve the dispute in accordance with UN principles and the UK's treaty obligations.*

*As I was the first secretary responsible in the UK Mission for colonial affairs, my Mission boss invited me to suggest how we might respond to the cleverly drafted Spanish draft resolution. After mulling over several possible options, none of which had much attraction, I suggested that Britain should adopt the following strategy. We should table our own draft resolution, setting out the UK position in the most uncompromising terms. This would create the impression that the Spanish and British rival draft resolutions were at each end of the political and international spectrum. We should then encourage our friends in one of the Nordic UN Missions to table a resolution which would represent a kind of compromise between the UK and Spanish drafts, while in practice not damaging our position on Gibraltar nearly as badly as the Spanish draft would do if it was adopted. Most importantly it would include an affirmation that the colonial people of Gibraltar were entitled to the benefit of the principle of self-determination.*

*We could realistically hope that this Nordic "compromise" text would attract the votes of UN members who had no wish to be drawn into a quarrel between Britain and Spain or to have to take sides on the issue, and so would welcome the opportunity to support a "neutral" compromise. I had already discussed this strategy in a non-committal way with a middle-ranking friend in one of the Nordic delegations, who had thought it might work, especially as if successful it would represent a setback for the unloved Franco régime in Madrid. My Nordic friend had promised to put the idea to his chief in New York who he hoped might then put it to his government.*

*Our suggested strategy was approved both by my own Permanent Representative and later by the FCO in London. My Nordic friend and I met very discreetly and drafted the Nordic "compromise" resolution together. All that remained was to persuade the relevant Nordic government to go along with the plan and table our "compromise" resolution in its own name. Messages flew back and forth between London, New York and the Nordic capital concerned. Eventually the then British Foreign Secretary telephoned his opposite number, the Nordic foreign minister, in the middle of the night from his bedroom and finally got his agreement to collaborate in our manoeuvre. The Nordic delegation, with the support of a few other Nordics and some Commonwealth delegations whom we had quietly lined up, duly tabled their draft "compromise" resolution.*

*In the end it all came to pieces over a procedural technicality. When there are several alternative resolutions on the table on the same subject, all saying contradictory things, the normal rule is that the resolution that was the first to be tabled is voted on first, then the second, and so on. The Nordics put down a procedural motion proposing that their "compromise" resolution, although the third to be tabled, should be voted on first. If this had happened, and their resolution had received a majority of the votes, the Spanish and British drafts would have been withdrawn. But Spain had done its homework, too, and had mustered a large collection of votes from nearly all the Latin American Spanish-speaking countries (which normally voted automatically in support of Spain unless their own contrary interests were involved) and from a large number of "non-aligned" African and Asian countries which could always be relied on to vote against "colonialism" and the colonial powers, regardless of the rights and wrongs of the specific issue in question—namely, the right of the Gibraltarians to decide their own future and not to be handed over against their will to the fascist government in Madrid or any other kind of Spanish government. The Nordic motion for priority for their own draft resolution was narrowly but decisively defeated, so the Spanish draft resolu-*

*tion was voted on first and approved by a modest majority. The Nordic and British draft resolutions accordingly fell away and were withdrawn.*

*It was undoubtedly a success for Spain, not because Spain had the better arguments (it didn't), but because of the tendency at the UN for countries with no particular stake in a problem and with no national interests of their own involved, to vote with their geographical, linguistic, and cultural friends, or else on the basis of some doctrinaire approach which might in fact be irrelevant to the issue in question. For a good example of this tendency beyond the United Nations, you need look no further than the Eurovision Song Contest.*

***Postscript:*** *Since the restoration of democracy in Spain (1975–1978) and Spain's accession to the European Community (now the EU) in 1986, both the UK and Spanish governments have generally adopted a more cooperative and conciliatory attitude to the Gibraltar problem, including agreement to hold talks on regional cooperation (but not on sovereignty over Gibraltar) in which representatives of the Gibraltarians would participate. Spain continues to protest against any visits to Gibraltar by British nuclear submarines or members of the British royal family despite implicitly accepting the validity of the Treaty of Utrecht ceding sovereignty to Britain "in perpetuity," while Britain has pledged never to "enter into an agreement on sovereignty without the agreement of the Government of Gibraltar and their people." The latter continue to vote almost unanimously in periodic referendums to remain British. More recently (mid-2013) Spain has resumed its harassment of people waiting to cross the Spanish-Gibraltarian border in both directions by imposing long bureaucratic delays, apparently in the context of a complex dispute over the demarcation of Gibraltar's territorial waters and its implications for Spanish fishermen.*

At a noisy cheerful buffet dinner given by Adam's opposite number in the UN Mission of 'Aranda' (the small independent Commonwealth African country next door to the French-speaking west African state of 'Trepegal'), Adam began talking to Louis, a Trepegalese member of the UN Secretariat of about the same age as himself. Louis was sitting somewhat apart from the noisier of the revellers, watching the proceedings with benevolent amusement. It emerged that Louis worked in the UN Secretariat's section dealing with Security Council affairs, which was also Adam's own area in the UK Mission. Adam asked what it was like working in the Secretariat and having to be scrupulously neutral as between the conflicting objectives of the great powers which dominated the Council. Adam had put his question in French, but Louis replied in fluent English.

"It's not so bad, in effect. In the Secretariat we are working for the UN Secretary-General, whose only prejudice (if one may call it that) is in favour of peace and whose only obligation is to uphold the Charter. So we are the servants of all the members of the Organisation and the servants of none of them. We take our orders from the Secretary-General and our guidance from the Charter, from no one else and from nowhere else. It is, you know, kind of liberating."

Adam looked quizzical. "You make it sound very high-minded."

"Well, things are not always as they should be," said Louis. "Some Secretariat officers are far too close to their fellow citizens in the national delegations, telling them things that should remain secret inside the Secretariat and keeping much too close to them socially. For instance, if you were a first secretary in the Trepegalese delegation, I would not wish to be seen talking to you like this. People might get the wrong idea."

Adam wanted to know what kind of secrets there were in the Secretariat which its officers were not supposed to pass on to their compatriots in the national Missions, or indeed to anyone else.

"Well, for example, the Secretary-General might be planning to launch a new initiative at the right moment in the attempt to resolve a dispute by offering his good offices as a kind of mediator on the basis of principles that he would set out. Obviously the principles would not be completely to the liking of either side in the dispute and it might be that one side would not want the Secretary-General to intervene in this way. Sometimes it suits one side best if the dispute is not resolved, for example, if that side is in possession of disputed territory, or fears being put under international pressure to make a big compromise in the interests of peace. If that side learns in advance from a Secretariat officer what the Secretary-General is planning to do, it might take some action to prevent him from taking that initiative, such as issuing a press statement questioning the Secretary-General's impartiality on the issue and suggesting that he should not get involved in it.

"Or a Secretariat officer might pass on to his compatriots in his country's mission a secret intelligence briefing received by the Secretary-General which puts another UN member country in a bad light. The

Secretariat officer's national mission can then use that information to the disadvantage of the other country, which will then blame the Secretary-General for leaking the secret briefing to their enemy. This might prejudice the Secretary-General's ability to act as a neutral arbitrator between the two quarrelling governments."

Adam nodded. "Yes, I can see that. Obviously I had better make friends with some fellow Brits in the Secretariat and see if I can pick up some useful bits of secret information from them."

"You won't get very far if you do. Your Mission are always complaining that they get more useful guidance and private briefing from Russian or Chinese people in the Secretariat than they ever get from their fellow British—how to say it? your fellow Brits?"

"'Fellow Brits' is right. Why is that?"

"Because your fellow-Brits have too high principles. They will talk to anyone except their own, that is to say, 'fellow-Brits.'"

"But it must be fantastic to work in the Secretariat with the brightest and most idealistic people from all over the world, all working for peace."

"I would like that to be true," Louis said. "Unfortunately, too many governments of the world send to the UN Secretariat their laziest, most incompetent, most disloyal people, their failed politicians or else the nephews and sons-in-law of their Presidents. They want to get them as far away from their own capitals as possible, you understand it. Half of my dear Secretariat colleagues have tried and failed to overthrow their own governments and they are very happy to end up in New York instead of in front of a firing squad, believe me."

Adam protested: "But why does the Secretary-General accept such people onto his staff?"

"He has no choice. Each country has a quota of Secretariat posts that it can fill with its citizens, even if they can barely read and write. They can be very corrupt and not intellectually able enough to do the job, but once they have been nominated, they have a comfortable well-paid tax free job for life here in New York. So the rest of us must work three times as hard and three times as long to make up for the lazy, the incompetent, and the corrupt—who sometimes include our bosses that we work for. Everyone knows this but no one does anything about it."

"So how did you get a Trepegal quota place in the Secretariat, Louis?" asked Adam. "By passing a competitive examination?"

"*Non, pas de tout,*" Louis said. "In Trepegal which I love as a Frenchman loves France—a big mystery but they do—there is no competitive examination anymore. I got into the UN Secretariat because my great-uncle is a government minister and I wanted to work far away from the internal politics of my homeland."

Adam was learning fast.

At the UN, especially in the Security Council, Adam also rapidly learned the importance of fast, accurate drafting—drafting speeches that he himself would deliver in the committees and working groups in which he often represented Britain, or drafting speeches for more senior members of the Mission to deliver, usually after fiddling (pointlessly, as Adam thought) with Adam's finely honed arguments. Adam was also often involved in the collective drafting of resolutions and consensuses, and amendments to resolutions and consensuses, on which so much seemed to depend.

"One of the great things about a posting at the UN is that virtually everyone in the delegation, however junior, gets some first-hand experience of real-life negotiation, which is at the heart of diplomacy," Rob told Adam. "That's quite rare for junior or middle-ranking officers in an ordinary bilateral embassy or high commission. So make the most of it while you're here, my lad. And one of the key rules you'll soon pick up in negotiating is that the delegation that's first with a text on paper starts with a huge advantage."

Rob, a counsellor with three years' UN experience already behind him, had a gift for suggesting a word or a phrase to substitute for the wording in some draft resolution which other Security Council members were prevented by their doctrinal positions, or by their governments' instructions, from swallowing. Sometimes Rob's suggestion would be accepted because it meant subtly different things to different Missions and their governments.

"When that's the key to shifting everyone towards an acceptable solution," Rob said, "you just have to make sure no one wrecks it by asking for a definition of the word or phrase you're proposing, or else tries to amend it themselves to remove the ambiguity, or to stop the other side stipulating that their acceptance is conditional on their particular interpretation being adopted as the only valid one."

"I thought diplomatic language always had to be clear and unambiguous," Adam objected.

"Quite right, my boy," Rob said, grinning. "Usually clarity and unambiguity are among the great diplomatic virtues. But remember Henry Kissinger's useful principle: when a negotiation of a particularly thorny problem in international affairs seems to have come to a halt, it's often because the negotiators have rushed at the most difficult element in the problem in the hope of settling that first, whereas generally it's wise to put the really difficult bits aside for the time being, pick out the easier elements first and concentrate on getting agreement on those. If even a little progress can be made on the easier parts, it can create a momentum that will help to keep the talks going until it's time to tackle the big issue. Diplomats sometimes develop a certain respect, sometimes even a friendship with other diplomats across the table who may privately be suffering the same headaches. In the end frustration makes them willing to consider accepting a compromise just to get the negotiating process started again. And it can all start with someone like you, Adam, scribbling an ingenious formula on his yellow legal pad, showing it to his own immediate boss and—if it's all about a really big crisis that ministers at home are taking an active interest in—watching while the suggested formula is considered in London, which gives us the nod to try out on the other side a new form of words that was originally your own brainchild."

"And if it's ambiguous, meaning different things to different people?"

"That may be the price of agreement on a different and more important principle that both sides can accept and which can be the basis for agreement later on the more difficult aspects of the problem. Remember that the historic Security Council resolution 242,[2] laying down the principles of a two-state solution of the Arab-Israel dispute, would never have been adopted if anyone had insisted on including an unambiguous definition of a key phrase. The resolution calls on everyone to recognise the right of Israel to exist within secure borders—in return for which Israel promises to withdraw from 'territories' that it had occupied in the 1967 war. It doesn't say 'the' territories, which would clearly mean all the territories; but nor does it say 'some' territories. In the Russian-language text of the resolution, Russian of course being one of the official UN languages, it just says 'territories,' which can be translated as 'the' territories or as simply 'territories' because Russian doesn't have a definite article."

"So it was agreed, formally or tacitly (I'm not sure which), that Russian would be regarded as the official language of the resolution, so everyone could interpret 'territories' in the way that suited them. It just means that there's still no agreement on whether the resolution requires Israel to withdraw from all or just some of the occupied territories: but the constructive ambiguity on that one point allowed the Security Council to agree *unanimously* on all the other important principles in the resolution, which was a huge advance. Plus, of course, it reflected general agreement that at least some Israeli withdrawal from occupied territories must be an ingredient in the settlement. The whole resolution was essentially the work of our UK delegation here in New York. One of my predecessors as the counsellor for Security Council affairs drew up a first draft and took it round all the Security Council member Missions, who of course had to seek instructions on it from their capitals. The UK Mission kept on plugging away at it, accepting small changes in some places and resisting them in others, until in the end every single Security Council delegation voted in favour of the final draft. It just shows how the work of a single diplomat, perhaps supported by one or two others, can occasionally change the world, and make the difference between war and peace. Keep at it, Adam, m'lad, and one day it might be your name up in lights. Not many people can say that!"

(No, thought Adam seditiously, and after all these years since resolution 242, we're still no nearer to a solution of the problems of the Middle East.)

The longer Adam was working at the UK Mission to the UN, the more he was struck by the importance of language in this remarkable body—so much like a World Parliament in some respects, not so different from a World Government in others (with the Security Council having sweeping powers of coercion in certain circumstances), yet in other ways little more than a futile talking-shop, designed to give the smaller and weaker countries an opportunity to lecture those bigger and more powerful than themselves. In the Security Council, though, on which Adam's efforts were focused, the resolutions passed by the Council often virtually created new and binding international law, and the interpretation of those resolutions by lawyers and governments around the world for decades to come would depend to a great extent on the speeches made in the debates in the Council preceding and immediately following the passage of each resolution. So words really mattered, and so did the interpretations of potentially ambiguous passages in Security Council resolutions placed on the public record by its members.

Diplomats working out of their embassies abroad could generally rely on the tradition that almost everything they wrote or said would be treated as private and confidential, between the embassy and its own government or between the embassy and the government to which it was accredited. Of course when an ambassador or an embassy information officer gave an interview to the local television station or newspaper, or a speech to the local Rotary Club or Elks, the text would be public property: but in those circumstances it was rarely that anything new or really significant would be said, and no one would think it necessary to crawl over every word of the article or interview in search of some hidden significance. At the United Nations (and most other international bodies), by contrast, every speech or statement in the Security Council, the General Assembly, and their numerous committees and working groups was published verbatim, usually in the five working languages of the UN: and the same was true of their resolutions and agreed statements. In this well-lit goldfish bowl, the slightest verbal indiscretion could have frightening consequences. The informal discussions among Security Council delegations leading up to a resolution were generally agreed to be off the record and in confidence (although there is some dispute about whether such discussions can be used to interpret the intended meaning of passages in the resolutions that result from them, despite the absence of any official records of what is said at them). But once the Council goes into formal session, everything said at the meeting and every document used by the Council is on the record, just as everything said by a U.S. Congressman appears in the Congressional Record, and everything said by an MP in the UK parliament is published in *Hansard*. Some diplomats, accustomed to a degree of leeway in their diplomatic correspondence and conversations, find this aspect of multilateral diplomacy disturbing. One consequence of the public openness of formal UN proceedings is that the heads of delegations, "Permanent Representatives" and ambassadors to the United Nations, especially the ambassadors of the five permanent members of the Security Council, often act more like politicians than officials or diplomats, frequently giving press conferences on current crises which are transmitted all over the world, and giving highly political interviews to the television and radio stations and newspapers of their own countries.

To be an effective "perm rep" at the UN, Adam reflected, you needed to have lots of self-confidence, to be ready to take risks, to be a little bit flamboyant. Sometimes one's political masters back home or visiting New York for the General Assembly in the autumn could be seen to be uncomfortable at finding their ambassadors better known to the local media and more in demand for interviews than themselves.

Whether diplomat or politician, at the UN you had to watch your words if you wanted to keep out of trouble. Adam had been in the UK seat at a General Assembly committee meeting at which the Russian representative, talking about an obscure British colonial territory, had used a quotation in Russian from a poem by Pushkin to the effect that there must be something seriously wrong in another unnamed country. The UN interpreter, simultaneously translating from Russian to English in her glass booth high above the committee chamber, had enterprisingly substituted for the Pushkin quotation the similar quotation from Shakespeare's *Hamlet*: "There's something rotten in the state of Denmark." The Danish delegate, listening to the English translation through his earphones, had immediately demanded the right of reply, speaking in English.

"Mr. Chairman, it's most unfortunate that the distinguished representative of the Soviet Union should make this unprovoked attack on my country, especially at a time when the prime minister of the Soviet Union is about to pay an official visit to Copenhagen. I shall of course report the matter immediately to my government, which will no doubt wish to have an explanation of these unfriendly remarks by the distinguished Soviet representative. Meanwhile, speaking entirely personally and without instructions, I would like to assure my Soviet colleague in this committee that there is absolutely nothing rotten in my country, which had been much looking forward to his prime minister's visit—until this afternoon. Thank you, Mr. Chairman."

The unfortunate Russian, who of course had not even mentioned Denmark in his speech in the original Russian, and naturally had not heard the English translation of his own speech, was bewildered and appalled. Adam, as the representative of the country of Shakespeare whose reference to Denmark in *Hamlet* had caused the misunderstanding, guessed what had happened and asked for the floor to clear it up, much to the relief of the Soviet delegate (and that of the young woman interpreting from Russian to English in her glass box). After the meeting, the Danish delegate to the committee, chatting to Adam in the delegates' bar, refused to say whether he had genuinely believed that the Russian had referred disparagingly to Denmark in the Russian original of his speech, or whether he had simply been exercising his Danish sense of humour to cause a little temporary embarrassment to the representative of the Soviet superpower. From the Dane's mischievous grin, however, Adam was able to make a pretty good guess about what had happened. In this case it had been the interpreter who had been too clever in thinking of an English equivalent to the Russian quotation. But it could easily have been a delegate, a diplomat from one of the UN Missions, using a familiar English quotation without thinking how it would be translated into the other languages.

At the UN, every word matters.

## NOTES

1.  http://news.bbc.co.uk/1/hi/in_depth/middle_east/israel_and_the_palestinians/key_documents/1639522.stm.

2.  http://unispal.un.org/unispal.nsf/0/7D35E1F729DF491C85256EE700686136.

# 7

# DIPLOMACY IN A HOSTILE COUNTRY

*Life behind enemy lines. Conducting mainly adversarial relations with
a hostile, authoritarian régime; personal and official security.*

The purpose of diplomacy is often thought of as the establishment of
friendly relations between countries and governments. In general friendly
international relations are obviously a good thing: the less conflict and
animosity there is in international affairs, the better the prospects for
peace and mutually beneficial collaboration between nation states and
their peoples. In one category of bilateral relations, such as those within
the EU and the Commonwealth or between Britain and the United States,
friendly relations are almost a given, despite such occasional spats and
misunderstandings (or, more seriously, conflicts of interest) as may occur
between even the best of friends on the personal level. In a second category, bilateral relations may be cool, even suspicious, and prone to misunderstandings; but both sides can be assumed to want as far as possible
to avoid conflict and to collaborate with each other when mutual interests
make collaboration possible. In this category, the diplomats of both countries may expect reasonably easy access to each other's foreign ministries
and perhaps other government departments. Contacts between diplomats
and officials or ministers will usually be courteous, civil, even guardedly
friendly, while probably lacking the warmth of relationships in the first
category.

But in a third category, relations with the diplomat's host country are
actively hostile and mutually suspicious, either because of a clash of
national interests over a specific dispute, such as the question of sove-

reigny over the Falkland Islands, or because of a clash of ideologies as between the two countries and governments, typically where the régime of one is communist (China, North Korea, the Warsaw Pact countries before 1988–1990) or simply despotic, and the other is based on free market capitalism, liberal or otherwise. In such cases basic courtesy is generally observed in diplomats' relations with the other side's officials, but there's no mistaking the adversarial character of the relationship. Neither side has any particular interest in fostering "friendly relations" with the other; indeed, each may be actively seeking to score points off the other, or even to undermine the other government's hold on power, for example, by openly or surreptitiously supporting local dissidents and (probably clandestine) anti-government groups. Here both governments will profess allegiance to the principle of non-interference by diplomats or others in each other's internal affairs, as laid down in the Vienna Convention on Diplomatic Relations and the United Nations Charter, while simultaneously citing such lofty principles as human rights, the prevention of humanitarian disaster or self-determination and decolonisation as justification for as much discreet or open interference as each thinks it can get away with.

It was the third or adversarial kind of bilateral relationship in which Adam knew he would be working when he arrived in 'Sifimar,' capital of communist-ruled 'Boronia' in eastern Europe, to take up his position as a counsellor (on his promotion from first secretary) and the ambassador's deputy, a few years before the almost entirely unpredicted collapse of communism in the Soviet Union and the rest of eastern Europe. Boronia was at that time the most reliably loyal of the allies and client states of the Soviet Union, easily keeping under control such tiny groups of anti-communist dissidents as managed to keep functioning.

Shortly before leaving London, Adam received a briefing on security in posts behind the iron curtain from the head of security department in the FCO, Andrew Hill, someone whom Adam knew and liked since the days when they had served together at the UN in New York.

"Look, Adam, you've been in the Service for long enough to know the form in communist countries where security is concerned—security for Britain and your own personal security," Andrew began. "The basic things to keep in mind in Boronia are that the Boronians regard us as an enemy, dedicated to the overthrow of their system, so they are intensely suspicious of us, and they will do everything they can to steal our secrets so that they can find out our real intentions and take steps to frustrate us. Their main modus operandi is to compromise our diplomats and politicians in some ingenious way so that they can be blackmailed into betraying our secrets to them, for fear of exposure of some personal weakness or error of judgement if they refuse to collaborate with them."

"Naturally, the moment anyone succumbs to this blackmail and agrees to give them some official information, he's done for. However trivial the original misjudgement or character flaw that has laid him open to blackmail (and believe you me, very few of us have led such saintly lives that we are not vulnerable to blackmail sooner or later), it's that first act of collaboration that gives them control over you, perhaps for life. They will ask you initially for some completely harmless piece of information, like a list of the names of all the UK-based staff at the embassy—information that they can easily get from any reference book or website. But once you have handed it over, thinking that giving it to them can't do any harm, they have got you. You have been blackmailed into giving information to a communist government, so if you're found out, then or later, you'll lose your security clearance and probably have to resign from the Service. Actually you'll be lucky not to be prosecuted under the Official Secrets Act, whether or not the information you gave them was technically classified.

"And bear in mind that the Boronians play a very long game. They'll compromise some quite junior politician or diplomat at a time when he may have little or no information of value to give them, and then wait, perhaps for years, until he—or she—has reached a senior position with access to classified information and to other senior people about whom they want information. Then they will reel him in."

Adam had heard most of this before as part of the briefing before his security clearance was upgraded and before each of his foreign postings. But the knowledge that he would be on communist soil within a few weeks, and in a senior position in the embassy that would automatically make him a prime target for a security attack by the much respected Boronian intelligence service, concentrated his mind wonderfully.

"Andrew, what are the precautions you recommend against being set up by the Boronian spooks—apart from living a life of stifling probity, never having too much to drink and never speculatively eying a pretty girl in case she turns out to be some kind of Boronian Mata Hari?" Adam asked.

He knew what Andrew's answer would be. "It's obvious. Rule 1: Don't do anything that you'd be embarrassed to find your parents or wife or children reading about in a Sunday newspaper. Rule 2: If you've already done something that you are keen to keep secret from your parents, wife, etc., don't go on doing it. Rule 3: If someone finds out about your secret and threatens to expose you unless you agree to do something for him that you don't want to do, come clean at once with me (I mean whoever is head of security department), or your ambassador, or someone else in authority before the situation spirals out of control. You never know: it might be possible to turn the situation to advantage. We might ask you to go along with the blackmailer, whether the Boronian Intelligence Service or the KGB or whoever else, while actually continuing to work for us. We might be able to use you to pass bogus information to your supposed controller so that we can draw conclusions from the use he makes of it."

"Rule 3(a): Even if you can't bring yourself to come clean with us after the first blackmailing approach, even if you have started to pass classified information to your blackmailer, it's still not too late to spill the beans with us and face the music. In fact, it's never too late. It's the only way to wake up from a nightmare that can only become more and more destructive. However foolish or misguided you may have been, there's always your life and your self-respect to be rescued. OK?"

"OK," Adam said, reflecting on the aspects of his life that could lay him open to blackmail by some colonel in Boronian intelligence. From now on, he promised himself, his life would be beyond reproach, transparent, and open in every respect—for the duration of his Sifimar posting, anyway. After all, it would only be for three years.

### As an example:

*A year or two after I had joined the Colonial Office as a very junior home civil servant, the time came when my work required a higher level of security clearance than I had needed until then. For this purpose I was interviewed by some kind of security official, an elderly man who looked like (and no doubt was) a somewhat seedy retired army Major. The Major was clearly troubled by my record of student political activism in the Labour party interest, surely in his eyes evidence of potential treachery on my part if he gave me the higher security clearance that I needed and if consequently I were to come into the possession of a higher class of government secrets. He ques-*

*tioned me at length about my attitude to the British constitution, democracy, and the threat of Soviet communism. I answered all these questions truthfully if sometimes in a nuanced or qualified way, and, I thought, without giving any hostages to fortune.*

*Finally, baffled, the Major put the killer question.*

*"Mr. Barder, tell me honestly: do you believe in our country's Royal Family?"*

*I looked him straight in the eye. "Yes, sir, I truly do," I said solemnly. "I'm absolutely convinced that they exist."*

*"I'm very glad to hear you say that," said the Major. "I think that removes any remaining doubts I might have had about your loyalty. I have no further questions. I confess that you're a bit of a mystery to me, Mr. Barder, but I don't think you're going to let me down. Good day to you."*

*So I got my higher security clearance. But I was disappointed to find that even though my total loyalty was now guaranteed, there were yet higher grades of clearance that were still beyond me. At the time, I used to attend periodically the meetings of a committee, or sub-sub-committee, whose task was to assess both unclassified information and secret intelligence about the area of west Africa that I was then concerned with, in the context of possible threats to British security. I would arrive at the underground bunker where these meetings took place before my item had been reached, and would be made to wait outside until it was time for me to be allowed in. Often the door into the bunker was left slightly ajar and I would see the preparations being made for my entry, mainly consisting of large black curtains being drawn across the wall of maps facing the committee's members so that I should not be given any clues to the area discussed before I was admitted. A large notice was also pinned to the black curtains reminding all those present that the level of security of the discussion of the next item had been reduced to Class B. My ears were obviously not to be sullied by discussion of Class C intelligence with which I was still not to be entrusted, even though in the discussion of my item the principal provider of classified information about my particular area, and sometimes the only such provider, would be myself.*

*I should of course acknowledge that security clearances conducted by the likes of my Major are a thing of the past. It's all a much more serious business these days.*

Adam's ambassador took him on his forthcoming call on the head of the Western European Department in the Boronian MFA (Ministry of

Foreign Affairs) in order to introduce him. Adam was struck by the superficial formality of the occasion. The Boronian diplomat had previously served as his country's ambassador to Belgium and was therefore entitled to be addressed as "Mr. Ambassador" (but not "Your Excellency") for the rest of his life, American style. Adam's ambassador accordingly greeted him formally.

"I'm glad to see you, Mr. Ambassador. It's some time since we had a talk."

"Indeed, Your Excellency," replied the Boronian. "And this is your new deputy, I take it?"

Adam was formally introduced.

"You are welcome to Sifimar, Mr. Counsellor. I hope your arrival will mark a pronounced improvement in the relations between our two countries."

The British ambassador's eyebrows went up in an expression of exaggerated surprise.

"Oh! Are they really so bad, then, Mr. Ambassador? Do you have any complaint about anything? I had the impression that our relations were currently normal; not especially warm, but considering the differences between our systems of government, not especially cool, either?"

The Boronian leaned forward and fixed his British opposite number with an expressionless stare.

"My minister has been struck by the increasing number of anti-Boronian articles that have been appearing in your English newspapers, Your Excellency. There was even a whole BBC television programme devoted to malicious slander of my country. We desire to have normal or even friendly relations with England—"

"Britain," murmured His Excellency.

"—but it is hardly possible when there is this campaign against us."

"Mr. Ambassador, you have served in western Europe, and you know very well that my government has no control over what our newspapers or the BBC say about Boronia—or any other subject, come to that."

"Come, come, Your Excellency. Of course I know that this is your official line. But we are both adults, we know that your government can orchestrate a campaign against anyone whose ideology it dislikes. We do not overlook that the BBC is financed by your Foreign & Commonwealth Office. I think you have a saying that he who pays the piper . . ."

"I'm disappointed that your experience in Belgium has not given you a better understanding of the realities of a free and independent press in a democratic country like mine, Mr. Ambassador. As for the BBC, the Foreign & Commonwealth Office does indeed handle the budget of the World Service of the BBC,[1] but not that of the BBC itself. And even the World Service would not dream of allowing the FCO to influence the contents of what it broadcasts: the FCO decides only in which languages the World Service broadcasts and the hours allotted to each language. If you have a complaint against the BBC or against a British newspaper, for example, if you think reporting of your country's affairs has been unfair or inaccurate, you have an immediate remedy: your embassy in London is free to make a formal complaint to the editor or the BBC producer concerned, and if you are not satisfied with the response, you can take the matter up with the Independent Press Complaints Commission, which will investigate the matter, and if your complaint is upheld, the BBC or the newspaper will be obliged to publish a correction and, if necessary, an apology. I have noticed that you have no such system here in Boronia, Mr. Ambassador. That seems to me regrettable."

"Your Excellency, I'm very disappointed that you try to avoid your government's responsibility in this way. If your government is sincere in saying it wants good relations between our countries, clearly it is for your ministers and your FCO to take up the slanders against Boronia in your British Broadcasting Company—"

"Corporation," said His Excellency.

"—and make sure that it doesn't happen again. Also those responsible should naturally be disciplined."

"Mr. Ambassador, I hear what you say, and I shall of course report what you have said to my government. But I have no doubt that my government's response will be to endorse my own purely personal reaction just now. I can give you no assurance that my government can or will take any action designed to influence the contents of our newspapers or of BBC programmes. The right course is for your embassy in London to take the matter up with the BBC and the newspapers concerned."

On their way down to the ambassador's official car, a Jaguar with the Union flag flying on its front near-side wing, waiting to take the two diplomats back to their embassy, Adam remarked on his impression that the conversation had had a ritual air about it: both sides were going through the motions of complaining and rejecting the complaint, each knowing the other's position perfectly well, but each somehow compelled to act out its allotted script.

"That's very true, Adam. A lot of our exchanges with Boronian officialdom are rather like that. Occasionally the mask drops slightly, and your Boronian interlocutor will give you the equivalent of a wink, as much as to say: 'You understand that I have to make this complaint so that I can tell my minister and the foreign relations division of the Party that I have done so, but you know very well that I know it's nonsense.' These guys have to live and function on two levels: the level of officials having to conform with the party line and their ministers' instructions, and the level of highly educated, well-read Europeans privately recognising reality. If ever they allow the two levels to clash in their heads, they're liable either to have a nervous breakdown or to defect to the west. Or both. We have no alternative to going along with this empty ritual. There's a danger of humiliating these people if we make it clear that we know that on one level they are spouting doctrinaire nonsense and that on another level *they* know it, too. If we confront them with that, it could be the end of our relationship with them, which would mean the end of any possibility of doing business with them or of influencing their behaviour to even the most marginal degree. You have to feel sorry for them, really. Most of them are not bad people; they try to do the best they can for their country within the bounds of a pernicious system."

He interrupted himself: "But we mustn't continue this discussion in the car: Igor, my Boronian driver, is a splendid chap, as loyal as the day is long, but like all our Boronian staff he has to make regular reports to his Boronian intelligence bosses on everything I've done, everywhere I've been, and everything he's overheard me say while he's been driving me."

As soon as Adam and the ambassador appeared on the steps of the ministry, Igor jumped out of the Jaguar and stood holding the rear offside passenger door open for His Britannic Excellency. Adam nipped round to the other side and got in to sit next to the ambassador in the back seat. A mere counsellor, as he knew from long experience by now, could be assumed to know how to open a car door for himself.

### As an example:

*Most British diplomatic posts[2] celebrate Britain's National Day by holding The Queen's Birthday Party (QBP), the biggest function in the British diplomatic year. It generally takes place in June, although the Queen's real birthday is in April. June is, however, a more sensible time of year in most parts of the world for a big outdoor drinks party and reception, to which by convention the ambassador invites all the embassy's contacts from every walk of life, including the entire government of the host country, members of opposition parties (to the extent that these are not in prison at the time), top business tycoons, editors and columnists of the local press, television stars of the leading current affairs programmes, mayors and chiefs, local writers and artists, and most or even all of the British expatriate community, depending on its size (exclusion from the QBP being for almost any Brit in a small expatriate community a trigger for bitter resentment and hostility to the embassy, the ambassador, and his entire staff). Preparations for the QBP begin many weeks beforehand, with specific duties to be performed at it allocated to every member of the embassy staff and all their wives or husbands.*

*I arrived in Warsaw as the British ambassador only a few weeks before the date set for the embassy's QBP. Poland was still enduring the humiliations of Soviet domination with a reluctantly conformist communist party and government, despised by a handsome majority of the doggedly Catholic and deeply patriotic population. During a brief period of détente some years earlier, the communist government had recognised Solidarity as a valid trade union, and implicitly as a political movement, and had started talks with its leadership, including its President, Lech Wałęsa, about a possible power-sharing settlement, but before long the Russians became panicky about this obvious threat to the basic doctrine of the supremacy of the communist party, and under the threat of a Soviet military invasion, the Polish government broke off the talks, declared martial law, banned Solidarity, and for a time imprisoned Wałęsa and some of his colleagues. Wałęsa was later released and returned to his old job as an electrician in the Gdansk shipyards, to which a succession of western ambassadors (including later myself) drove in their official cars to pay him homage, much to the irritation of the Polish authorities.*

*I was able to present my credentials from the Queen to the President of Poland quite soon after my arrival, and was thus able to function as ambassador almost from the beginning. A few days after I had presented my credentials, I received a summons from the head of the western department of the Polish foreign ministry, a Mr. Wyschynski (not his real name). It turned out that this was no mere courtesy call.*

*"Your Excellency, I am sorry to have to raise with you a sensitive matter on your very first call at the ministry," Mr. Wyschynski said*

*with a hint of embarrassment. He was a large, portly, rather friendly, Dickensian figure.*

*"No problem, Mr. Wyschynski," I said, curious to know what sensitive matter was so urgent that it justified departure from the tradition that an ambassador's first call on the MFA (Ministry of Foreign Affairs) is a purely social call for mutual introductions and a general conversation at which matters of substance are not usually raised.*

*"It concerns Your Excellency's forthcoming National Day reception: I believe it is called in your country the 'QBP,' always a memorable event in the Polish calendar."*

*"Yes?" I said, surprised.*

*"Yes. My minister has specifically asked me to tell you that it will make a very poor first impression here of Your Excellency if invitations to your 'QBP' are to be sent to members of an illegal and irresponsible group of misguided Polish people who have unfortunately banded together to try to subvert our socialist constitution and the leading role of the Polish Workers' Party—the party which western observers sometimes refer to as the communist party. These dissident criminal elements are of no political significance and if certain western diplomatic quarters persist in treating them as if they represented some quasi-legitimate element in Polish public opinion, those western diplomatic quarters are deluding themselves and misleading their own governments."*

*I said that I understood perfectly that this was the position of the Polish government with regard to the Solidarity trade union movement and its supporters, but I was not clear what any of this had to do with my national day party.*

*"I must be blunt with you, Your Excellency: I must tell you that if we discover that invitations to your 'QBP' have been sent to any of these antisocial elements despite their complete lack of political status and their criminal subversive tendencies, no member of the Polish government or party and no official of this ministry will feel able to attend. We would much regret it if we are forced to forego our attendance at Your Excellency's always most enjoyable function, but we would be left with no choice in the matter. My minister has instructed me to make our position absolutely clear on this point. It is purely a friendly warning, meant to avoid embarrassment through any possible misunderstanding. I am sure Your Excellency will accept it in that spirit."*

*"Mr. Wyschynski," I said in a tone of deep disappointment. "First, you must know that no ambassador of a self-respecting country can*

*allow another government to influence the invitation list for his coun-*
*try's national day reception, still less to try to veto the sending of*
*invitations to any particular category of guests. Secondly, you must*
*also know that it is a legitimate function of a diplomatic mission to*
*maintain lawful contacts with all shades of the host country's opinion,*
*including those who may be critical of their government. I'm sure the*
*Polish embassy in London is in touch with members of Her Majesty's*
*Loyal Opposition, not least because they may one day form a govern-*
*ment in Britain after winning a democratic election. Thirdly, neither I*
*nor my government shares your view of the insignificance in Polish*
*public life of your Solidarity movement, which as you well remember*
*was briefly officially recognised only a few years ago and was ac-*
*cepted as a negotiating partner by your government. Fourthly, I must*
*tell you that the invitations to the Queen's Birthday Party were sent*
*out this morning after I had personally approved the list. You would*
*scarcely expect me to tell any of those whom I have invited that I have*
*had to withdraw their invitations in response to representations from*
*the Polish government. And fifth and last: I shall greatly regret it if the*
*distinguished head of western department in the MFA and the many*
*colleagues of his whom I have invited to my reception find it impos-*
*sible to accept your and their invitations. You will be greatly missed, I*
*assure you. But the decision is entirely yours and I wouldn't dream of*
*seeking to influence it either way. Please explain my position frankly*
*to your minister, with my compliments. I much look forward to my first*
*call on him, which I hope will take place before I see him again at the*
*QBP."*

*"Your Excellency," Mr. Wyschynski said wryly, "I have to admit*
*that your response is not entirely unexpected, even though I may have*
*taken you by surprise with my démarche and left you no time to seek*
*instructions from your government or to prepare your answer. I shall*
*report faithfully to my minister what you have said."*

*"Indeed. I have been speaking purely personally and without in-*
*structions from my government: that must be obvious, for the reason*
*that you have so tactfully mentioned. I shall promptly report our con-*
*versation to my government and if London takes a different view from*
*mine, I shall immediately inform you and ask you to pass the informa-*
*tion to your minister. But I shall be extremely surprised if my govern-*
*ment takes a different view."*

*It hardly needs saying that at the QBP a few weeks later the Resi-*
*dence garden was swarming with government ministers and MFA offi-*
*cials, as well as nearly all the well-known Solidarity spokesmen and*

*activists based in Warsaw. My wife and I were stuck in the entrance to the garden at the end of the receiving line, welcoming and later saying goodbye to the guests as they queued outside to shake our hands on arrival, and queued inside to shake our hands again to say goodbye. But it was reliably reported to me afterwards by at least half a dozen of the guests that Mr. Wyschynski had been spotted in a far corner of the garden, almost obscured by a huge tree, deep in conversation with the official spokesman of the banned Solidarity movement. One of the many functions of these occasions, tedious though they are for those unable to leave the receiving line, is to provide a discreet meeting-place for people who are otherwise inhibited from meeting one another in public. When Mr. Wyschynski joined the line of guests waiting to say goodbye, and his turn came to shake hands with a word of thanks "for a most successful party, as always," I thought I caught the merest hint of a wink as he and his wife walked away to his car. But I probably imagined it.*

*The Poles were always the least obedient and submissive of the client states of the former Soviet Union. Their officials had to go through the motions, if only to stave off a Soviet military invasion and occupation, but it was clear that in many cases their hearts were not really in it.*

## NOTES

1.   Much more recently the arrangements for funding the BBC World Service have been transferred from the Foreign & Commonwealth Office to the BBC proper, which means that the cost of the World Service is now met from television license fees like that of the rest of the BBC.

2.   In the Queen's fifteen other realms (such as Canada and Australia) it's up to the country's own government to celebrate their Queen's official birthday, not for the British high commission. So the British high commissions in, for example, Ottawa or Canberra do not hold an annual "QBP."

# 8

# DEALING WITH FOREIGNERS

*Getting to know key host country nationals, private, and official; spotting and cultivating key contacts; potential rewards. Official visits. Relations with diplomats of other countries.*

Adam was first appointed a head of mission, at the relatively early age of forty-eight, as Ambassador to 'Noridan,' a vast north African Muslim state of some strategic importance. This was also a promotion, since the Noridan ambassadorship was at the level of Director (then called Assistant Under-Secretary of State or AUS), one rung up from Adam's previous grade of Counsellor. At that time the compulsory retirement age was sixty, although a number of diplomatic service officers found themselves forced to retire before their sixtieth birthdays if there was no suitable job on the horizon for them by the time they were fifty-six or fifty-seven. When Adam's appointment to 'Khaliman,' the Noridanese capital, was announced, his then line manager, the supervising Director in the Foreign & Commonwealth Office, congratulated him and reminded him that at this grade he was likely to remain a head of mission now for the next twelve years, apart from any home posting in the Foreign & Commonwealth Office in London as a Director or above. His annual reports would no longer be written by his ambassador: he would be writing the annual reports on his own senior embassy officers, and reports on himself would be written by the relevant supervising Director far away in London.

Adam was lucky to be given a date soon after his arrival in Khaliman for the presentation of his credentials to the Noridanese President, the ceremony that frees a newly arrived ambassador to begin to function. His credentials, or "letters of credence," signed by the Queen and written in standard flowery antique language, addressed the Noridanese President as Her Majesty's "good friend," the term used in all such documents, even when addressed to the most bloodthirsty and corrupt dictators on the planet. Those addressed to other Kings and Queens, refer to "My Brother/ Sister and dear Cousin" or to "Your Highness," depending on the close-ness of the dynasty to the House of Windsor (Britain's royal family), some of whom may be quite literally cousins of the royal signatory. The nominal purpose of the credentials is to assure the receiving head of state that the new ambassador has the full confidence of the Queen and her government and is an all-round admirable person. The ceremony is large-ly ceremonial and while there is often little or no substance, there may on occasions be nuggets worth reporting back to the new ambassador's foreign ministry at home. Moreover, its atmosphere and the presence or absence of personal chemistry between the head of state and the new ambassador may set the tone for their relationship for the rest of the ambassador's tour of duty.

Adam, never having served as ambassador to a royal court, had had no need to equip himself with diplomatic uniform, gold braid, fringed epau-lettes, plumed hat, and sword, so he performed his part in the ceremony wearing a dark grey lounge suit. He inspected the Presidential Guard of Honour before being led into the Presidential Palace by the Noridanese Chief of Protocol, who had briefed him the previous day on what he would be required by local protocol and tradition. The elderly, heavily built President, standing in elaborate military uniform on a dais in front of a rather monarchical-looking throne, his face grave and unsmiling, waited for Adam at the far end of an ornately decorated room. Adam handed over his credentials letter with a brief neck-bow. The President murmured a word of thanks and passed the letter, without reading it, to the Chief of Protocol standing behind and to one side of him. Short formal speeches were then exchanged, Adam and the President each assuring the other of his earnest desire to improve yet further the already friendly relations existing between their two countries, while promoting the causes of world peace and the eradication of poverty and hunger throughout the world.

The Chief of Protocol then beckoned forward the four most senior members of Adam's staff who had been watching the presentation from the back of the room, for Adam to present them to the President. Adam and the President, accompanied by a Noridanese interpreter and the Chief of Protocol, then retired to a smaller drawing room where they sat down and were offered glasses of warm Coca-Cola (Adam accepted his but didn't drink it). After a brief exchange of politenesses, the President rose and extended his hand to Adam who hastily got up and shook it. The President then withdrew, Adam was taken to yet another room where his four embassy colleagues were waiting, each with his or her warm Coke, and the five of them were led out to where the Foreign Ministry's Protocol Department cars were waiting to take them back to the British embassy, Adam's ambassadorial Union flag[1] now fluttering on the off-side wing of his car. Adam was now a fully-fledged, duly accredited British Ambassador. His first act in this capacity was to send a telegram to the Secretary of State in London saying so, and adding some personal impressions of his first encounter with the Noridanese Head of State.

Rules of protocol are changing all the time, mostly (in Adam's opinion as he looked back years later on his first few weeks as a head of mission) in the direction of becoming less formal, more relaxed, and less burdensome. Nowhere has this gradual change been more welcome to practising diplomats than in the duty laid on newly arrived heads of mission, whether ambassadors or high commissioners, to pay introductory calls on some (nowadays) or all (in Adam's early days) of his diplomatic colleagues. In more recent times the practice has developed of the new ambassador making introductory calls only on those fellow members of the local diplomatic corps with whom he will have the closest and most substantive relations. Thus during his first few weeks after presenting his credentials a new British ambassador will naturally call on the Dean of the local Corps, his other European Union and Commonwealth colleagues, and on the American, Russian, and Chinese ambassadors. In a capital city where a large number of countries are represented, calls on even that limited selection of colleagues will be remarkably time-consuming, and not all of them will be equally rewarding.

When Adam began his ambassadorial career, the burden of courtesy calls was incomparably heavier than it is now, and the demands of internationally accepted protocol were inexorable. Adam's first few weeks after he had presented his credentials were occupied almost exclusively by a huge and obligatory programme of introductory calls on every one of his diplomatic colleagues, the bane of the life of a head of mission in those rigidly protocolaire times. Then as now, Adam's first call was necessarily on the Dean of the Diplomatic Corps—the longest-serving foreign ambassador in Khaliman. Seniority among heads of mission in any post is determined either by the ambassador's date of arrival or, more usually, by the date on which he or she presented credentials. The size, power, and importance of the ambassador's country have nothing to do with it. A newly accredited American ambassador is the most junior diplomat in the Corps, and the ambassador of Malta who has been there longer than anyone else is the most senior. As Dean he is the representative of the whole local Diplomatic Corps in its dealings with the Ministry of Foreign Affairs (MFA) and the rest of the host government. The Dean also represents the Corps at ceremonies to welcome or say farewell to visiting dignitaries, at state funerals and weddings, and other such formal occasions, although for the most important of these the presence of the entire Corps may be required (as Adam was chagrined to discover in the coming days). He formulated for himself a rule of thumb on this: the more insignificant the country and the more authoritarian its régime, the more frequently its rulers demand that all the ambassadors accredited to it turn out for its numerous ceremonial occasions, generally making them sit on benches in the hot sun in some vast open-air parade ground, in strict order of seniority, waiting for several hours for the local bigwigs to arrive, then for several more hours while quasi-military ceremonies were conducted, then for a couple more hours waiting for the President or Vice-President and his (or in rare cases her) entourage to leave.

For the moment, however, introductory calls would be the order of the day for Adam. The Dean, an elderly Maltese, stressed that Adam and, where appropriate, his wife, should call on every other ambassador, as far as possible in their order of seniority, ending with the Chargés d'Affaires (ambassadors' deputies occupying their ambassadors' places during the absence of their bosses from the country). The dean warned that failure to pay an introductory call on any ambassador, however irrelevant his country, would be taken as a slight that could mar Adam's reputation in the Corps throughout his time in Khaliman. Such a minatory warning would strike a modern diplomat as both impractical and absurd. For Adam, it had to be taken seriously, for at that time it reflected virtually universal practice.

"You said that I should be accompanied on my calls by my wife 'when appropriate,'" Adam said. "When will that be appropriate?" Adam could well imagine how Eve would react to the news that she would be required to spend several hours a day, for weeks to come, accompanying him on an endless series of calls on other ambassadors and their wives, many of them certainly people with nothing much of interest to say.

"When your secretary telephones to arrange a time and a date for each call, she should ask whether it would be appropriate for your wife to accompany you," replied the Maltese. "Some of our Muslim colleagues will prefer your wife to pay a separate call on their wives. As you will understand, they can be quite uneasy in mixed company. There's sometimes a problem over a Muslim Excellency not being able to shake the hand of a woman, however eminent."

"What happens when the ambassador paying the call is a woman?"

The Dean smiled. "Fortunately, Mr. Ambassador, that does not appear to arise in Your Excellency's case."

Adam was even more dismayed by the thought of having to ask Eve to pay separate calls, on her own, on some of the Muslim ambassadresses. [2] She was more than capable of carrying off such occasions without the smallest embarrassment, but she was also capable of reminding Adam, if and when the occasion arose, that she was neither employed nor paid by Her Britannic Majesty or her government and that even such a grand personage as the Maltese ambassador to the Islamic Republic of Noridan was in no position to give her orders. But in the end she would comply, with a reasonably good grace.

There was worse to come. "Your Excellency should bear in mind," said the Dean, "that some of our colleagues will ask, towards the end of your call, when it would be convenient for them to pay a return call on Your Excellency."

"With their wives, no doubt," said Adam.

"Of course—when appropriate. However, if you are reluctant to double the amount of time you have to spend on your own calls by accepting return calls as well, it's quite in order to say that you hope His Excellency will be willing to defer his return call until a later date, when Your Excellency will have completed Your Excellency's programme of introductory calls. It will be mutually understood in such a case that the deferment will be indefinite." The dean smiled a conspiratorial smile. Adam later found, to his infinite relief, that even in that hidebound era no one ever actually insisted on paying a return call following his own introductory call. A few of his more ancient colleagues insisted on making a ritual enquiry as to when a return call would be convenient, but no such nonsensical event ever took place. Similarly, Eve found that in practice she hardly ever had to call on any other ambassadress on her own, although she dutifully accompanied Adam on many, perhaps most, of his own calls. This tiresome convention too is now a thing of the past.

Adam had to overcome a powerful urge to ask the Dean, who was after all a Commonwealth colleague, to stop calling him Your Excellency or Mr. Ambassador and to call him Adam. But he sensed that that would have to come later, if at all. This occasion had to be solemn; it was, after all, part of the Dean's *raison d'être*. Adam was relieved to find that nearly all his diplomatic colleagues were automatically on first-name terms with Eve and himself from the time of their first meetings, whether formal or social.

A feature of Adam's (and usually also Eve's) calls on his diplomatic colleagues in those early weeks was the production by a uniformed maid of a large plate of their host countries' local delicacies, often sticky lumps of some indeterminate substance flavoured with an anonymous sugary coating. Pressed to take the third, fourth, and subsequent helpings of the hosts' local dish, Adam and Eve both learned to decline without causing offence. Repeated glasses of some fiery alcoholic liquid, produced only in their hosts' country, were more difficult to refuse, even at 10 o'clock in the morning.

At last the ordeal by introductory call on their colleagues in the Corps was over. Adam had accepted the Dean's advice not to omit a single ambassador or chargé, however obscure the country he or she represented. The Australian ambassador had mentioned, during their call on him and his wife, that their United States' colleague, an emaciated businessman who owed his ambassadorial status and life-long title to his success in having raised several millions of dollars for his president's election campaign, had given considerable and widespread offence in the Corps by failing to pay introductory calls on several of his colleagues from the more insignificant countries, although despite the grumbling it seemed to be reluctantly accepted that such arrogance was only to be expected of the representative of a super-power. (On the other hand, the jovial Russian ambassador had conscientiously called on every one of his colleagues.)

Another area in which customary international practice has relaxed over the years since Adam's induction into the ambassadorial world is that of attendance by heads of mission at National Day receptions. Nowadays, especially in big posts with a large diplomatic corps—well over one hundred embassies or high commissions in some of them—it is generally accepted that it's impossible for every ambassador to attend every single national day function. In some capitals, such functions may take place almost every week-day evening, sometimes with three or four on the same evening. As with introductory calls on first arrival, heads of mission are nowadays bound—and permitted—to be selective about the functions they will attend in person. They may send a member of their embassy staff to represent them at the rest. Adam's experience, however, in an earlier era allowed him no such leeway. It was made clear to him by the Dean and by some other friendly colleagues that his own personal appearance at every national day function would be *de rigueur*; to send one of his staff to represent him would be taken as a calculated snub, not just to the host country's ambassador but also to its head of state whom he represented.

During the three weeks following Adam's presentation of credentials, there had been four national day parties, big evening receptions each at the relevant ambassador's residence, which Eve and Adam had been obliged to attend. Three of these had marked the national days of minor countries which Adam understood to be the only functions given by their ambassadors during the year. The Australian ambassador had warned Adam that there were five or six ambassadors in Khaliman—those of Britain, France, Germany, Russia, China, and Saudi Arabia—whose failure even to put in an appearance at any national day reception would be certain to be noticed and to give offence. Everyone knew that the Americans were often represented at such occasions by the ambassador's deputy or even one of the embassy's Counsellors; this was widely deemed to be another example of superpower arrogance, but only to be expected. There were more than ninety embassies in Khaliman (including most Muslim countries and many other Africans as well as the bulk of the Europeans and a few from Latin America and Asia). Each of these would hold a national day reception during each year: that meant up to ninety obligatory evenings out annually for Eve and Adam, without counting the numerous other evening receptions and dinners that would crowd into their diaries, along with almost as many lunches. The only bright spot on the horizon was that the horrors of the working breakfast had not yet crossed the Atlantic to Noridan.

Not all the introductory calls on Corps colleagues were a waste of Adam's professional time; nor were all the national day parties. Most of his Commonwealth and EEC (now EU) colleagues gave him useful insights into the political and economic scene in Noridan, and tips on how to circumnavigate the many pitfalls lying in wait in Khaliman for newly arrived diplomats and their spouses. Several soon became firm friends and invaluable sources of sensitive information. After a few months Adam was able and glad to reciprocate as he built up his collection of local contacts. In the case of his EEC colleagues, the exchange of information took place not only informally on social occasions such as receptions, lunches, and dinners, but also more formally at the monthly meetings of EEC ambassadors. Adam found that at these meetings the most useful information tended to be provided by his German and French colleagues, and often the Dane and the Belgian: most of the rest spent more time listening and taking copious notes than contributing anything themselves. Meetings of all the ambassadors of Commonwealth countries took place more rarely and were in general less productive, although obviously much valued by the ambassadors of the smaller Commonwealth countries. At both EEC and Commonwealth ambassadors' meetings some participants seemed to have few local contacts, depending for their reporting to their governments mainly on what they were able to pick up from the EEC or Commonwealth meetings and from conversations at parties with other diplomats. Before long Adam became a net contributor, although he generally came away with at least one nugget of news that justified a reporting telegram to London (with Adam's own assessment of its implications and reliability in each case). The members of Adam's embassy staff similarly often gleaned valuable information from their Commonwealth and European opposite numbers in other embassies. But much more (and more reliable) information came from the Noridanian contacts whom all of them zealously cultivated at their various levels, the youngest of these, such as students, often being the most daringly frank.

**As an example:**

*Diplomatic missions often seek to improve and lighten their relations with the people and dignitaries of the host country by arranging events that will be enjoyed by local people and involve friendly contacts with local government officials, the host country's military officers, local business and media people, and others with whom contacts made in the context of the event may prove useful later. For example, a goodwill visit by a ship of the Royal Navy to a port of a foreign or Commonwealth country can be a powerful demonstration of British goodwill. If enough local people can be involved in it, and if it's properly covered by local television, radio, and the press, it can give a long-lasting and favourable impression of British friendliness, smartness, and efficiency: very useful for raising the profile of both the British embassy or high commission and of Britain itself. During my time as British high commissioner in Australia a Royal Navy destroyer, HMS Valorous (not its real name), paid a three-day visit to the northern Australian port of Darwin, on the Timor Sea, much closer to Indonesia than to Sydney or Canberra. J. and I flew up to Darwin for the visit. The high commission information officer and my Naval Adviser (Commonwealth equivalent of Naval Attaché) had flown up a week earlier to set up the arrangements in accordance with guidance notes sent by the Ministry of Defence in London.*

*Under the plan for the visit, J. and I were to be flown out to Valorous in the ship's small Lynx helicopter so that we would be on board during the last hour or so before the ship reached Darwin. The Mayor of Darwin and his wife had also been invited to fly out to Valorous with us. The four of us gathered at the side of the Darwin port's helicopter pad to watch the little Lynx come in from far out to sea, hover for a moment over the landing pad, twirl a little, descend, and land. The helicopter pilot, in full flying gear, climbed out, saluted the party smartly, and came with us into the small VIP lounge in the main port building to brief us. Introducing himself as Lionel, the pilot took his four passengers through the emergency drill to be followed "in the highly unlikely event of us having to ditch in the sea": unhook and remove the big headphones and microphone used to communicate with the pilot and co-pilot, undo the star-shaped safety harness by rotating the metal fastener over the tummy, shrug off the harness, push out the plastic window beside the passenger seat, and crawl through it into the sea, trusting to the buoyancy of the flying suit that each passenger would wear to keep afloat until rescued. "The only slight snag," Lionel warned, "is that you'll only have three minutes at most to do all that before the helicopter turns upside down, because of the weight of the engines and rotors above the fuselage. Once that happens, you're suspended upside down below the waterline and it all gets a lot more tricky. Any questions?"*

*There was a stunned silence.*

*"All right, then: here are your flying suits. As soon as you've got them on, we'll board the Lynx and get going."*

*We hugely (if tremulously) admired the way Lionel hovered the helicopter above the big destroyer once we reached her far out on the horizon, matching the ship's speed and direction through the water and positioning the Lynx precisely above* Valorous's *tiny helicopter pad, marked with its big H. We didn't know whether to be reassured or alarmed by the sight of the ship's fire-fighting team, in full firemen's kit, gathered round the landing pad, pointing thick hoses at the centre of the pad as the helicopter, still moving forward at the same pace as the ship, gradually lost height and settled gently on the dead centre of the pad. We heard Lionel shut off the engine and the gradual fading of the noise of the rotors as the fire-fighting team put down their hoses and came forward to lash the Lynx firmly to the deck. What amazing skills people like Lionel possess! But we were secretly relieved to know that we would be returning to dry land aboard a substantial Royal Navy ship, and not in the little Lynx.*

*After J. and I and the Mayor and Mayoress had been introduced to the Captain of* Valorous *and had a welcoming drink in his stateroom, the Captain and I went through the arrangements for the ship's arrival ceremony together, and then discussed the programme of events for the ship's officers and ratings that had been arranged for them during the three-day visit—football matches, a banquet given by the Mayor, a disco for the entire crew to meet the local youth sightseeing with a visit to the famous Kakadu national park, a visit to the Darwin brewery, a debate and quiz at the university, and conducted tours of* Valorous. *Satisfied with these plans, the Captain invited his four visitors to have a look round* Valorous *while we waited for her to arrive at Darwin and for us to disembark. Walking round the deck with one of the ship's officers and the Darwin Mayor (by now a good friend), we came across Lionel, who had piloted the helicopter that had brought us out to the ship. I greeted him warmly, congratulating him on the extraordinary skill he had exhibited, not only in flying us out across the water, but especially in landing the little helicopter with such precision in a high wind on the deck of a moving ship, without mishap.*

*"Tell me, Lionel," I said, "all that emergency drill that has to be carried out in less than three minutes if you ditch in the sea—have you ever had to do that for real?"*

*"No, no," laughed Lionel. "Not for real, I'm glad to say. Of course I had to practise doing it many times in the big tank in a mock-up of a helicopter during training, as we all do."*

*"And did you manage to get out before the three minutes were up and the machine turned turtle in the water?" I enquired.*

*"No, never," Lionel replied. "No one does. It's absolutely impossible."*

*On the arrival of* Valorous *at Darwin, and as the senior representative of Britain in Australia, I was ceremonially piped ashore by a smartly turned-out rating playing what looked and sounded like a superior tin whistle, while the Captain, standing to attention on the other side of the top of the gangway, saluted J. and myself as we left the ship. Of course it was the office I held that was being formally acknowledged in this traditional way, not myself personally. Nevertheless it was a proud and memorable moment for both of us—if no more memorable than our flight in the Lynx.*

Much more valuable than meetings with his fellow diplomats for the collection of information and insights about Noridan was Adam's growing portfolio of contacts with Noridanese decision-makers and opinion-formers. His calls on the ambassadors and their spouses once completed, Adam turned to much more useful and congenial introductory calls on Noridanese ministers and their officials, newspaper editors and commentators, senior army, navy and air force officers, business and trade union leaders, bankers, and (with great caution) a few independent political activists. Adam was surprised and gratified to find that most of these were not only ready but often also eager to entrust to him confidences which, if he had leaked them to others, would have caused them severe embarrassment, or occasionally much worse. Some government ministers would voice scathing criticisms of aspects of their government's policies and even of their government colleagues, but only in one-on-one conversations or in the intimacy of their house, Eve's and Adam's official Residence but also, for the time being, their personal and family home.

Adam came to realise that Britain was one of only a limited handful of countries whose diplomats were felt to be trustworthy recipients of highly sensitive information and opinions. But while he was off to a flying start as the new British ambassador, and therefore *prima facie* trustworthy, he had to earn future confidences by himself being personally discreet. He must take care to respect the confidences entrusted to him, show consistency in his own communications, and be seen as an accurate and reliable exponent of his government's policies and intentions. Above all he must never be caught out in malicious gossip, tricky behaviour, or, above all, lies. It was tacitly assumed that he would report to London even the most sensitive of private revelations, insights, and opinions, and that they would go no further. Occasionally, in fact, Adam would share some of these with the most obviously trustworthy of his Commonwealth or European colleagues, or with his American opposite number, usually in exchange for equally valuable insights and revelations in return. But his own reliability as a recipient of confidences enabled him to build up close relationships with some of his Noridanese officials and other contacts, and some of these stood him in surprisingly good stead when he was in need.

### As an example:

*At the height of the Ethiopian famine in 1984, as the international relief effort was beginning to show results in relieving hunger, deaths from starvation and sicknesses associated with malnutrition and deprivation on a colossal scale, it became apparent that there were millions of Ethiopians in the central and northern highlands who were living many miles from any navigable road, many too weak to walk hundreds of miles to the nearest feeding centre or clinic, and thus impossible to reach with supplies of food and medicines by normal means. The United Nations Relief Coordinator and some of the heads of UN agencies and NGOs[3] (including Britain's Oxfam, Red Cross, and Save the Children, among many others) began to make enquiries about the possibility of air transport being made available for delivering relief supplies from the Ethiopian ports direct to remote airstrips in the mountainous famine areas.*

*At the same time, public opinion in Britain, stirred and shaken by vivid television reports of the famine and its pitiful victims, was increasing pressure on the government to step up its contribution to the famine relief effort. British ministers decided that an offer of Royal Air Force transport aircraft to transport relief supplies would amount to a dramatic high-profile gesture as well as filling a genuine and pressing need. As the British ambassador to Ethiopia at the time, on my first head of mission posting and still wet behind the gills, I was instructed to approach the Ethiopian government with this offer. My government at home immediately gave enormous publicity to my delivery of our offer, without waiting to hear whether the Ethiopian government would accept it.*

*As I had predicted beforehand to London, our offer presented the Ethiopian leadership, party and government, with a major political and ideological problem. The régime was both military and (nominally) communist, repressive and authoritarian, its top leaders ferociously anti-western and wholly dependent on Soviet military support for its resistance to several armed secessionist rebel movements around its periphery. To the hard-liners in the party and government, the idea of a NATO western air force such as the RAF being allowed to operate conspicuously inside Ethiopia in a famine relief role was almost unthinkable; I knew from several good sources that the Russians were actively encouraging the Ethiopians to reject our offer. Other Ethiopian government leaders were less doctrinaire and more pragmatic: they argued that to reject an offer of sorely needed help just because it came from a western NATO government would do irreparable harm to the international (almost entirely western) relief effort on whose continuation the survival of around nine million sick and hungry Ethiopians depended.*

*I was under increasingly urgent pressure from London, including from No. 10 Downing Street, to extract an Ethiopian reply to our offer of RAF transport aircraft for delivering relief supplies. I spent hours and days visiting ministers' offices and on the telephone to other contacts in the frantic effort to get an answer. Under growing media pressure at home, the British government decided to mobilise the first three Hercules (C130) aircraft, fill them with grain and medical supplies, and send them halfway to Ethiopia to await the Ethiopian reply at the British sovereign military base on Cyprus at Akrotiri. Still I could get no answer as the argument raged within the Ethiopian leadership.*

*At this point I received an unexpected telephone call from a senior contact in the ruling Ethiopian communist party. He was a party boss with whom I had had some friendly conversations at various official Ethiopian government functions, and who had cautiously uttered to me some faintly liberal opinions, always in strict confidence. His secret telephone call was to tell me that it was proving impossible to resolve the argument within the leadership between the hawks who wanted to reject the British offer of RAF aircraft, and the pragmatists who thought rejection would be disastrous. Since no agreement on the issue was in sight, it followed that I would never get a reply to our offer to transmit to my government. But then came the jewel in the message: if our aircraft were to arrive at the capital, Addis Ababa, they would not be prevented from landing and they would then be tacitly, but not officially, allowed to operate relief flights into the remote famine areas.*

*Was this the definite answer I had been pressing for?*

*"That's very welcome news," I said. "May I take that as a definite promise?"*

*"You understand that it's unofficial. I don't have permission to speak to you like this, Mr. Ambassador—my life would be in danger if our conversation became known. But yes, it's almost certain. That's all I can say. Goodbye."*

*And he hung up, that terrible "almost" ringing in my ears.*

*Taking a deep breath and crossing my fingers, I reported this unofficial (and obviously deniable) message to London and added my personal recommendation that the aircraft should now leave Cyprus, come to Addis Ababa, establish their operational base and start flying supplies to the famine areas, even though the Ethiopian authorities had still not officially accepted our offer nor authorised the arrival of the RAF. Within an hour I received an answering telegram from London asking for my definite confirmation that if the aircraft flew to Addis Ababa, they would not be prevented from landing. The telegram reminded me of what I already knew all too well: that if the C130s arrived over the Ethiopian capital only to find oil drums blocking the runway, or, even more horrendously, if one of them were to be shot down as a hostile military aircraft entering Ethiopian airspace without Ethiopian government permission, it would be a public relations as well as a human catastrophe. London's telegram made it very clear that if I had any reservations or hesitation about my prediction and recommendation, I should state them now so that the whole operation could be called off before even more serious harm was done.*

*I had no time to ponder the dilemma: the C130s were starting their engines on the Akrotiri airfield amid a huge UK press and television presence. What was at stake was more than my reputation for reliability in London and the future of my diplomatic career: it was potentially the lives of hundreds of thousands, perhaps millions, of sick and starving Ethiopians. Yet the basis for going ahead was nothing firmer than a secret telephone call from a communist party boss who had been speaking unofficially and without authority and who would unhesitatingly deny having telephoned me at all if I were ever to quote him as the basis for mounting the operation. I swallowed hard and sent a telegram confirming my recommendation that the C130s should now fly to Ethiopia, claiming to have more confidence than I really felt that they would encounter no resistance to landing at Addis Ababa and beginning operations. My recommendation was accepted and the air-craft were cleared for take-off.*

*On the bright sunny cool Saturday morning of November 3, 1984, my wife and I stood on the airfield at Addis Ababa, waiting for the arrival of the huge C130s. There was no sign of obstruction on the airstrip. Moments before the appointed time, two specks appeared in the sky, then a third. The specks grew into aircraft, and eventually we could make out the familiar RAF concentric rings markings, then huge banners painted on the fuselages proclaiming them to be carrying "Ethiopian famine relief supplies." One after another the transport planes landed and taxied to the terminal where an advance guard of the RAF, pre-positioned in case the operation were to go ahead, was waiting for them. Operation Bushel had begun.*

*The RAF were to stay in Ethiopia for fourteen months, delivering grain and medical supplies, tents and blankets, and other desperately needed supplies to needy people all over northern Ethiopia, flying every single day (including Sundays and Christmas Day) in harsh and dangerous conditions, without losing a single aircraft or crew or harming a single Ethiopian. They carried out difficult and dangerous low-level air drops of supplies to areas where there was not even a gravel airstrip at which a C130 could land. They were later joined by the West German Luftwaffe, flying slightly smaller transport aircraft, and later still by a squadron of the Polish air force flying ancient Soviet-made helicopters which landed at the sites of the RAF air drops to clear the DZ (dropping zone) of people and ensure that the supplies dropped would be collected for orderly distribution and not seized by the healthiest and fittest of the local people. So we had two NATO air forces (the RAF and the Luftwaffe) who had been enemies in the sec-ond world war, collaborating in a humanitarian cause with a Warsaw Pact air force from Poland, now ranged against NATO, but brave allies of the RAF against the Germans during the war. Professional and personal relations between all the crews—British, German, and Polish—in those cold war days were movingly close and comradely as they all collaborated in a great humanitarian enterprise.*

*Ethiopians in Addis Ababa would wave to the RAF C130s as they took off each morning to fly to the ports and load up with grain and other supplies, credibly reported as saying: "The Russian planes bring us guns and bombs, the English bring us food and medicines." Travel-ling often on the C130s to visit the feeding centres and clinics run by British NGOs in distant parts of the country, watching the daring low-altitude air drops and the landings of the heavily loaded aircraft at*

*impossibly short, often soft, gravel, or grass runways in remote moun-*
*tainous areas, my wife and I saw more of Ethiopia than, probably, any*
*of our predecessors.*

    *My gamble paid off handsomely. But I, more than almost anyone*
*else, knew what a gamble it had been.*

## NOTES

1.   A British ambassador's flag is the Union flag with the royal coat of arms
at the centre, signifying that the ambassador is the personal representative of his
or her Sovereign as well as of his government and of his country as a whole.
High Commissioners, however, fly an ordinary Union flag without the royal coat
of arms, since many of them represent Britain in another of the Queen's realms,
and the representative of the Queen can't present credentials to another representative of the same Queen (namely, the Governor-General). Such anomalies and
differences keep protocol departments the world over happy and occupied.

2.   A male ambassador's wife is an ambassadress. His female equivalent is
also an ambassador. There is no word (yet) for the husband of a female ambassador, a rapidly increasing species, no doubt because when these nomenclatures
came into general use, the species did not yet exist.

3.   Non-government organisations such as famine relief charities and human
rights organizations.

# 9

# DEALING WITH THE FOREIGN MINISTRY FROM ABROAD

*Dealing with the diplomat's own Foreign Ministry. Influencing foreign policy; relations with the geographical department in the diplomat's home capital; seeking, receiving, and obeying instructions.*

From his earliest experiences while serving in overseas posts as a junior diplomat, Adam had come to understand that the relationship between his embassy or high commission abroad and the Foreign & Commonwealth Office in London was almost as sensitive and important as the one with his host government. What was more, relations between the embassy and other departments in Whitehall could be even trickier.

Dick Grant, the British ambassador when Adam was a Counsellor at the embassy in 'Pazalia' was habitually caustic about the stream of messages from the Foreign & Commonwealth Office in London, containing guidance on policy issues and instructions on arcane questions of procedure, and above all about the incessant stream of questionnaires to be completed by all posts around the world. The ambassador would select the most offensive or obviously redundant of these and read them out with extravagantly pedantic emphasis at his daily morning meeting, radiating fastidious distaste. He was equally critical of some of the instructions specifically issued to the embassy.

One day at the ambassador's morning meeting Adam reported that he had received instructions from the Pazalia desk officer in the FCO (Chris Boardman, a relatively junior First Secretary) to lobby the Pazalian government to persuade it to vote for a draft resolution on equal rights for women at the General Assembly of the United Nations, then in session in New York. The United Kingdom was one of the high-minded sponsors of the draft resolution, a document whose purpose was manifestly noble but whose specific wording was ambiguous, woolly, and open to a number of perfectly rational objections, being clearly the result of argument and compromises when the text had been negotiated by the sponsor governments. Adam knew from the reporting telegrams from the UK Mission to the UN in New York that the Permanent Representative of Pazalia at the UN was one of many who had already expressed their reservations about some of the wording of the draft resolution, warning that unless the text was amended to take account of their criticisms, they would be unable to vote for it. The fact that many of the draft's critics were representatives of Muslim countries, including Pazalia, was universally noted but also by general tacit consent never mentioned.

"It's a bit peculiar, really," Adam told the meeting. "The Office has instructed us to lobby the Pazalians to vote for the resolution but apparently we and the other sponsors refuse to amend the resolution to take account of the criticisms that the Pazalians and others have made of it."

"Typical of the Office these days, I'm afraid," growled the ambassador. "I suppose the human rights fanatics in London have sent out these instructions without bothering to find out from United Nations Department which governments have already criticised the draft resolution or refused to vote for it unless it's amended. It's a complete waste of time to lobby the MFA here if we can't promise that the draft will be amended. Who sent us these pathetic instructions, Adam?"

"Sir, they're in an email to me from Chris Boardman—the Pazalia desk officer in Central Asia Department."

"Ah, yes," muttered the ambassador. "He was the one who was out here last month on a familiarisation visit, wasn't he?"

"That's right, sir."

"In that case, I'm not surprised. I wasn't impressed by young Boardman. Seems as if he hasn't done his homework before firing off absurd instructions to us. Better send him a telegram pointing out that it's a waste of time telling the Pazalians to vote for the resolution if we aren't prepared to amend it."

Ed Sorenson, the ambassador's deputy, chipped in. "Dick, I wonder whether it's really necessary to go back to the Office on this one?"

As the number two in the embassy, Sorenson was the only member of its staff who publicly addressed the ambassador by his first name. He continued:

"It's a pretty marginal issue, and if we do query the instructions, it will be the fourth time in as many weeks that we have gone back to London questioning instructions instead of biting our lips and carrying them out, whatever we might think of some of them. We'll begin to get a reputation in the Office for being unnecessarily picky. They're desperately over-worked in London, as we know, and every time we go back to them with queries on our instructions, it just makes extra work for them. Why don't we let Adam deliver a short Third Person Note to Western Department at the MFA expressing HBMG's hope that Pazalia will vote for the resolution despite the reservations about some aspects of it which we realise have been expressed by the Perm Rep of Pazalia at the UN?"

"I suppose you have a point, Ed," the ambassador conceded. "But things have come to a pretty pass when we can't point out that the instructions we've received from some ignorant teenager in the Department are rubbish and that if we obey them we'll make ourselves look ridiculous. What do you think, Adam?"

"Well, of course, instructions from the Office are instructions, whoever approved them, sir," Adam pointed out. He had no need to tell his ambassador that even if their instructions had been authorised and sent out by a junior officer in the Department and never seen by the Secretary of State (or, much of the time, by anyone else), that was beside the point. Overseas posts, even the grandest of ambassadors, are not entitled to look behind their instructions to see whether they have been approved at a sufficiently senior level before deciding whether to comply with them, although it sometimes happens. All instructions to overseas posts are deemed to have come from the Foreign Secretary himself.

"Ours not to question why: ours but to do and look daft," said the ambassador. "OK, Adam, we'd better do as we're told. But for God's sake make it clear to the Pazalians that we do know what the Pazalia position is on this damned resolution. Otherwise we'll be made to look like real amateurs. Then when you report to the Office that you have acted as instructed, please tell your young friend Boardman that in the circumstances his instructions were nonsense. Make sure we earn some credits for obeying stupid instructions—for the umpteenth time."

"Right, sir," Adam said. "Will do."

Young Chris Boardman's visit to the embassy had been a bit of a disaster, Adam reflected as he drafted his Note Verbale about the UN resolution. As the Pazalia desk officer, Boardman, although only a relatively junior and inexperienced First Secretary, was the most senior officer in the whole of the Foreign & Commonwealth Office dealing exclusively with Pazalia and all aspects of Britain's relations with it. At a time when his boss, the head of Central Asia Department and a Counsellor, had only recently assumed charge of the department, Boardman found himself in effect the British government's expert on Pazalia. His new head of department had oversight of fifteen different countries, of which Pazalia was by no means the most important. He had appealed to Boardman to refer upwards to him only the most serious issues, to enable him to devote more time to a crisis in another part of his parish. No doubt that was why Boardman had sent off the instructions on the UN resolutions without apparently consulting anyone else.

Boardman had arrived at the embassy a few weeks earlier for his familiarisation visit. Adam had been responsible for organising his programme, which had included calls on Boardman's opposite number in the Pazalia MFA, i.e., the UK desk officer in the ministry's Western Europe Department; on the two most prominent British businessmen in Pazalia; on an influential political commentator writing in the principal Pazalia newspaper; and on an official in the Pazalia Defence Ministry responsible for liaison with defence attachés in the embassies accredited to the country. Boardman also accompanied the embassy number two, Ed Sorenson, on a routine call on the head of Western Europe Department in the MFA. Sorenson had given a lunch for Boardman to meet assorted local figures, including two ambassadors of friendly countries, one a Commonwealth diplomat and the other a member of the EEC—now the EU—ambassadors' group. Adam took him to call on the European Commission Delegate (effectively the ambassador of the EEC to Pazalia) and also arranged a picnic for Boardman to see the embassy at play. Boardman had a long talk with the ambassador, attended by Adam, and an even longer one with Ed Sorenson with no one else present. On all these occasions Boardman, no doubt overawed by so much high-level attention, had seemed to be tongue-tied in the presence of Pazalians. Whoever was accompanying him from the embassy had had to do most of the talking to avoid embarrassing gaps in the conversation, leaving his Pazalian host wondering about the purpose of the call.

From the embassy's point of view, the visit of the Pazalia desk officer from the FCO had provided an opportunity to air some complaints about the way the department in London handled its relations with Pazalia and also the way it handled its relations with the embassy. Most of these complaints were relatively minor: frequent failures to acknowledge or to comment on reports from the embassy, long delays in responding to requests for instructions, sometimes on urgent issues; a tendency to disregard the embassy's recommendations on policy matters without fully explaining the basis for rejecting them; a failure to secure a place in the Office's visitors programme for an official visit to London by the Pazalia foreign minister, a visit for which the embassy had been pressing for years; and failure to persuade the UK Chancellor of the Exchequer to invite the Pazalia finance minister to pay a courtesy call on him while the latter was on a private visit to Britain (to see his younger son into his first term at Eton, Britain's most exclusive private school). Adam, Sorenson, and the ambassador tried to impress on the unfortunate Boardman that his department appeared to underrate the strategic importance of Pazalia and the potential benefits to UK interests of upgrading bilateral relations.

Boardman had responded by promising to convey these complaints and disappointments to his head of department at home, while at the same time pleading the extreme pressure of work in the office, aggravated by under-staffing, which made it difficult, sometimes impossible, to respond as promptly as they would have liked to the constant flow of information and requests coming in from the embassy. (Adam thought he caught a hint here that the embassy could usefully send a little less material to London.) As for the importance to be attached to relations with Pazalia, Boardman assured everyone that he and his head of department invariably battled strenuously for more resources of time and effort to be devoted to Pazalia, as to the other countries for which the department was responsible, but it had to be remembered that the senior management of the Office had to take a global view and that a host of factors had to be taken into account in determining priorities as between countries, especially when the FCO's workload was constantly being increased and its staffing levels and budget constantly and arbitrarily reduced.

Adam privately thought these explanations pretty convincing—especially as he was expecting a home posting as a head of department in the

FCO when his Pazalia posting came to an end in a year's time. Ed Soren-son was also cautiously sympathetic to Boardman's case. But the ambas-sador, Dick Grant, was dismissive.

"The Office is constantly whingeing about being overworked and understaffed. That's always the excuse for incompetence and indolence. It's the fault of our top management—the PUS[1] and the Directors-Gener-al[2] —for never having the guts to stand up to FCO ministers and the Treasury. They're too wet to refuse to take on new responsibilities with-out insisting on the extra resources we need to discharge them. And what does young Boardman know about Pazalia's importance in the scheme of things? God knows, we've explained it to him and his useless masters often enough. All this tosh about other factors that we're not supposed to know about! Heard it all before, far too many times."

Adam reflected that all over the world heads of mission were com-plaining to their geographical departments[3] that the Office was not pay-ing enough attention to their host countries, that their host governments' ministers were not being invited to pay official visits to London, and that their post budgets were inadequate for funding the ingenious activities that would make all the difference to their bilateral relations, all at mini-mal cost. And all over the world, heads of mission were receiving the same dusty answers from London.

Ed Sorenson gave Adam a surreptitious wink.

**As an example:**

*During my time as British high commissioner[4] in Nigeria, I be-came increasingly aware of a conflict between the policies of the Treasury and those of the Ministry of Defence (MoD) in Whitehall in regard to Nigeria. I reminded the relevant geographical department in the FCO (West African Department) that it had a duty to coordinate the policies of all Whitehall ministries towards the countries for which it was responsible, arbitrating and ironing out any inconsistencies as they appeared. This had no effect: HM Treasury and the MoD were notoriously disinclined to complicate their lives by consulting the FCO about their policies towards foreign or Commonwealth countries.*

*Matters came to a head when I received a long letter from the senior official heading the Defence Sales department of the MoD (De-fence Sales was later hived off into a quango, and, later still, privat-ised). The letter amounted to a prolonged rebuke, addressed to me personally. I was accused of a lamentable failure to exert myself con-*

*stantly in my contacts with the Nigerian Federal Government to press them to buy defence equipment from Britain—especially tanks and fighter aircraft, details of which had been sent to me as the basis for a sales drive which I had conspicuously failed to mount. The letter quoted extensive statistics to demonstrate that defence sales to Nigeria had fallen off dramatically since my arrival as high commissioner in Lagos some 18 months previously. My performance in this area was a matter of severe disappointment to the MoD in general, and Defence Sales in particular. If there were practical reasons for my failure, Defence Sales would be glad to know what they were, and what I was doing about them. I don't think the letter actually instructed me to pull my socks up and get on with selling tanks to the Nigerians, but that was certainly its general drift.*

*I wasn't inclined to take this without complaint. I dictated an almost equally long and equally blunt reply, recalling that because of Britain's substantial investment and trade stake in Nigeria, we had a clear national interest in Nigeria's economic development and the pursuit by its federal government of sound fiscal and economic policies. Accordingly we were providing Nigeria with a substantial aid programme, mostly in the form of balance of payments support, administered so as to ensure that as far as possible the foreign exchange which we were providing was used exclusively to buy new and additional imports that would contribute directly to economic and social development in Nigeria. I had been working closely with the head of overseas finance at the Treasury in London to make it clear to the Nigerians that the future of our aid programme depended on Nigeria continuing to pursue policies that would avoid waste and concentrate on promoting development, including poverty reduction programmes and the reduction of the ubiquitous corruption, then as now rife throughout the public and private sectors in Nigeria.*

*As part of this effort, I had established a close personal relationship with the Nigerian Minister of Finance, a powerful Northerner with a strong influence on government policy. He was collaborating closely with us in the effort to eliminate corruption and the waste of precious foreign currency on unnecessary imported goods.*

*On the possible purchase by the Nigerian federal government of British tanks and fighter aircraft, I recalled that a few years previously one of my predecessors had triumphantly succeeded in selling Nigeria substantial numbers of British-made tanks and fighter aircraft, together with a programme of technical assistance and training in how to use and maintain the new and expensive military hardware. The outcome of all this was instructive. The Nigerians had never had any occasion to use either their new tanks or the fighter aircraft, since Nigeria faced no military threat from its much smaller and weaker neighbours, or indeed from anyone else. British instructors had done their work, training scores of Nigerians in how to use and maintain the hardware. However, despite Nigeria being a major producer of crude oil, the Nigerian army and air force had proved unable to secure supplies of petrol or aviation fuel necessary for driving the tanks or flying the fighters: the distribution of oil was determined by bribes and deals, not by military need, real or imagined. The consequences were predictable: the tanks and the fighter aircraft were rusting away unused and unmaintained, no longer capable of being made serviceable even if the need for them should arise. All this had been reported to the MoD and the FCO by the high commission but the MoD had apparently drawn the sole conclusion that the time must be ripe to sell Nigeria fully functioning replacements. It was true that several thousands of jobs in Britain depended on selling tanks and aircraft to overseas customers. But I reminded the head of Defence Sales that despite some initial payments by the Nigerians for the tanks and fighters, later payments had dried up. The UK manufacturers had been insured against non-payment for their exports with Export Credit Guarantees Department (ECGD), then a department of the British government, which had been obliged to pay the British exporters the substantial amounts of money which the Nigerians should have paid for the hardware, but which they had failed to stump up.*

*I concluded from all this that it could not be in either Britain's or Nigeria's interest to sell to Nigeria military hardware which the Nigerians didn't need, could not afford, would never use, and would never pay for. The only consequences of such sales would be to effect a transfer of resources, via ECGD, from the UK taxpayer to the British arms manufacturers, and to demonstrate to the Nigerians that all our pious advice to the federal government to eliminate wasteful use of foreign exchange on unnecessary and expensive toys for the rich or the military, as a condition for our continuing our handsome aid programme, was hypocritical guff when it came to the export of military hardware from Britain.*

*My own view, I wrote, was that the whole idea of trying to sell these military goods to the Nigerians was fundamentally misconceived, that it was impossible to reconcile it with our aid and economic policies as managed by the Treasury at a senior level in regard to Nigeria, and that it should accordingly be abandoned. I hoped that the points I had made would be given proper consideration in Whitehall by all the departments concerned, including the FCO, the Overseas Development Administration (responsible for our aid programme) and the Treasury, as well as Defence Sales and the MoD itself. Following such consideration, I would need fresh instructions, which I would of course comply with, whatever they were. I sent copies of my letter to senior officials all over Whitehall.*

*When my Number Two in the high commission in Lagos saw his copy of my reply to Defence Sales, he congratulated me on such an eloquent career suicide note.*

*In the event, my letter was received in total and lasting silence. I never received a counter-blast from either Defence Sales or the FCO, nor a message of support from the Treasury. Years later I heard that my letter had caused something of a stir in Whitehall. An interdepartmental committee had been set up, I think at the behest of ministers, to discuss the issues I had raised (which of course were applicable to many other developing countries besides Nigeria) and to reach a consensus on any necessary changes of policy. Perhaps predictably, the committee failed to reach any consensus at all. The FCO proved quite unable to mediate between the Treasury and the Overseas Development Administration on the one hand and the MoD on the other. The committee continued to meet from time to time, but eventually it seems to have withered away without ever producing an agreed report to ministers. I never received the revised instructions which I had requested. But I was never again urged to work to promote sales of British military hardware to Nigeria.*

*Officials can occasionally be successful in challenging hallowed government policies and recommending alternatives, if only by default.*

## NOTES

1. The Permanent Under-Secretary of State and Head of the Diplomatic Service, the most senior official in the FCO and the whole Service.

2. Directors-General in the FCO were at that time called Deputy Under-Secretaries of State, or DUSs, responsible under the PUS for the efficient running of the Diplomatic Service and the FCO.

3. FCO geographical departments are responsible for relations with countries in a defined geographical area—in this case West Africa. Subject departments deal with specific areas of policy—economic and trade, defence, the Unit-

ed Nations, human rights, the environment—wherever in the world they arise. Most of an embassy's or high commission's dealings with London will generally be with the relevant geographical department and its supervising Assistant Under-Secretary (now called Director).

4. High Commissioner is the title given instead of "ambassador" to a head of mission representing one Commonwealth country in another Commonwealth country. High commissioners' functions are to all intents and purposes the same as those of ambassadors to foreign countries.

# 10

# ENTERTAINING AND BEING ENTERTAINED

*The purpose of socialising with local officials and other nationals; techniques, hazards, and successes; the wear and tear.*

From the time when Adam first toyed with the idea of applying to join the diplomatic service, he had worried about the social side of diplomatic life. Would it mean a lifetime of more or less elegant cocktail parties, candle-lit dinners, and catty small talk with bejewelled women and suave chinless men in evening dress? Adam had no particular inhibitions about chatting with strangers, but there must, he felt, be better ways of passing the time than engaging in vapid conversations with a lot of snobs and arrivistes. Later, when Adam proposed marriage to Eve, Eve had similar worries about the social implications of marrying a diplomat. Would she spend the next few decades worried that she might unwittingly commit an appalling faux pas on some glittering social occasion, humiliating Adam's ambassador and potentially ruining his own career? Would all the social life, all the gins and tonics and Ferrero Rochers, serve any discernible purpose?

Experience quite soon dispelled some, but by no means all, of these concerns in both Adam's and Eve's minds. Adam, and to some extent Eve, at first felt intimidated by the upper-class fripperies of much diplomatic social life, then came to resent them, and later despised them as faintly absurd relics of a bygone age and a long gone class system. They gave numerous dinner parties over the years, but never asked their guests to wear black tie and dinner jackets, or the female equivalents. At their "drinks parties" (diplomats never seemed to call them "cocktail parties") they rarely served champagne or cheaper variants of it, fearing to be thought pretentious if they did. They avoided, as far as they could, inviting to their lunch or dinner tables local people whose status depended mainly or entirely on their wealth or aristocratic origins, or both, while lacking influence or interesting or provocative views, and being unlikely sources of insights and information. Later still, challenged by their children on the snobby style of life that they seemed to have adopted, they came to realise that internationally accepted rules of protocol actually served a purpose in avoiding the embarrassments and humiliations that would flow from a diplomatic social world without them.

When attending other people's drinks parties, national day receptions, lunches, and dinners, Eve and Adam of course had no control over the style of entertaining that they would have to endure, nor over the quality of the other guests. Both of them spent long, arid hours making pointless conversation with uninteresting and sometimes unpleasant people with whom they had nothing in common.

Returning with Eve late one night in Khaliman from an interminable black tie dinner given by the Austrian ambassador for a visiting Austrian government minister, Adam, now HM Ambassador to Noridan, expressed his disillusionment to Eve as they changed out of their evening dress in the cavernous master bedroom of the Residence.

"Don't you sometimes wonder why we go on doing this, Eve?"

"Of course I do. Often. But it's all part of the job—your job, I mean. It goes with the territory."

"But we could have a different kind of life if I had an ordinary nine-to-five job that I could take off with my raincoat every evening when I got home. We could have an early night whenever we wanted, we could have scrambled egg and a cup of coffee instead of the interminable mushroom soup and coq-au-vin followed by sugary cheesecake, all washed down with countless glasses of indifferent wine, night after bloody night. Wouldn't that be marvellous?"

"Oh, come on, Adam," Eve said. "You know you'd miss the buzz from getting the foreign minister in a corner at some national day reception and bending his ear with some foreign policy issue that you would never be able to tackle him with in working hours. And us two having half an hour alone with the Queen when you were appointed an ambassador. And both of us chatting on equal terms over a Scotch with a group of visiting British MPs who are staying with us in the Residence and who are dying to tell you all the malicious gossip circulating at Westminster about who's plotting against the prime minister and who's secretly sabotaging some government Bill. And talking to a member of the royal family in the back of the Jaguar after meeting her on arrival at the airport, to find out what she's going to want for breakfast next morning."

"How fascinating *that* conversation was," Adam remarks, pulling his black tie bow apart and unbuttoning his dress shirt. "Two poached eggs on brown toast, if I remember rightly."

"Well, some of our official visitors are more interesting than others. But now you've experienced these things—"

"Now that *we've* experienced them," Adam corrected her.

"All right, we: now that *we've* experienced these things, wouldn't we find almost any other kind of life tame and colourless?"

"Well, I might have agreed with you," Adam said, "if I didn't face the prospect of having to go out to a lunch given by the Dean tomorrow for the Vice President of Costa Rica who's here on an official visit for some unfathomable reason, then to a drinks party in the evening to celebrate the birthday of the younger daughter of the governor of the Bank of Noridan (where the strongest drink available will be orange juice, of course), followed by a stag dinner with all the EU ambos to meet the Danish Deputy Minister for Women who's here on a fact-finding visit, God help us."

"You won't mind meeting that particular visitor," Eve remarked, wriggling out of her long pencil skirt. "She's a very attractive blonde aged 23, I'm told."

"All right, but by the time I get home tomorrow evening I'll have had far too much to eat and rather more to drink than I should, and I'll have been on duty from around 7:30 in the morning until nearly midnight."

"Oh, you poor thing," said Eve sarcastically. "Our friends at home must feel *so* sorry for you, being forced to spend your days wining and dining with beautiful Danish blondes at the EU's expense."

"Actually," Adam admitted, "I think I might meet some interesting people at the Bank Governor's do—some of the Finance Ministry people who play hard to get when you try to call on them during office hours. There could be some useful contacts to be made there."

"Oh, do you think one of them might offer you a job, then?"

"Fat chance!" Adam laughed. "But you never know when having a contact in the finance ministry might come in handy one day, when you want some sensitive financial information in a hurry or when you want someone from the Finance ministry to come to lunch and meet your visiting Under-Secretary from the Treasury in London. It's much easier to winkle out some key bit of information from a Noridanese minister or official when you've met him socially and had a friendly chat with him about his family and his recent visit to London, than if your only contact has been chilly and official—or than if you haven't had any previous contact at all."

"So all our drinks party and lunch and dinner commitments aren't such a waste of time after all," Eve pointed out.

"Sixty per cent of them are," grumbled Adam. "The trouble is, you never know in advance which the useful forty per cent are going to be."

"As I said before," Eve said, "it's all part and parcel of your job. It's what lubricates diplomacy the whole world over. We shouldn't knock it."

"All right," Adam agreed. "I could do without the Vice President of Costa Rica tomorrow, all the same."

**As an example:**

*Soon after my arrival in Addis Ababa as ambassador to Ethiopia, a member of the embassy's Ethiopian staff happened to mention that, according to a mutual friend of his, the Minister of Finance in the Ethiopian government was an avid fan of Manchester United, a prominent English football team. Although the government's finance ministry was less powerful than the financial section of the ruling Ethiopian communist party, the ministry and its minister were not to be lightly dismissed as potential sources of information and influence. So I asked the FCO information department if it could lend me a couple of videos of football matches spectacularly won by Manchester United. Some weeks later the two video tapes arrived in the diplomatic bag.*

*The Ethiopian régime was a brutal military communist dictatorship with no pretence of being democratic and deeply in hock to the Soviet Union, on which it depended for military support against a number of armed secessionist movements around its borders. It was also strongly anti-western. Contacts between government or party officials and western embassies were accordingly rare and generally limited to frigid official exchanges. One day, however, I spotted the Finance Minister, Bellew Bekele (not his real name), in a row of government ministers on the VIP stand in Revolution Square to which the entire diplo-*

*matic corps had been summoned to witness an enormous military pa-
rade to mark some anniversary of the revolution in which the Emperor
Haile Selassie had been deposed (and later murdered). Ambassadors,
including me, were seated on benches immediately behind the ministers. I managed to sit myself down immediately behind Ato[1] Bellew.
Shortly after the parade had begun, the minister turned round to wave
to someone at the back of the VIP stand, and I managed to catch his
eye.*

*"Minister," I said, "I'm very glad to meet you! I'm the British
ambassador. I wanted to mention Manchester United to Your Excellency."*

*"Manchester United?" said the minister.*

*"Yes—I happen to have some very nice videos of two Manchester
United matches that I think Your Excellency would be interested to see
if you could spare the time to come round one evening, very informally, for some supper and to watch the videos."*

*"Well," Bellew said cautiously, "I'm very busy just now, but per-
haps some time . . . "*

*"Just get your secretary to telephone mine to fix a date whenever
it's convenient to you," I suggested.*

*"I'm much obliged to you, Mr. Ambassador," the minister said,
turning back to watch the parade.*

*A month or so later, and rather to my surprise, my secretary had a
call from the finance minister's office. The minister and his wife were
pleased to accept my invitation and would arrive at my Residence at
7:30 pm the following Thursday. Fortunately and somewhat surprisingly there was nothing in my diary for that evening. My secretary
called back to confirm to the minister's office that we were looking
forward to meeting them on Thursday.*

*The four of us—the minister and I and our wives—spent a pleasant
evening together and once the ice was broken by the showing of the
first video tape before we sat down to a deliberately unostentatious
supper, we were soon chatting freely about our families, a recent
political crisis in Britain, the British royal family, and the forthcoming
American presidential election. After supper we watched most of the
second video. Before Bellew and his wife got up to leave, amid profuse
expressions of appreciation of a most enjoyable evening, he asked
whether as a special favour he could borrow the videos, against a firm
promise to return them after his son, another Man U fan, had seen
them. I willingly handed over the two boxes. On an impulse the minister fished out of his pocket his card with his private address and*

*telephone number and gave it to me "in case you should ever need to get in touch again"; and he and Mrs. Bellew vanished into the night.*

*Nearly a year later, we were visited by a team from a leading British construction company (let's call them Barlows), led by its Chief Executive, who after many years of intricate argument had finally been invited to discuss an issue of compensation with the Ethiopian government. After the communist revolution, Barlows' Ethiopian branch, which had been active in Ethiopia during the time of the Emperor, had been nationalised and its offices and other assets confiscated by the new régime, with an offer of compensation that was at once rejected by Barlows, with the support of the British government, as derisory. Barlows' demand for adequate compensation and Ethiopia's refusal to discuss it had become a running sore in relations between the two countries and governments. Like my predecessors, I had repeatedly nagged the Ethiopian government through its foreign ministry to invite Barlows to Ethiopia to see whether the issue could be resolved. There were various complicating factors needing to be settled before there could be a discussion of a figure for total compensation that both sides could agree upon.*

*Rod Johnson, the Barlows' Chief Executive, came to see me with his two colleagues on the evening before the meetings with the Ethiopian team were to begin. We had a useful discussion of Barlows' most promising tactics and I made some suggestions about Ethiopian susceptibilities and objectives. Johnson said he would like to look in each evening as the negotiations went on to brief me on how the day had gone and to continue our discussion of tactics.*

*Next evening Johnson duly arrived at the Residence, now in pessimistic mood. The talks had not gone well. The Ethiopian side had refused to discuss a figure for compensation until various other matters had been settled, and their position on these seemed uncompromisingly rigid. Johnson described which of these issues was a sticking-point for Barlows and which might allow for some flexibility. I undertook to see what I could find out about the Ethiopian position. Johnson had mentioned that Bellew Bekele, the minister of finance, had been present throughout the talks although he had not personally contributed to them. I found Bellew's private telephone number on the card he had given me when he had come to the Residence for dinner and the Manchester United videos, and called him. He answered the telephone himself, and agreed that it could be useful if we were to keep in touch about the Barlows negotiations, unofficially and off the record, in the hope of dispelling any possible misunderstandings. Silently encour-*

*aged by Johnson, I suggested to the minister some of the issues that I thought might be capable of resolution first, if both sides were willing to show flexibility. Bellew took note of these and in return suggested which of the points that I had listed might be able to be dealt with flexibly on the Ethiopian side also. We agreed that it would be helpful if the talks next day could focus on those issues on which both sides seemed able to be flexible. Once these were agreed, the talks could move on to the more difficult areas.*

*Next day considerable progress was made at the talks. After they had ended for the day, Johnson came to see me and report, as on the previous day, and I telephoned Ato Bellew again. We had another useful exchange, hinting again at areas where some compromises seemed possible. The process continued on the same lines for two weeks. At the conclusion of the talks agreement had been reached on all the main issues, including a provisional figure for compensation to be paid to Barlows, subject to the settlement of a couple of outstanding matters which it had been agreed could be sorted out during the following month in London.*

*At the beginning of the talks neither side had expected them to reach a substantive agreement on any of the principal issues: several further rounds of negotiations at a later stage had seemed inevitable, even supposing that the current talks were not to break down completely. It didn't seem unduly far-fetched to credit Manchester United with the unexpected success. After the Barlows team had gone home to celebrate, I telephoned the finance minister on his private line one more time to thank him for his help, which I said had been the key to the eventual agreement.*

*"Don't thank me, Mr. Ambassador," the finance minister said. "Thank Manchester United."*

Eve and Adam were back at home in London on their mid-tour leave from Khaliman after their first eighteen months of a three-year posting there. Their old friends, Peter and Nora, had come to supper with them, the first time they had seen each other since Adam had gone to Noridan on his first ambassadorial appointment.

Eve joked about not having to worry about the way her dinner guests were placed at the table according to their order of precedence, for the first time in eighteen months. Correct placement was always a worry at one's own dinner and lunch parties, as she and Adam knew from their previous postings.

"Heavens, Eve," Nora said incredulously: "you don't bother about that obsolete stuff, do you? People must think you're terribly old-fashioned."

"We certainly do," Adam said. "We'd cause frightful embarrassment all round if we didn't. People can tell at once whether they have been allocated to the right chair at the table corresponding to their seniority in the order of precedence. Each country publishes its list of orders of precedence and among diplomats everyone knows that precedence depends on the date on which the ambassador presented his or her credentials to the head of state. If someone lower in the pecking order is sitting in the senior lady's place, the senior lady is likely to take it as a personal insult, she won't know what to do about it, and the less senior lady occupying the wrong place is going to be seriously embarrassed, too. No one can possibly benefit from such a situation."

"But why can't you let everyone sit wherever they like? That's what real people do, and it works all right," Peter said.

Eve pointed out that the kind of people she and Adam often entertained in Noridan were not "real people," but other diplomats, government officials and ministers, generals and admirals, bishops and newspaper editors, politicians and writers and business people and their spouses and partners, from different countries all over the world.

"It's essential to have internationally understood rules about *placement* at the meal table, who is the senior guest, who leaves the dinner party first (the senior guest and his or her partner, obviously), and such quite minor matters," Eve explained. "If you ignore these rules of protocol, you just cause everyone anxiety and concern. If the senior couple have not each been seated on the right-hand side of the host and hostess at the table, it will create doubt about which couple is the most senior (or the guests of honour, which comes to the same thing). And that means that no one is sure when they are free to leave at the end of the dinner. No one wants to appear ignorant or arrogant by saying goodbye and leaving before the senior guests have left."

Adam added: "It's equally important that the senior guests know who they are, and that no other guests can leave before them. If the senior lady is talking and talking and having a lovely time, she may forget that she's preventing anyone else from leaving."

Peter said: "But that doesn't explain why everyone has to dress up in the same fancy dress for every function—black tie, lounge suit, and so on. That's crazy."

Adam replied that the case for rules on dress was the same as for *placement*. If the invitation card gave no indication of the grade of attire to be worn, some would arrive in casual gear, others in smart dresses and suits, others again in dinner jackets and black tie. The most formally dressed would be embarrassed at having misread the nature of the occasion, and the most informally dressed, seeing others in black tie, would fear that their hosts will be upset at being taken for granted.

Nora said: "Anyone would think that the only point of being a diplomat is not to embarrass anyone."

"Well, that's actually quite important if people are to be relaxed and enjoy the party without fear of committing a faux pas," Adam replied. "Everyone knows the story, true or not, of the diplomatic guest at a formal dinner, believing himself to have been seated in a more lowly place than his importance entitled him to, picking up his empty soup-bowl, turning it upside down on the table, and walking out. We have never seen that happen, but we did have one guest, a junior diplomat of another European country, ostentatiously not drinking his soup, and when Eve enquired whether there was a problem with it, pointing silently to his table setting from which a soup spoon had been accidentally omitted. He had regarded it as beneath his dignity to ask for a soup spoon as soon as he saw that he hadn't got one, and also because that might have been taken as an insult to his hostess."

"Perhaps the poor guy was just too embarrassed to ask for a spoon. You both live in a funny world if these are the only things that matter to everyone," Peter said caustically.

"Of course they aren't the only things that matter," Eve said, now getting cross. "But they do matter, and there's a good reason for them, as you get to realise after a while. They soon become second nature and then you're free to worry about more important things, like why the Residence cook has over-boiled the sprouts."

"The *Residence cook*?" exclaimed Peter and Nora simultaneously. "You have a *cook*?"

"Of course we do," Eve said. "You don't seem to realise that what we call the Residence—which is what everyone calls the place where an ambassador lives, even if it's only a mud hut—is not just our cosy little home: it's a fully functional hotel and restaurant for the hundreds or even the thousands of people who come to eat and drink in it and the dozens and dozens of official visitors who come to stay in it. It would be literally impossible to run a hotel and restaurant without any staff."

"You mean you have maids and waiters and bottle-washers as well as this cook?" asked Nora, her voice rising.

"Of course. We have a butler, too, whose job is to manage the running of the Residence and to supervise the other Residence staff."

"Good grief," muttered Peter. "I'll need to watch my Ps and Qs if we ever come out to Noridan to stay with you. A *butler*!"

"Come on," Eve said, "time to eat. You can sit here, Peter . . ."

"He certainly can't," Nora said. "I'm senior to him so that's *my* place."

### As an example:

*While I was working in the Foreign & Commonwealth Office in London as a first secretary and assistant head of an African department, I was nominated to take part as the junior member of a small FCO team visiting Madrid for annual Anglo-Spanish talks about Africa. The briefing telegram from Madrid before we left London said specifically that there was no need for us to take dinner jackets. However, on the way in to the Residence from the airport, the ambassador mentioned casually that he looked forward to seeing the three of us at a dinner party he was giving at the Residence the following evening for some Spanish friends and contacts: he was sure we would enjoy meeting them.*

*"Dress for your dinner, Richard?" asked the leader of our team.*

*"Oh, black tie," the ambassador replied. "That's taken for granted here in the diplomatic world and the smart set's social scene."*

*My heart sank. I said, "I'm afraid I didn't bring mine. We were told we wouldn't need it. So I'm afraid I'll have to skip your dinner, Ambassador."*

*"No, no, not at all," said the ambassador. "A dark suit will be perfectly acceptable. Might raise a few bejewelled Spanish eyebrows, but we needn't worry about that. Or you might be able to borrow a dinner jacket from someone in the embassy. Afraid my spare one wouldn't fit you." He was about 6' 2"; I'm a fraction over 5' 9".*

*Enquiries in the embassy produced only one offer, from the kindly registry clerk, who was short and tubby. There was ample room for two of me in the trousers. I looked like a circus clown in them. But to be the only guest at the ambassador's dinner in a lounge suit seemed likely to be even more humiliating than attending in my clown's outfit, which would be largely invisible once we sat down at the table to eat.*

*So I went as a clown. As the most junior of all the diners I was correctly seated halfway between the host at one end and the hostess at the other, with heavily bejewelled Spanish ladies on each side of me. Up and down the table vigorous conversations were taking place, all in fluent Spanish. Neither of my bejewelled neighbours spoke or understood English, and I had (and have) no Spanish, so both very sensibly ignored me and struck up conversations with their other neighbours. I made a mental note to avoid a posting to Madrid, or any other Spanish-speaking post, like the plague, or Spanish flu. But I greatly appreciated the kindness of the tubby registry clerk.*

Adam found that the rules governing the entertainment allowance for a head of mission had kept changing. In the past an ambassador or high commissioner had received all his allowances rolled into one, called his *"frais"* (short for *"frais de représentation,"* or "expenses of representation") and paid monthly. Then *frais* was disaggregated into all its component parts, as was the case with diplomatic staff below the head of mission. There was an overseas allowance (to compensate British diplomats serving abroad for the extra cost of living away from home). A difficult post allowance was payable in some places, such as hostile totalitarian states or developing countries with bad climates, very few western cultural opportunities, poor or non-existent medical and educational facilities, serious insecurity both indoors and out, and chronic shortages of basic things such as food, imposing the additional cost of having to import almost everything from toilet paper to beef. There was a married allowance (two cost more than one). For parents there were boarding school allowance, covering only the average cost of a UK boarding school despite the fact that nearly all diplomatic service parents send their children to schools that are considerably more expensive than the national average (standards of care and teaching at average and below-average schools being mostly unacceptable). There were language allowances for those who had studied a hard language which they were currently using as part of the job, and had passed an FCO examination in it. And, not least, there was the entertainment allowance.

Until his first overseas posting, Adam had thought that all these allowances sounded reasonably generous. Surely, he thought, it must be possible to save some of this money by spending thriftily; entertaining must be something of which one could do as much or as little as one liked. He was swiftly disabused of such ideas when he experienced his first Foreign

& Commonwealth Office Inspection. He was still unmarried—he met and married Eve only later—and had not taken very seriously the advice he had received from his head of chancery to keep careful and detailed records of everything he spent, both on his own personal needs and pleasures and also on official entertaining. His allowances interview with the visiting inspectors, members of the diplomatic service like himself but doing a stint as inspectors instead of a regular posting, was somewhat choppy. The FCO has long since abandoned the old system of three-yearly inspections of all UK overseas posts by teams of diplomatic service officers dispatched from London with instructions, implicit or explicit, to reduce allowances wherever possible in order to save money for the FCO's ever-shrinking budget. No doubt the inspection system was terminated because it was proving too expensive, although British diplomatic service officers at all levels remain strictly accountable for the way they spend their allowances. But when Adam was posted overseas for the first time, to Côte Noire in west Africa, the FCO Inspectorate was still going strong. When the FCO team was accompanied by an additional inspector from the Treasury (the UK's Ministry of Finance, answering the question: "Who inspects the inspectors?"), the posts to be visited knew that an even more rigorous examination of their allowances was in store for them. Such was the case when it was the turn of the small British embassy in Côte Noire to be inspected.

"May we start by going through your entertainment expenditure accounts, Adam?" suggested the junior of the three FCO inspectors.

"Well, look, Jasper, I only have these rather rough notes of my entertainment spending which I've had to reconstruct largely from memory. I hadn't realised—"

"Your posting instructions told you very clearly to keep careful records of all your spending, you know."

"Yes, I realise that now, but it's my first overseas posting, and . . ."

"Right. We'll have to manage as best we can with these rather scrappy notes. I see there's a rather large figure here for 'wines and spirits.' You need to break that down into alcohol consumed in the context of official entertaining, and alcohol consumed privately, that's to say by yourself and your friends in your leisure time or at any office party that you may have given. You'll have to be careful to get that breakdown right. You have quite a generous entertainment allowance, I see—I can't imagine what the last inspection of this post three years ago thought it was doing, setting your predecessor's allowance so high. We'll have to go through all your entertainment records for the past year so that I can judge what was really essential, whether any of it looks a bit frivolous, and whether you were spending unnecessarily lavishly even on the essential and useful entertaining, so that I can fix your new allowances at a more realistic rate. For example, I see that you have an item here for 'cigars.' Unless your official guests smoked a phenomenal number of your cigars, it looks as if you have been offering them inappropriately expensive cigars relative to your rather junior grade. The allowances are calculated on the basis that only heads of mission would normally buy and offer Cuban cigars; below that level officers are expected to offer much cheaper brands."

Adam did vaguely remember, now Jasper had said it, that someone had warned him, when he put in his six-monthly order for imports of wines, spirits, and tobacco, that his entertainment allowance wasn't meant to cover Cuban cigars. He had thought at the time that to offer lesser cigars would make him look miserly in the eyes of his official guests, so he had ordered fine Havanas and hoped for the best.

"I'm puzzled by this item in your entertainment allowance account for imported soap," remarked Jasper. "You may think I'm nit-picking, but we need to make sure that local allowances aren't inflated by officers importing unnecessarily expensive items when perfectly adequate equivalents can easily be bought in the local market. Janet, our excellent inspection secretary, got on a local bus yesterday to visit a very picturesque market a little way out—"

"I'm told she went out to what we call the camel market, about four miles from the embassy," said Adam. "It's not safe to take a car out there if you're driving on your own, and even more risky to come back on a crowded bus carrying a load of tempting shopping. Virtually no one from the embassies shops there. You really have to shop at the so-called midtown market where prices are admittedly higher and there's a smaller choice of products, but at least it's fairly safe."

"Well, Janet had no problems going out to the camel market, and the soap there was almost exactly a tenth of what you're paying for fancy bars of Imperial Leather imported from London or the diplomatic suppliers in Copenhagen. Can you give me any reason why the British taxpayer should pay so much over the odds for your soap, Adam?"

"Jasper," said Adam, exasperated, "have you actually *seen* the local soap? Or *smelled* it? Or tried to wash your hands with it?"

"Well, if you're that fastidious about your soap," the inspector said primly, "you're at liberty to import the most expensive soap you can find; just don't claim the cost of it on your entertainment allowance, even if you have had a dozen official visitors billeted on you for weeks at a time—however unlikely that might be at your level."

"Let them eat cake," Adam muttered, getting angry.

"Exactly. Now, about these rather expensive imported cocktail nuts that you're claiming for. I have two problems with these. First, Janet found very cheap and quite acceptable peanuts on sale locally—"

"At the camel market, I suppose. I hope she had an armed escort. A second secretary at the Nigerian embassy was attacked and shot by an armed robber just behind the camel market only last month. She very nearly died. The American embassy doctor saved her life, actually."

"How very sad. Of course the same kind of thing happens all the time in Tooting,[2] but we aren't afraid to go to Tooting for our shopping. Yes, Janet got the nuts at the camel market, reached by an extraordinarily cheap bus ride. Secondly, you don't seem to have distinguished between the imported fancy nuts that you have used for official entertaining, and the ones you have bought for yourself and your friends. Obviously the private nuts don't qualify for entertainment allowance."

"Obviously," Adam agreed. "I'll do a breakdown and let you have a revised figure."

"Thank you," Jasper said. "Now, you have this item for candles— quite expensive imported candles. Janet tells us—"

"Strike out the candles," Adam said. "I'll donate them to HMG out of my own pocket. Look, it's nearly time for lunch. Can I offer you—what would you like?—"

"A glass of sherry?" suggested Jasper.

"No, I was going to offer you a glass of water—local water, straight from the tap. So much cheaper than the fancy imported bottled stuff. Of course, you might easily catch typhoid from it, but what the hell! Got to think of the British taxpayer, haven't we?"

**As an example:**

   *During a particularly draconian visitation by a team of FCO inspectors to Canberra, the Australian federal capital, where I was a Counsellor and head of chancery in the British high commission, the Academy of St. Martin-in-the-Fields with their distinguished founder and conductor Sir Neville Marriner and Lady Marriner, along with the*

*Early Music Consort, with its co-founder David Munrow, two famous British orchestras and conductors, were touring Australia and the far East under the auspices of the British Council. The two orchestras gave a concert in the Australian capital, Canberra, before a large and enthusiastic audience which included half the Australian federal government and most of Canberra's artistic and musical elite. My boss, the British high commissioner, had indicated to me a fortnight earlier that he would appreciate it if J and I were to give a big buffet supper after the concert for both the orchestras and their conductors and managers, at which they could meet a selection of prominent and other local people, thus lifting Britain's prestige in Canberra by a few much needed notches. It was made clear that the high commissioner's Residence would not be available for such a function on that particular evening. Obviously I had no alternative but to agree, dreading what J would say when I broke the news to her.*

*J spent most of the next two weeks shopping and preparing for the buffet supper, recruiting for the evening a small team of capable Australian domestic helps who would arrive at our house shortly before the guests were due to arrive, soon after the end of the concert, dish up the numerous dishes that J had already prepared, serve it to the hundred or so guests at a signal from J, clear away the cutlery and crockery towards the end of the party, wash it up and go home before the last of the guests had departed. J had also been involved in the tricky task of drawing up the guest list in such a way that those Australian dignitaries not invited would not feel insulted by their exclusion, and those invited were unlikely to include anyone who would drink too much and pick a fight with the leader of the second violins or, worse, with Sir Neville Marriner. The guest list included the three FCO Inspectors and their intimidating lady secretary, in accordance with the tradition that visiting inspectors were included in any official entertaining that took place during their visit, to enable them to judge the quality and especially the cost, either excessively lavish or satisfactorily frugal, of the post's entertainment performance.*

*The supper went extremely well, the British musicians glad to relax after the concert and to chat with their enthusiastic Australian admirers, the Australian guests fascinated to meet and talk to such celebrities as Marriner and Munrow. The wine and Foster's flowed freely and J's excellent food, hot and cold and plentiful, vanished in record time. Eventually the buses arrived to take the orchestras back to their hotel and the Australians began to leave, thanking J effusively for a memorable evening. At last only a few high commission colleagues and their spouses were left, along with J and me—and the four FCO inspectors. I thanked the high commission colleagues for conscientiously helping out with keeping the guests fed, their glasses filled and suitable company provided, and urged them and the inspectors to stay on for a nightcap before they went home—normal practice after a big party. The colleagues settled into the easy chairs with glasses of Scotch or brandy. The inspectors also sat themselves down but the leader of the inspection team, whom I will call Algernon, refused to drink anything stronger than water ("no ice, thank you"), as he had done throughout the evening. Algernon moved from the chair he had been sitting in to be next to J, an exhausted but happy hostess.*

*"I see that you had caterers to provide the food, prepare and cook it, serve it, and clear away afterwards. That must have been quite expensive?" said Algernon, eyebrows raised interrogatively.*

*J explained that on the contrary, she had done everything herself right up to the moment when the guests were about to arrive. The Australian lady that helps had been in the house for less than the duration of the supper. J herself had spent not hours but many days planning, shopping, preparing, cooking, and finally rushing back to the house before the end of the concert to be there before the first guests arrived. She would still have to put away the mountain of cutlery and crockery before she could go to bed, well after midnight, with a clear conscience. She was understandably and visibly exhausted.*

*"Tell me," said the senior inspector, staring at J through the thick lenses of his National Health Service spectacles, "do you think that this evening's function was a good use of British public funds?"*

*With the utmost difficulty, J restrained herself from bursting into tears.*

Adam was uncomfortably aware of his heavy dependence on Eve for the whole of the social side of his life as a diplomat serving abroad, especially for the entertaining that he and Eve did together as part of their job, and also as an indispensable companion at the numerous official functions that he and Eve inevitably had to attend. This was true both when Adam was an officer of middling seniority in the embassy or high commission to which he was posted, and later when he served as a head of mission himself, first as an ambassador to a foreign country and later when he was British high commissioner in a Commonwealth country, performing the same functions.

For Adam and for most of his diplomatic service colleagues of the same generation, entertaining and being entertained were essential elements in the vital task of establishing a personal relationship with the movers and shakers, the decision makers and influence wielders, in the countries where he served. Only when a personal relationship had been established could Adam create the kind of mutual trust that enabled his contacts to talk frankly to him, to seek his advice on often surprisingly *sensitive local issues, and* to take him seriously when he urged a course of action on them which would serve both Britain's and the host country's interests, perhaps in the face of a hostile public opinion and a sceptical press. It was easier for him to ask the editor of the leading national newspaper to publish an article by Adam (and signed by his ambassador or himself) setting out the British government's policy on some contentious current issue, if the editor had been to lunch with Adam at his house a couple of weeks earlier and found him to be good company, willing to talk freely, and without the stuffiness or pomposity that many people associate with their idea of a diplomat.

Adam knew that many of his opposite numbers in other embassies did little or no entertaining apart from holding an annual national day reception, and were rarely to be seen at diplomatic social functions. They relied on visits to the offices of ministers and officials to establish their contacts, and in consequence their relationships with local people tended to be stiff and formal. Those who did sometimes entertain their local contacts often took them out to local restaurants where it was in practice impossible to hold a frank and sensitive conversation. Some local figures were nervous about being seen publicly to be accepting hospitality in a restaurant or hotel from a foreign diplomat, fearing that they would seem to be accepting a kind of bribe in exchange for some favor.

It was inconceivable to Adam that he could achieve even a half of what he did without the active help and support of Eve. He knew of British ambassadors, both men and women, who were unmarried and who got by with the help of a resident housekeeper, paid by the FCO, to do some parts of what Eve did all the time with no formal recognition of her work and no payment from official funds. Towards the end of Adam's career, the FCO introduced a limited system of payments for spouses who did work in entertaining that would otherwise have been done by caterers or other domestic servants, the cost of which would have been unquestioningly accepted as a charge on the officer's entertainment allowance.

But initially this didn't apply to the wives of heads of mission who enjoyed (if that was the word) the services of a Residence staff whose salaries were met from public funds, although later they too qualified for a small allowance, subject to stringent conditions. In fact when Eve came to be the chatelaine of her husband's ambassadorial Residence, she soon learned that the management of the Residence staff added appreciably to her workload: she found herself mediating between the cook and the butler in their quarrel over which of them was responsible for locking up the kitchen at the weekend, persuading the housemaid to send her ailing husband, one of the Residence gardeners, to the doctor when she found him coughing up blood, persuading the aging steward to stop hiding the keys to the wine cellar in a flowerpot in the Residence grounds where no one else could find it, and trying to get the cook to try out a new and unfamiliar recipe for a dinner she and Adam were giving for a visiting British minister. Sometimes she felt it would be easier and quicker to do all these things herself instead of having to exercise all her diplomatic skills just to keep the house running smoothly.

Eve had the residence accounts to be kept and checked every week, the petty cash to be doled out and accounted for, the six monthly food order from home to be planned and paid for, the wines to be selected and imported on the basis of a rough calculation of probable needs in the coming months, the flowers to be selected and brought into the house from the grounds by the gardeners for the guest bedrooms when official visitors from London were coming to stay, the tactful guidance to be given to the numerous official houseguests on how much to tip the Residence staff on their departure, for refunding from their travel allowances when they got home (an invidious practice now sensibly discontinued). Sometimes Eve was tempted to stop doing any of these things, letting the house run itself while she hid in their tiny private flat at the top of the house and curled up with a good book and a stiff gin and tonic. But she knew that would be a recipe for disaster.

Above all Eve hated the knowledge that she and Adam were never alone in their own home. Any fierce argument between them would be overheard in the kitchen, embarrassing the cook and the butler. Adam couldn't risk venturing out of their enormous bedroom in his underpants to retrieve a book he had inadvertently left in the drawing-room downstairs without the risk of being seen by a horribly embarrassed maid. When their children came to live in the Residence during the school holidays, they found it unbearably frustrating not to be able to wander into the cavernous kitchens to raid the massive refrigerators and freezers or to fry themselves some bacon: one of the staff would invariably rush in and insist on providing whatever Anne or Ian had wanted, sitting them down in the long dining-room and bringing them huge slabs of bacon on a silver tray. It didn't feel like home. It was like having to run a medium-sized hotel and restaurant and living on the premises, provided with the services of the hotel staff but denied any vestige of privacy and given the unwanted responsibility for managing the enterprise, staff, accounting and all. Eve remarked that her home was more like Fawlty Towers[3] than the Ritz.

Yet all this, both Adam and Eve fully realised, constituted what the world would regard, with some justice, as an enormous privilege. The two of them were living a kind of cheap imitation of the luxurious life-style of the filthy rich around the world. Their friends at home displayed a mixture of envy, disbelief, amusement, and prim disapproval when they were home on leave and described life in the Residence.

By the time Adam and Eve were coming to the end of their third and final posting as a head of mission and his official but unpaid spouse, Eve was counting the days to the time when she and Adam could leave their luxurious prison, go back to their modest suburban house in Wimbledon, have a boiled egg and an early night if they felt like it, and become real people again.

*Postscript*: Like so many of Adam's other experiences during his decades in the diplomatic service, the pattern of official entertaining by diplomats, especially British diplomats, was constantly changing, and continued to change after he retired. Some of these changes were dictated by the constant and continuing squeeze on the FCO's budget: the pressure for savings was unremitting. Others reflected the more relaxed and informal manners of later years, and a less deferential attitude towards authority on the part of a younger generation. During most of Adam's time in the diplomatic service, even quite junior diplomatic staff were generally housed in reasonably generous accommodations when serving overseas, mostly quite close to the city centre and to the inner suburbs where influential local people—senior officials and ministers, newspaper editors, bankers, and businessmen—tend to live. Latterly, however, the FCO was forced by budgetary constraints, or anyway opted, to sell many of these desirable staff houses, even sometimes including ambassadorial residences, buying instead much more modest homes in more distant and cheaper suburbs. This made it much harder for junior staff to entertain local contacts at home: busy local decision-makers and opinion-formers had no time to find their way out to remote areas on the fringes of the capital in order to have lunch or even dinner in some modest bungalow or apartment.

Another factor for change had been the revolution in attitudes to the role of wives (and other women). In Adam's later years in the service, it could no longer be assumed that if a career sacrifice had to be made, it was automatically the wife who made it: the husband's career was no longer invariably regarded as paramount. Some diplomats' wives chose to stay at home and pursue their careers rather than accompanying their diplomat husbands on overseas postings, especially the more challenging ones. Even when the wife gave up her career and accompanied her husband on a foreign posting, there was no longer a presumption that if her husband, a junior diplomatic officer, was ordered, say, to contribute two dozen strawberry tarts to the refreshments needed for the Queen's Birthday Party, his wife would uncomplainingly buckle down to making them: the increasing likelihood was that, when told of the demand, she would merely laugh and make it clear that she had better things to do. Whereas in earlier years responsibility for entertaining official visitors—MPs, officials from Whitehall, cultural groups—would be farmed out to members of the ambassador's diplomatic staff, suggestions for such delegation began to fall on deaf ears. In his last head of mission posting, Adam had suggested at his morning meeting that a delegation of six visiting British MPs should be invited to an early evening reception at the Residence to meet local dignitaries, and then split up into three couples, each to be invited to dinner with the political Counsellor and two First Secretaries respectively. One of the designated First Secretaries had replied without a trace of apology that "if these MPs are worth being officially entertained at all, they are worth being entertained to dinner at the Residence." So that was that.

Whereas in earlier days it had been taken for granted that it was a natural part of the embassy's responsibilities to arrange a suitable function even for non-governmental visitors from home—an orchestra or choir, a theatre group, a distinguished writer and her partner, a football team—such entertaining became the exception rather than the rule: unless such expenditure could be squared with the post's formally approved annual objectives, such visitors increasingly had to fend for themselves, unless there was a local office of the British Council with some surplus cash in its budget to take care of them.

It has gradually become the common understanding, also, that the Residence, with its big kitchen and experienced domestic staff, is primarily the post's official entertainment centre, and only secondarily the home of the ambassador and his family. Staff below the level of the head of mission might take their official contacts out for a drink or for a meal at a local restaurant: but the idea that they might entertain at their homes has, Adam came to realise, largely died out. What were the Residence cook, butler, and other domestic servants employed for if not to manage the post's entertaining? Embassy officers and especially their spouses, male and female, took it for granted that the ambassador and his wife (or her husband) could leave all the hard work of hosting receptions, lunches, and dinners to the Residence servants. Only when they *became heads* of mission themselves did they begin to realise how big a toll such constant official entertaining inevitably took on the head of mission and his or her spouse, despite having staff available to do the cooking, serving, and washing up.

The ultimate nail in the coffin of the old system was the decay and eventual expiry, unlamented, of FCO inspections of posts with their minute scrutiny of every last detail of official expenditure, including on entertainment, and their function of fixing the entertainment allowances of every diplomatic officer for the ensuing three or four years. An entertainment budget was fixed for each post as a whole: it was left to the post to decide how to spend it and how to divide it up among members of its staff as and when the need arose. The sense of individual obligation to spend one's own individual entertainment allowance in the most productive and economical way disappeared. British diplomats, newly appointed to their first head of mission posts with heavy entertainment responsibilities, arrived in the Residence with virtually no experience of official entertaining, its benefits and pitfalls, from earlier service in lower grades.

After Adam had retired, Eve received with mixed feelings the news, relayed by a friend married to a still serving British head of mission, that in some posts the ambassadress or high commissioner's wife had applied successfully for the paid post of "Residence Manager," whose functions sounded identical to those performed by Eve for many years on a pro bono basis—i.e., unpaid. Eve wondered how far the salary paid to such a

Residence Manager would compensate for the penalties of becoming an employee of the government: someone, somewhere (presumably the relatively junior post Administration Officer? or the head of mission, also by definition the Residence Manager's spouse?) would have to be her line manager, needing to be satisfied that the Residence Manager was carrying out the duties listed in her job description to an acceptable level of efficiency, putting in the requisite hours in the job, not being unduly frequently absent with her husband on tour up-country or on an official visit to London, and otherwise justifying being paid the Queen's Shilling for what she would have been doing anyway. Eve supposed that the same line manager would be obliged to write an annual report on the Residence Manager's performance, to be discussed with her in minute and embarrassing detail. What would happen if the Residence Manager/head of mission's wife was assessed as incompetent and a poor value for the taxpayer's money, with the unavoidable implication that she should be given the sack? Could a paid Residence Manager who was also the ambassador's wife resign from the job, but stay on in the Residence as His Excellency's wife? On balance, Eve concluded that it had probably been better doing the job in the way she had thought best, answerable to no one, and unpaid.

Adam respected and supported many of the attitudinal and procedural changes that had caused this revolution in the modes of diplomatic entertaining. But he also regretted the loss of experience in official entertaining at home that he and Eve had acquired in their overseas posts before he became a head of mission himself. The intimacy and privacy of dinner round a First Secretary's table in his own dining-room could powerfully influence the nature of his relations with a local contact; a meal in a restaurant could never be the same thing. Even the relative formality of the Residence, with Residence staff hovering, was inimical to intimacy. Entertaining prominent British visitors from the worlds of culture, sport, and the arts had provided both Eve and Adam with some fascinating and memorable moments, and even some lasting friendships far away from the arid air of diplomacy and government. Change had been inevitable, and in many ways healthy. But, Adam thought sadly, like all welcome change, it had come at a price.

## NOTES

1. "Ato" is the Amharic equivalent of "Mr."

2. Tooting is a south London suburb with a large and vibrant population of Asian origin, and many other immigrants or descendants of immigrants.

3. *Fawlty Towers* was a celebrated British television comedy of the late 1970s, frequently re-broadcast, about a small hilariously mismanaged hotel at a seaside resort on the south coast of England.

# 11

# SERVICE IN THE FCO AT HOME

*A home posting in the diplomat's foreign ministry. Dealing with overseas posts, with senior officials of the Ministry, with the diplomat's own Foreign Minister and other ministers.*

When Adam, after his posting as a Counsellor in the embassy in 'Pazalia', was appointed to be head of a Foreign & Commonwealth Office department, still as a Counsellor, he found, to his considerable satisfaction, that he was able to have far more direct influence on foreign policy, if only in a limited sphere, than in any of his previous posts. Much later, as he looked back on his career immediately before his retirement, he thought that as a head of department in London he had probably had more say in policy questions affecting his parish than an ambassador or high commissioner in charge of his own post overseas, mainly because of being so much closer to the seat of power, with regular access to ministers both on paper and face to face.

As head of the FCO's North African Department, Adam was responsible for relations with nine states that included three significant oil-producing countries. All nine shared many characteristics with the states of the Arab and other Muslim middle east, and most identified strongly with them. At the same time, all of them were members of the Organisation of African Unity (OAU, later the African Union) and most were as active in inter-African politics as in the cauldron of the middle east. There were British embassies in all nine of Adam's countries, all headed by ambassadors of varying seniority and experience, and—as Adam was soon to discover—of varying ability. Some of these Adam knew from earlier postings; others he knew only by name, although after familiarisation visits to all his posts Adam soon got to know them all personally, and equally importantly, all his ambassadors soon knew him. When one or the other came home on mid-tour leave, or at the beginning or end of a posting, Adam would always take him or her out to lunch for a convivial review of relations between his own department and the ambassador's post. Most were senior to him, both by length of service and by grade; the rest were also Counsellors but with the added clout of having been appointed heads of mission. All of them, however, understood that regardless of formal grade, Adam, as a senior FCO officer working for the Foreign Secretary, would always have the last word, and that he had immediate access to the levers of power if he cared to use them (he did).

Adam's own immediate boss was the Director (then called Assistant Under-Secretary of State) for Africa, Giles Farmer, back in London after a spell as ambassador to Ethiopia. Giles supervised the work of all four of the FCO's African departments. He, in turn, was nominally responsible to a Director-General (then called a Deputy Under-Secretary or DUS), the next grade up from Director, although in practice the Director-General, as a member of the FCO's Board of Management, was mainly immersed in the overall policies and management of the Office, and rarely interposed himself between Giles Farmer and the Secretary of State or other FCO ministers in their day-to-day work. The Director-General did, however, routinely see copies of all communications passing between Farmer and ministers and would occasionally add his own views or comments to the debate, especially if the issues raised questions of significance going wider than Africa. When a ministerial decision, usually in the form of ministerial approval of a recommendation by the department, was needed urgently, Adam would put his recommendation, with the reasons for it and an analysis of possible alternatives, direct to the minister's private office, with copies to Farmer as his Director and to the supervising Director-General, as well as to any other heads of department whose parishes might be affected. Often issues were resolved by a short meeting in the office of the junior FCO minister responsible to the Foreign Secretary for relations with African countries. These meetings would commonly be attended by Adam and Giles Farmer and often also by representatives of a subject department with an interest in the matter to be discussed, and sometimes by the minister's political adviser, who kept an eye on implications for the minister's political party and in parliament of what was going on.

Adam was supported by the Assistant (i.e., assistant head),[1] a senior first secretary, Tom Longhurst, who had served in the embassy in Noridan, one of Adam's north African countries, and so had a good feel for the problems of the area; and by four desk officers, all first secretaries. Three of the desk officers were responsible for two each of the department's nine countries, and the other for three. Two of the desk officers were, in turn, supported by a second secretary each, and another by a new entrant in his first job in the Office; one of Adam's duties was to oversee the work experience of the new entrant and to ensure that it provided the maximum benefit as training. Adam was the only member of the department to have his own Personal Assistant, in effect his secretary, Marilyn, an efficient and alert young woman whose numerous duties included acting as Adam's eyes and ears, giving him early and discreet warning of inter-personal or other frictions in the department, any overloading of one desk compared with the others, discontents over some aspect of the way the department was being run, or resentment on the part of a hard-pressed desk officer of what might be perceived as a lack of appreciation on Adam's (or Tom Longhurst's) part of the good work he or she was doing and their long working hours.

Adam's clout as a head of department derived from the fact that he was the senior British government official with a detailed knowledge and understanding of the affairs of each of his nine countries in the context of north Africa collectively. His supervising Director, Giles Farmer, had a wider view of African policy generally, but he could never have the detailed knowledge and command of detail that Adam had as a result of his constant exposure to advice and information from his nine UK embassies, from the nine countries' embassies in London, from the steady flow across his desk of intelligence reports, many of them highly classified, from his regular meetings and social functions with academic and media experts on his parish, from his background reading, from FCO Research Department background papers, and from his own occasional visits to his posts. Moreover, when it came to policy decisions, he enjoyed the substantial advantage over everyone else that under normal day-to-day FCO procedures it was Adam who determined what recommendation on any particular issue his department was to submit for approval, if necessary after informal consultation with Farmer and perhaps with the private office; the more senior Directors and Directors-General generally responded to Adam's recommendations, rather than making their own. Adam rapidly learned that whoever is the first to have something on paper for discussion has the advantage over everyone else whose ideas are not yet formed, or still inchoate and in gestation.

Only the most important decisions would go as high as ministers for decision. Once Adam had won the confidence of Giles Farmer and ministers for his generally sound judgment, he was increasingly able to make everyday decisions on policy issues himself, usually after discussion with Tom, the assistant head and Adam's deputy, and the relevant desk officers. Once he had made his decision on some policy question, it generally issued to overseas posts over the name of the Secretary of State, even though the Secretary of State would usually never have seen it. Even the most senior and powerful British ambassador in charge of an overseas post was bound by the rule that a decision or instruction emanating from the Foreign & Commonwealth Office in London had the authority of the Secretary of State, regardless of the level at which it had been approved. If time permitted, it was always open to an ambassador to question his instructions—once; but if his objections were overruled by the Office, at whatever level, his duty was to act in accordance with his instructions, whatever he thought of them. (Of course it took an exceptionally bold and confident head of department to overrule on his own authority the objections of a very senior ambassador in a major overseas post: in that situation the objections would almost certainly be considered by a Director-General or even ministers. But even then the advice of the head of department would carry considerable weight.)

Not all of Adam's policy advice was produced in response to requests from posts or to the pressure of outside events. Several times during his time as head of the North African department he devised proposals for changes of policy affecting his parish, and discussed them informally with others in the Office who might have a view (often including the Secretary of State's political adviser, who could helpfully advise on ways to frame policy proposals in a way likely to be acceptable to his minister), before embodying his ideas in a formal submission. This document would set out the problem and the proposed solution or change of policy recommended: lay out the arguments for and against it; discuss possible alternatives and the reasons for not preferring them; and end with a precise recommendation. Important and relevant texts would be attached as appendices. The submission would go to Farmer as Adam's immediate superior but with copies to the private office, the junior minister responsible for Africa, the Permanent Secretary, the Director-General, perhaps to one of the Office's Legal Advisers, and to any other interested departments. Any of these would be free to send their comments, whether supportive or critical, to all the other recipients. If the issues were important enough, the submission might be considered at a meeting, chaired by Farmer, the Director-General or a minister. By no means all of Adam's personal policy initiatives were eventually approved, at any rate in their original form; but some were, and these became the policy of Her Britannic Majesty's Government. Although he didn't know it at the time, Adam was never to have such personal influence on foreign policy again, however many more promotions he was to enjoy. But it was an influence confined to a narrow geographical sphere. Adam was sufficiently realistic to venture only very rarely, and then with extreme caution, into global foreign policy issues outside north Africa.

Running his own department was, Adam knew, good preparation for running an embassy, further from the centre of power in London but with much less day-to-day supervision from above and greater freedom to determine which areas of policy he would concentrate on. Heads of department were often promoted at the end of their home postings and appointed to one of their own posts as a head of mission.

Early in Adam's second year as head of the department, he was chosen by the Office's administration as one of three department heads whose department's work was to be analysed by a firm of management consultants, hired at the urging of the Board of Management to recommend ways in which the Office's work could be streamlined and speeded up. A keen young couple, Damian and Zoe, came to interview him in his office. He had been warned to set aside most of a day for the interview, including a period in which Damian and Zoe would silently observe him at work. They had been security-cleared and were permitted to take notes although Adam was assured that their notes would be shredded before their report was submitted.

"Hi, Adam," Damian and Zoe said simultaneously, settling themselves into the chairs facing Adam's desk. Zoe introduced herself and Damian; she was evidently in charge. She kept on nodding vigorously, without any obvious reason, which Adam found distracting until he realised that she was doing it to shake her long blonde hair out of her eyes. She wore almost invisible glasses to write her notes but hastily removed them whenever she was not writing. Adam knew that both were British citizens although they both spoke with faintly American accents and used faintly American idioms.

"Adam, we'd love you to talk us through a typical event involving you and your division—"

"Department," Adam said.

"Department, OK, so we can see how many stages it goes through before a decision is made on it. You know, in a place like this where procedures are obviously ossified, we can often find ways to carve out whole layers of management."

Adam reckoned she was about twenty-eight. Damian looked even younger. He wore bright red braces (which he no doubt referred to by their American name, "suspenders," despite that term's very different connotation in British English), not to stop his trousers falling down, Adam guessed, but more as a kind of badge.

"Right," Adam said. "Well, let me tell you what's happening at the moment about a routine task we've been given by the Secretary of State's private office."

"Hold it right there," Damian said. "Who is this Secretary of State and if his office is private, what's it doing getting involved in official business? Can't we chop this private office out of the loop right away?"

Adam spent a few minutes explaining about the Foreign Secretary and his "private" secretaries, then returned to the task being handled by his department.

"The Secretary of State has had a letter from a back-bench MP, enclosing a letter the MP has received from one of his constituents whose son is working for a British NGO in Noridan in north Africa. The constituent has been told by his son that the security situation in the far south of Noridan is very bad, with a lot of activity by local armed rebels who want independence for the south of the country. There are a dozen or so Brits working with this NGO and they're afraid that some of them may be taken hostage by the rebels. The constituent wants his MP to find out what the British government is doing to improve the security situation there and to give better protection to Brits for whose protection the father reckons HMG is responsible. The covering letter from the MP to the Secretary of State is in the usual form, simply asking for advice on how he should reply to his constituent. The private office have shown the MP's letter to the Secretary of State so that he's aware of it, in case he bumps into the MP when he's across the road in the Palace of Westminster,[2] and they then referred it to my department to submit a draft reply to the MP for the Secretary of State's signature. The private office has set us a 5-day deadline for a draft reply, to be submitted through my Director, Giles Farmer. This is probably one of maybe 30 or 40 MPs' letters to FCO ministers received every day, and almost all of them will have been sent out to departments for draft replies in the same way."

After another pause for explanations of terminology, Zoe asked what Adam had done with the private office's request for a draft reply to the MP.

"As we have got a few days to produce the draft," Adam replied, "and since it's a fairly straightforward matter, I've asked my Noridan desk officer to get our young new entrant to have a first go at drafting a reply from the Secretary of State to the MP. I gave the desk officer a quick steer on what the reply should say and the desk officer will flesh out that guidance with the new entrant before he tries his hand at a draft. It will be good training for him. Unless he's a very quick learner, which he may well be, I'll probably need to re-write his draft, but he's a smart cookie so I'm expecting the main points of the draft reply to be there when he produces it."

"You're saying this is a simple routine task, Adam," said Damian, "yet from what you say it's going to involve the new entrant, your desk officer, yourself, your Director person Farmer, the private secretaries—let's say two of them—and the Foreign Sec. That's seven guys just to handle this simple routine task, that right?"

"Well, yes," Adam admitted, "except that at least two of the seven will not be guys but gi—er, women. But that's because there's no special urgency and I'm using the exercise partly for training purposes—good practice for the desk officer and the new entrant."

"OK, so what would be different if it was really urgent?"

"One of the private secretaries would probably ask me to pop down for a word about it. I would go down to the private office, and discuss with the private secretary how best to handle it in the time available. If it was important enough for the Secretary of State to want to be involved personally, and so urgent that action would need to be taken the same day, I'd probably come back upstairs and dictate a quick first draft to my

PA which I would submit to Giles Farmer with copies going direct to the private office, the Director-General, and any other FCO departments who might want to comment or make suggestions. That wouldn't need to take more than half an hour. When Farmer got my submission he'd have a word with the private office and they'd agree that the Secretary of State would have a short meeting with all of us, perhaps immediately after lunch, to consider my recommendation and for the Secretary of State to make a decision on it. If no one had any major difficulty with my submission, the whole thing could be wrapped up by around 2:30 pm. Of course if it was a really major issue requiring consultation with other government departments in Whitehall, perhaps with Number Ten Downing Street,[3] and probably also with three or four of our embassies in the area concerned, it would all take longer, but with our modern high-speed communications it could probably still be wrapped up within a day if necessary."

"I thought," said Zoe, polishing her glasses with the edge of her sleeve, "that you guys could never do anything without the agreement of the Americans first."

"We often consult the Americans on major policy issues, naturally," said Adam primly. "And in the same way, the Americans often consult us. How else can I help you?"

**As an example:**

*I was head of the Southern African Department in the Foreign & Commonwealth Office for four years during the time of the apartheid régime in South Africa and the prolonged, increasingly intricate multilateral negotiations leading eventually to the independence of Namibia. All of us in the department were kept frenetically busy with both the problems of UK relations with the white South African régime, then an international pariah, and the Namibia negotiations, involving continuous bargaining with South Africa, a dozen other African governments, the internal political parties in Namibia, various UN bodies including the United Nations Secretary-General and the secretariat, and the other four members of the so-called Namibia Contact Group or Western Five (the US, Canada, France, Germany, and UK).*

*The political staff of the British embassy in South Africa, alternating like the South African government between Pretoria and Cape Town, were keen and hyperactive and of exceptionally high calibre, from the ambassador down to a pair of brilliant first secretaries, who did a superlatively good job in cultivating contacts in the black and "coloured" opposition and civil rights movements while maintaining good workmanlike if necessarily often adversarial relations with the South African government, not an easy tight-rope to walk. Both in the context of managing our contacts with apartheid and in that of the Namibian negotiations, every tidbit of gossip or confidential information about South Africa and its government was of paramount interest to us in London as part of the basis for developing policy in a fast-moving situation.*

*The volume of information, much of it pure gold, and policy suggestions and criticisms reaching us daily from the embassy in Cape Town/Pretoria grew and grew. Soon the ambassador there introduced a programme of papers on different aspects of the South African scene researched and written by the two Stakhanovite[4] first secretaries. Every couple of weeks another of these would thump into my In Tray with a request from its authors for urgent comments. All these papers deserved careful study and constructive responses, but there never seemed to be time to sit down and read them carefully amid the never-ending blizzard of telegrams generated by the Namibia negotiations, the need to respond promptly to a massive pressure of enquiries and protests from parliament and the media over our South Africa policies, and the constant demand for briefs for ministers, the UK Mission at the UN, UK delegations to conferences at which apartheid and Namibia were certain to come up, not to mention the ordinary management of our relations with the other, smaller countries in southern Africa for which the department was also responsible. We began to notice tactful expressions of disappointment from the embassy in Cape Town/Pretoria at our increasingly frequent failure to comment promptly, or at all, on the embassy's vast and high-grade output, sometimes noting that we had omitted even to thank its authors for the latest research paper or to promise comments "when things quieten down," which of course they never did.*

*Eventually, in despair, I wrote to the ambassador to apologise humbly for these failings on the department's part. I explained that the level of staffing in the department was barely enough to cope with the most urgent (but not necessarily the most important) day-to-day pressures from all sides, not just from South Africa. I expressed warm and genuine appreciation for the extraordinarily high-quality material flowing out of the embassy, but concluded by admitting that my department in the FCO was simply incapable of processing all of it at a speed and in a depth that the embassy's diligent authors had every right to expect. I suggested a new régime of restraint on the embassy's part, under which they would send us in future only material for which we had explicitly asked or of obvious relevance to urgent current business, archiving the rest for future use as and when required. I signed and despatched this letter with considerable trepidation. No one likes to be told that much of the material he produces is not read and is not regarded as sufficiently relevant to current business to be needed by its intended recipient.*

*My trepidation proved to be fully justified. My letter caused a very bad reaction when it landed in the ambassador's In Tray, a reaction compounded of anguish and rage. Within days the ambassador was on the telephone to me, expressing both emotions with practised eloquence. My letter, he said, had caused a crisis in relations between the embassy and the department and it needed urgently to be resolved. How soon could I fly out to Cape Town for urgent discussions aimed at removing mutual misunderstandings?*

*I arrived in Cape Town early the following week, leaving my long-suffering assistant head of department to hold the fort during my absence. I was welcomed at the airport by the ambassador's number two, who happened also to be my immediate predecessor as head of the Southern African Department, and driven in an embassy car with him to the embassy. On the way the number two warned me that I was in for a difficult time. My letter had not gone down well. He was too modest and courteous to say what both of us were thinking—that when he had been head of the department in London, he had somehow managed to cope with all the material reaching him from the embassy. If he and his department could do it, why couldn't I? There were answers to that question, but it would not have been tactful to mention the explosion of work, especially on Namibia, since my predecessor's time as head of the department. Many more governments had become involved in the negotiations, many more UK posts needed to be consulted or were now flooding us with their ideas and criticisms, and I was constantly having to fly to meetings of the Five (the "Namibia Contact Group") held in turn in Washington, Ottawa, Bonn (then the West German capital), Paris, and London. The international protests against our policies on apartheid had rapidly mounted and had to be addressed. And the volume of telegrams, letters, and research papers sent to the department by the embassy in South Africa had more than doubled since I had become head of the department.*

*On our arrival at the embassy, I was taken straight in to an expectant meeting of the entire diplomatic staff, presided over by the ambassador (himself several grades senior to me, older and much more*

*experienced). The ambassador started by expressing in predictable but
civil and moderate terms the whole embassy's dismay over my letter.
Others followed, some less moderately. The number two, my predecessor, remained tactfully silent. When everyone had had their say, I
defended my letter. I said that the situation in the department had
simply become untenable. We could all work 24 hours a day, seven
days a week, and we still wouldn't be able to cope at all adequately
with the volume of work that confronted us. We were in no way blam-
ing the embassy for this situation: far from it. On the contrary, we
appreciated, admired, and greatly benefited from its work. But something had to be done to reduce to more manageable proportions the
volume of material sent to the department; otherwise we would miss
something really vital and there would be a major disaster. I had not
enjoyed writing as I had done, but the only alternative—doing nothing—was simply not an option. Our friends and colleagues in the
embassy were free to blame me personally for the department's shortcomings if they liked, but I had to tell them frankly that if they continued to overload us, however brilliant their product, much of their work
would be filed away in the FCO's Research Department, unread, un-
acknowledged, and, when it was needed, unused.*

*The atmosphere slowly began to brighten. After some further dis-
cussion, the meeting broke up and I was allowed to unpack and have a
shower after the long flight. That evening there was a barbecue for the
whole staff and myself in the gardens of the ambassador's Residence,
at which a great deal of excellent South African wine was consumed
and the entire party was overwhelmed by a wave of general benevo-
lence. I flew home two days later after making some illuminating calls
on South African ministers and officials, visiting a black township and
meeting some leaders of the (banned) ANC. From the time of my
return to the Office, the volume of material reaching us from the embassy in Cape Town fell by about 40 percent. My letter of thanks to the
ambassador for his and his colleagues' hospitality and understanding
was unusually deeply felt.*

Adam hated having to write annual confidential reports on those who
worked for him. The guidance notes on how to write such reports occupied twenty-two full-sized pages of small print. The form itself ran to
sixteen pages. Reporting officers were exhorted to be utterly frank in
recording their subjects' weaknesses as well as their strengths. The officer reported on was entitled, indeed instructed, to read every word of the
report on him. He was required to fill in a page of the report saying

whether he agreed with the comments on him and if so what he intended to do to remedy any defects. He had to fill in another half-page assessing how well or badly he felt the reporting officer had managed him during the year: had he offered constant guidance, criticism and encouragement? It was generally assumed that this victim's assessment of the management qualities of the boss served no useful purpose except as an opportunity to avenge a poor report. No one knew whether the Personnel Department took any notice of the worm's-eye view assessments of people's line managers.

The time had come for Adam to conduct his confidential report appraisal interview with his immediate deputy, Tom Longhurst. Adam's private view of Tom was that his overall performance was adequate, but no better than adequate. He recognised that Tom made a commendable effort, was conscientious and loyal, but basically he was not terribly bright. Adam was sure that Tom was acutely conscious of his limitations, indeed had a chip on his shoulder about them, and lacked self-confidence as a result. Adam knew that there was nothing that either he or Tom could do to improve Tom's performance. His analytical and communication shortcomings were congenital and incapable of remedy. At the same time, Adam felt strongly that there were plenty of jobs in the diplomatic service that could be done better by a conscientious plodder than by an intellectual firecracker. The Tom Longhursts of the Service, in Adam's view, provided a rock-like basis for the running of British diplomacy: the starry high-fliers needed them and depended on their inconspicuous support. The recently introduced doctrine now fashionable in the diplomatic service's management, according to which there should be no place for the average or below-average plodder, with the corollary that such people should be eased out as soon as it became clear that they were unqualified for promotion beyond their current grade or one grade higher, seemed to Adam not just inhumane but also seriously misconceived in terms of the efficient functioning of the Service. The steady removal of the below-average might, indeed inevitably would, drive up the level of the average, but it would eventually leave a Service of stars, half of whom would be compelled to spend their careers in humdrum jobs for which they would be over-qualified and therefore chronically dissatisfied.

Another factor weighed heavily with Tom, however improperly in the eyes of the Administration. Tom would still be working for and with Adam for another year at least, possibly two. Their relationship of mutual confidence was essential for the smooth running of Adam's department. If Adam were to write, and Tom be forced to read, an absolutely frank report spelling out Tom's intellectual and other deficiencies, their working relationship would almost certainly be irreparably damaged. If Tom's shortcomings had been of the kind that could be rectified by trying harder, working even longer hours, or going to night school, Adam would have accepted that it would be his distasteful duty to speak frankly about them and encourage Tom to take the necessary action to up-grade his performance. But this was clearly not the case.

The point about needing to protect the working relationship between reporting officer and officer reported on applied even more strongly to relationships between an officer and his line manager in an embassy overseas, especially in a small post where the relationship was social as well as professional, where both officers' spouses would be good friends (or enemies), where their small children probably went to school together and played together. On an overseas posting, it would seem to Adam impossible to tell his deputy in the morning that she lacked the intellectual equipment to get any further in the Service, and then to go sailing with her and her family in the afternoon, ignoring the angry resentful stare of her partner.

"Tom, hello, come in," Adam said, responding to Tom's knock on the door of his office. "Report time again, I'm afraid. Here it is" (tossing the bulky document to Tom) "—pretty much the same as last year, a good solid performance again, several real successes for which I've given you full and sincere credit, and absolutely indispensable support for me and the rest of the department, for which I've recorded my real gratitude. Your working relations with the rest of the department have been excellent and you've done sterling work in ensuring that our new entrant, Joey, gets maximum training value from his work in the department and learns all the necessary lessons from it. I know you haven't always agreed with the courses I've tried to set for the department when it comes to policy and I have valued the way in which you haven't hesitated to tell me frankly when you have thought I was wrong, but you have always loyally accepted my and the Office's decisions and done everything you can to make them work. You'll see that I've given you full marks on all those scores."

"Thanks very much, Adam," Tom said, embarrassed. "That sounds more than fair."

"Well, take it away and read it in slow time, and we'll have another word about it when you've read it. You know the routine: if there's anything in it that you think is unfair, say so frankly when you write in your own reactions to the report. You'll also need to write in the report your assessment of my own performance as your line manager, which you must do absolutely frankly. Then it goes up to Giles, as my own reporting officer, to be counter-signed."

"What have you said about my promotion prospects, Adam?" Tom asked just a little too anxiously.

"Well, you'll see when you read it, Tom. Basically I say that there are many jobs in your next promotion grade of Counsellor for which you would be very well qualified by your experience and talents and in which you would put in a good, solid, reliable performance. I'm sure that's right, too."

Tom's face fell slightly, but he said gamely: "Thanks very much for that, Adam. I know I'm not going to be fast-tracked for rapid promotion to Permanent Under-Secretary and Head of the Diplomatic Service, but I think I could do a good job in the Counsellor grade."

"Certainly you could, and I've tried to make that clear," Adam assured him. "Well, take the report away now and let me or Marilyn know when you've read and digested it, and we'll go through it together."

Adam felt no sense of guilt at his flagrant failure to write Tom's report with the brutal frankness demanded of him by the Office's administration. He realised that it could be attributed to cowardice on his part, but he was confident that it was in fact justified by the need to avoid wrecking Tom's fragile self-confidence and to protect his working relations with Tom for another year: and justified, too, by the benefit to the Service of giving full useful careers to loyal, unglamorous performers like Tom Longhurst.

**As an example:**

*There were several occasions when urgency required me, as head of the Southern African Department in the FCO, to short-circuit the normal procedures for submitting my recommendations through the hierarchy, but one in particular has stuck in the memory. The controversial and unpredictable South African foreign minister, "Puck" Hertzog (not his real name), had come up with a complex proposal for revising the agreed procedures for Namibia's progress to full independence from South African rule, the effect of which clearly implied prolonging South African control of Namibia and postponing the transfer of powers to a new independent Namibian government under the procedures laid down in the United Nations plan which South Africa had formally accepted. I have forgotten the details, but essentially Hertzog's proposals would include an international conference, probably not under UN auspices, to revise the road map in the existing UN plan and to agree on a new timetable for Namibian independence. Puck Hertzog had told the British ambassador that he was going to launch his new plan in a major speech in Geneva the following day in which he would say that he had given the British government advance notice of his proposals and that he was confident that they would win Britain's support. If, however, HMG were to decide before the Geneva speech not to back his proposals, Hertzog would postpone launching them and would reconsider them. The British ambassador had reported this by telephone to my Director (Assistant Under-Secretary), L.A., and in a telegram to the Secretary of State, and asked for immediate instructions. The ambassador had spelled out the pros and cons of Hertzog's big idea as he saw them, concluding that it might be worth further consideration.*

*L.A. asked me to go and see him urgently to discuss what we should recommend to the Secretary of State, whose private office (i.e. his private secretaries) were already agitating for a submission. We agreed quickly that for a number of reasons HMG should not support Hertzog's proposal. L.A. telephoned the private office and suggested that I should see the Secretary of State for five minutes to make our recommendation orally and explain the reasons for it. This was agreed, and five minutes later I was in the Secretary of State's large, beautiful, and ornate office overlooking St. James's park, accompanied by one of the private secretaries. Lord Carrington, most relaxed and urbane of ministers, was standing by the fire.*

*"So what's Puck up to now?" he asked me.*

*I gave him a rapid summary of Hertzog's proposal and explained why it needed a quick response by HMG.*

*"Puck wants more time running Namibia and suggests a vast conference to give it to him?"*

*I agreed that this was what Mr. Hertzog's proposal amounted to. I was about to list four or five reasons for declining to give it our support. This proved to be unnecessary.*

*"Ho bloody ho!" said Her Majesty's Principal Secretary of State for Foreign and Commonwealth Affairs, the Right Honourable Lord*

*Carrington, making it clear that no further discussion was necessary.*
*The British Government had made its decision.*

*It was the quickest, most explicit and pithiest ministerial verdict on*
*a submission that I ever experienced.*

Adam, with the other three heads of African departments in the FCO and
the Africa Director, Giles Farmer, flew to Abidjan, capital of the Ivory
Coast (or Côte d'Ivoire, as some of his colleagues insisted on calling it),
for a conference of all the UK heads of mission in Africa, chaired by the
junior FCO minister responsible for African matters, Laura Chessman.
The ambassador to the Ivory Coast, in whose Residence the conference
took place, happened also to be a woman, as was Mrs. Chessman's private secretary who accompanied her, so there was a pronounced feminist
tendency at the top table.

The ambassador and hostess to all the visitors, Maggie Ross, was
somewhat unusual, although probably not unique, among women heads
of mission in the British diplomatic service in having taken her husband,
Phil Ross, to Abidjan with her as an accompanying spouse. The conference was enlivened by Phil's account of a briefing meeting held in London, before he and Maggie had left for Abidjan, for spouses of newly
appointed heads of mission on their first such postings. The briefing was
given by the wife of the FCO Permanent Secretary and head of the diplomatic service, Lady Brimley, who had wide experience of life as an
ambassador's spouse before her husband had been elevated to his current
position. Not surprisingly, Mr. Ross was the only male present at the
briefing. Lady Brimley was delivering a warning about personal behaviour in an ambassador's residence where members of the residence domestic staff were liable to be performing their various duties anywhere in
the house at virtually any time of day or night.

"What this means for all of you," Lady Brimley warned the assembled
spouses, "is that you should never go down from your bedroom to the
kitchen or the dining room for breakfast wearing nothing but your night-
dress, as you might do at home in England. Remember always to put on
your négligée before you come out of the bedroom, in case members of
the residence staff are already up and about."

Phil Ross politely raised his hand.

"Yes, Mr. Ross?" Lady Brimley said.

"Er—I have a problem with the négligée . . ."

There were some feisty arguments during the business sessions of the regional heads of mission conference in Abidjan. Adam took the opportunity to air some of his pet heresies. At the session for discussion of trade issues, Adam denounced the system then current under which a certain amount of public money from the development aid programme was earmarked for aid projects in poor and developing countries which would support British exports, by tying the aid to the purchase of British goods and services and by other devices. Adam argued strenuously that this was a retrograde system which inevitably reduced the value of our aid to the developing country concerned: the recipient country should be allowed to spend the foreign exchange that we were providing in whatever overseas market offered the best value for money—which would not necessarily be Britain. Competitive tendering was an important way to ensure the best price and the most appropriate purchase, whereas tying procurement to goods and services bought from Britain made competitive tendering impossible except within Britain's internal market. If the British government wanted to spend public money on subsidies to British exporters, probably thereby discouraging their competitiveness and initiative, it should be done openly with ordinary taxpayers' money, separately from the aid programme and not at the expense of the developing country receiving our aid.

Now, in the early part of the twenty-first century, Adam's case against linking aid and trade has long been part of the accepted wisdom, and Britain has for many years stopped tying its development aid to British supplies or linking aid with trade in the way the old "Aid & Trade Provision" used to do. But at the time of the Abidjan conference, Adam's arguments were widely and officially regarded as heretical to the nth degree, amounting in the eyes of some of his diplomatic service colleagues almost to high treason. Propounding such an unpopular and, at the time, unorthodox view was obviously seen by some of his colleagues round the conference table as reckless in its apparent disregard for its effects on his career, especially when voiced at a meeting chaired by a minister. Adam felt the risk was justified, mainly by the knowledge that his forthcoming promotion and appointment as ambassador to Noridan had been presented for its approval to the government of Noridan in accordance with universal protocol, that that government had granted him *agrément*, that his appointment had been publicly announced, and that the dates had been fixed for his and Eve's audience with the Queen and for him to fly to Khaliman, Noridan's capital, two weeks thereafter. The post of ambassador to Noridan was not greatly sought after in the British diplomatic service, traditional old Foreign Office types regarding it as a hell-hole compared with such hallowed centres of old-fashioned diplomacy as Vienna or Paris. Some of Adam's colleagues had gone so far as to mix their congratulations with condolences on his first head of mission appointment, enquiring with mock curiosity what he had done to earn a "punishment" posting. Adam, who knew Noridan would be a challenge, welcomed the appointment and was convinced, or had convinced himself, that service there as ambassador would prove fascinating (as indeed it turned out to be). But now that the appointment was public knowledge and could not in practice be rescinded because of any behaviour on his part short of a conviction for manslaughter, he felt free to speak his mind, whatever the minister and his colleagues round the table thought of his views.

Adam's expectations of strong dissent were not disappointed. Ambassador after ambassador, head of department after head of department round the table asked for the floor to express shocked disagreement with everything Adam had said, although Adam's Director, Giles Farmer, tactfully remained silent. Some of the assembled ambassadors betrayed deep scepticism about the value of the British aid programme (which most of them were actively engaged in administering in their respective African countries). It would be absurdly quixotic, some suggested, for British taxpayers' money to be given to a poverty-stricken country, probably with a corrupt government, to enable it to buy goods and services from Germany, America, even Russia or China. Many of them asserted that the promotion of the UK's foreign exchange earnings had to have the highest priority in UK foreign policy, with the alleviation of the poverty of some of the poorest people in some of the poorest countries in the world coming far down the league table, although a few pointed out that selling British goods to a poor country that would pay for them with British aid money was not in itself going to solve the UK's balance of payments problem. The then ambassador to South Africa, a man of much weight and prestige in the service at the time, was especially scathing, delivering what was obviously meant to be a knock-out punch to Adam's propositions. After this no one else bothered to join in the general denunciation of Adam's heresy, and the minister, Mrs. Chessman, summed up briefly that Adam's point of view, although eloquently expressed, had received no support from the conference. Adam murmured to his neighbour at the table: "At least they can't punish me by sending me to Noridan."

After his return to London, and when the other participants in the conference had returned from the Ivory Coast to their respective posts, Adam received several private letters expressing agreement with his arguments against the Aid & Trade Provision and the tying of UK development aid to purchases of goods and services from Britain. Each letter concluded in varyingly apologetic terms with the explanation that the writer had seen no point in supporting Adam on this issue at the conference, since there was obviously no prospect that the policy would be reversed or even reconsidered.

## NOTES

1. This position no longer exists in the FCO.
2. Home of both houses of parliament.
3. Residence and office of the prime minister.
4. Term used in the Soviet Union for a worker so enthusiastic that he exceeded his work target. Named after Aleksei Stakhanov, who mined 102 tons of coal in less than six hours (fourteen times his quota).

# 12

# A DOG'S LIFE FOR THE SPOUSE AND THE KIDS?

*Sacrifices, demands, and pressures on the diplomat's spouse (husband or wife); rewards (some) and penalties (many); implications for the children, probably including boarding school. Staff morale in small difficult posts and big comfortable ones.*

Adam met, pursued, wooed, and wedded Eve while he was on home leave from Côte Noire. Much later, when they had two children and Adam had been promoted to his first ambassadorial post in Noridan, Eve agreed to do an interview on the Noridan television station's weekly magazine programme, *The Week in Noridan*. The interview was conducted in English for broadcast later with Arabic subtitles.

Maya, the interviewer, had been brought up in London where her father had been at the Noridanian embassy for many years, so she spoke fluent English. She started by asking how Eve had felt about marrying a diplomat.

"After I accepted Adam's proposal of marriage," Eve replied, "I lay awake all night worrying about the likely effects on my life and the lives of any children we might have, of spending most of the rest of our lives in foreign countries. I had a university degree and I had already embarked on a post-graduate course to qualify as a social worker, when we met at a dinner party given by a mutual friend. Adam, of course, was already in the Foreign Office but really still finding his feet as a diplomat. Neither of us had any family background of professional careers: actually, no one in Adam's or my family had been to university before us. I had chosen what looked like the most interesting and relevant of the limited career options that were open to women in Britain at that time."

"So did you have to give up any idea of being a social worker?" Maya asked.

"Well," Eve said, "that was one of the things that worried me about marrying a diplomat. Adam had never been all that single-minded about wanting a diplomatic career. Openings for male graduates in those days of full employment were much greater, and Adam, like most of his friends, had applied for a whole lot of graduate trainee jobs, hoping for a good offer somewhere along the way. So he had done the rounds applying for jobs in advertising, manufacturing industry, and so forth, most of them using similar assessment processes to recruit. He was genuinely surprised when the Foreign Office was one of the many employers offering him a job. You see, competition for the diplomatic service was so intense that he felt it would seem like hubris to turn it down. He never really thought at the time about what it would mean for a future wife, or even less about how it would affect any children he might have. So when he wanted to marry me, and I desperately wanted to marry him, it brought it home to both of us what this would mean for me, especially, and for our children when the time came."

Eve remembered that she hadn't had much time to decide whether to accept Adam's offer of marriage with all that it would mean for her future life. He had been due to return to Côte Noire three or four weeks later, and if he was to return with a wife it would mean a sea-change in the lifestyles of both of them.

"Eventually I told myself that I would always regret it if I turned down this chance not only to spend the rest of my life with Adam but also to have a more exciting life and see the world. I supposed that really it was because we were both so young and we thought that middle age and old age would never happen to us."

"What were your main worries about starting on life with a diplomat, Eve?" Maya asked.

"My main worries had been about what I then perceived as the social aspects of the life, the dreaded cocktail parties above all. Fortunately it didn't even occur to me then that as well as having to go to other people's parties I would have to give them myself, and dinner parties, too. And it genuinely didn't occur to either of us that Adam might one day become an ambassador. We both thought of ambassadors as different kinds of beings, with titles, and born to privilege, not at all ordinary people like us."

"What about having to give up your plans for a career of your own?"

"Well, I realised that if I was to go out to Côte Noire with Adam, and then afterwards to other countries abroad which he would be posted to, I would have to give up the job I was training for, but most women of that era gave up their jobs when they had children or if their husband's career pattern changed. What I realised only much later was that most of my women friends had gone back to work when their children started school. Then they had progressed from part-time to full-time jobs and often moved into some of the newer job fields which were in some cases very well paid. They had been double income families for most of their working lives and now, as they are coming up towards retirement, my old friends have their own pensions to look forward to as well as their husbands' pensions."

Eve confessed that she did sometimes regret that although she had been very much part of Adam's job and they had been glad to be a team for most of their lives, she had never experienced the financial independence enjoyed by many of her friends at home. And Adam was getting increasingly worried about the fact that if he died before Eve, she would receive only half of his Foreign & Commonwealth Office pension.

"These are things you don't really think about when you make these life-changing decisions so early in your life," Eve told her interviewer. Maya, who was probably less than half Eve's age, frowned.

"I suppose you're right," she said. "But surely leading the glamorous life of a diplomatic wife, and now being an ambassadress, has more than compensated?"

"Only up to a point," Eve said. "Our British friends have naturally envied us what seems like our luxurious lifestyle when they have visited us in some of our more comfortable foreign posts—they haven't usually come out to see us in places where you can't travel anywhere without running into alarming road blocks or where your cramped little apartment is overrun by mice and cockroaches. They haven't realised that treasury and foreign office inspectors used to decide what kind of housing and how much entertaining is appropriate to each particular grade and post, and then calculate to the last penny what allowances you are given to cover essential expenditure. That's all changed now, but the results are the same: the FCO budget is constantly being squeezed and at the same time there's more and more work to be done for less money, and that means reduced allowances and reduced living standards all round."

"Even if I had wanted to have some of Adam's income from his allowances as money that we could spend as we wished, it would have been impossible. Until quite recently I have always had to submit my regular accounts and sometimes we have had to repay any money left over if we have underspent. When that happened it made Adam worry that we must be falling down on our representational role. We aren't surprised that our friends who have chosen business careers based at home have in most cases earned salaries in a different league from Adam's: we always accepted that that was going to happen. But over the years we have realised that while Adam's contemporaries in the Home Civil Service have earned salaries much the same as his, many of their wives have had their own professional or private sector careers, so with their joint incomes their standard of living in the UK is much higher than anything that Adam and I can afford when Adam is working in the FCO in London on a home posting, and much higher than anything we will be able to afford in retirement."

"So do you think now that you shouldn't have married a diplomat?"

"Oh, no, not at all. Sometimes I have regretted that Adam had chosen to be a diplomat when he had so many other job offers that wouldn't have meant me having to give up my own career. But we have seen the world and lived life at an eventful and often exciting level even if it's sometimes been stressful, too. But most people get stressed; you don't have to be a diplomat or a diplomat's spouse to be occasionally 'stressed out,' as my daughter puts it."

Maya picked up Eve's reference to her daughter, and asked how life as a diplomatic couple had affected their children. In fact, it was the effect of Adam's job on the children which had always niggled away at her. They had both been born while she and Adam were overseas on postings and at a time when many of their friends from school and university were starting their families with lots of mutual support.

"The first major change was when we realised that we would need an au pair or nanny to help look after the children if I was to continue to play the part that in those days—not so much now—was expected of a diplomatic wife, even a quite junior diplomatic wife, in the embassy. Luckily we recruited a young woman who was a really nice, kind person and who was always very good with our kids. Even so, we both felt guilty about having this person looking after them evening after evening while we were out at receptions and dinners, or at home but doing our own entertaining and too distracted to give them the attention that was possible during our home postings."

"And another thing: I came to realise for the first time that Adam's life didn't change that much after he married me and we had the children. Admittedly every time he got a new posting he was working in a new place, with new colleagues and dealing with new subjects, really like starting a new job, but he was soon absorbed in a familiar routine, looked after by his PA, and it wasn't so different from his life before he was married. Meanwhile every time we moved to a new post I was having to find my way around a new city, often with people speaking an unfamiliar language, shop in strange shops, find friends and something for the children and me to do. But it was the effect on our children's lives and our relationship with them which was the most worrying aspect of our lives as diplomats."

"I thought people went in for diplomacy so that they would get an expensive high quality education at a top boarding school for their children without having to pay for it themselves?" Maya objected. "That was how my parents saw it when I went to snobby schools in London paid for by our government."

"That wasn't at all how we saw it," Eve replied. "If Adam had had an ordinary nine-to-five job in England we wouldn't have dreamed of sending our children away to boarding school in England."

"But you did, didn't you?" asked Maya.

"Once they reached secondary school age we did," said Eve. "When they were younger and coming with us wherever we went in the world, going to whatever local school there was, they had both become very upset each time we moved to a new post. They had to say goodbye to their school friends, which was always a wrench, and start again in new schools, sometimes with quite different systems of teaching. Our daughter told us that rather than change schools yet again she would rather go to boarding school like other children in the embassy. She would miss us, she said, but so long as she could be with us for the school holidays three times a year, wherever we were, she would be all right."

"There was also the danger that at some point we would be posted to a country where there quite simply wouldn't be a local school that they could go to. Even if there were adequate schools for them wherever we were, if they had to change schools every three or four years, with a different curriculum each time, and different standards of teaching, it would be very unlikely that they would get places at a reputable university in Britain when the time came. That would have been a very high price for them to pay so that we could have them with us all through their childhood. We felt they needed stability and I think we made the right choice: I hope they think so, too. They seem to be all right so far but there was a lot of heartbreak along the way."

"In what way heartbreak?" Maya asked.

"Well, for starters, waving goodbye for three long months to your twelve-year-old as she flies off in a plane for a 24-hour journey back to school on the other side of the world, I suppose. I used to clean the house obsessively with the radio on until we heard that she had landed safely in England. I sometimes thought that the friends who used to ferry them back and forth to London airport, and visited them at their schools at weekends or had them to stay at half-term, knew them better than we did. And we were always too far away to be there if they were ill or upset. Thank goodness for kind understanding friends!"

"So what would you say if you were asked to advise someone considering becoming a diplomatic wife—if that's what you call it?"

"Yes, that is what we call it, and in a way it's a full-time unpaid career in itself, or it used to be," said Eve thoughtfully. "I would say 'Go for it.' That's what Adam and I did and although I've stressed the doom and gloom bits, we've been in exciting places, we've been travellers and not tourists, as they say. We've met the great and the good, the celebs and the saints, and sometimes the crooks. And the children have shared some of that, broadening their horizons, while at the same time they have been able to put down roots at home in England, whereas Adam and I haven't—in many ways we're really still strangers in our own country."

"What did you mean by saying it used to be a career, being a diplomatic wife?"

"Well," Eve answered, "things have changed over the years. In most ways for the better, I suppose. Diplomatic wives are no longer bound to the Office and the Service as they used to be when I was first married to Adam. In those days wives were not allowed to work when overseas, even if the host country would allow them to. They were expected to take a very full part in the official entertaining programme of the embassy. Large groups of visiting British MPs, for example, might be invited to a drinks party given by the ambassador, but then more junior members of staff would each be allocated a few members of the MPs' group to entertain to dinner in their own homes, along with interesting and influential local people for them to meet. In countries where you couldn't hire domestic help, that would mean the wife doing the planning, the shopping, and then the cooking, even if she could hire staff just to serve and wash up. The MPs would leave at the end of the evening saying: "Wouldn't my wife like to have such help with the shopping and cooking!"

"Nowadays it seems increasingly that the ambassador and his wife will do both the drinks party and the dinner party afterwards at the Residence for the whole group, because we are the only ones in the embassy who have the full-time domestic staff, and often the wives of the rest of the embassy's diplomats don't see why they should have to do any official entertaining. It was damn hard work catering and cooking, often on quite a large scale. Once, long before Adam became a head of mission, we had a whole visiting English football team and its managers and directors and physios and half its fan club to supper in our house to meet all the local football enthusiasts. I had to do all the planning and shopping and cooking and then play the gracious hostess. That was quite a stressful day! But at least I got to meet famous sports personalities and MPs and lots of other interesting VIP official visitors long before Adam became an ambassador. I think in most posts the bulk of the entertaining nowadays is done in restaurants or in the Residence. It's not the same."

"You said that wives used not to be allowed to work. Are they allowed to work now?"

"Yes, sorry—I got carried away. Spouses (the right word now because quite a lot of women diplomats are accompanied by their husbands or male partners) are allowed to work unless the head of mission—the ambassador or high commissioner—has a very good reason to rule against a particular job. Of course the host country has to approve spouses of foreign diplomats getting local employment, and a lot of countries don't welcome foreigners coming in and taking jobs away from local people. But missions now often employ their spouses as locally engaged staff: some embassy visa sections, for example, are largely staffed by spouses. That all helps morale, and morale can be a real problem in difficult posts where the spouses can't work in the local economy and don't have a lot to do. In a few posts even the ambassador's wife has been able to get a paid job, as the Residence Manager, or some such title, which could mean being paid—not paid much, but paid—to do what she would have been doing anyway."

"Do you see any other improvements in diplomatic life?"

"I think so much better communications above anything else. If we had been able to Skype or email our children when they were at school it would have made such a difference. Not so many years ago it used to be a major feat to get through on the telephone from some parts of the world, which could be really distressing if someone—child or parent—was unwell or in some kind of distress. Now anyone can make instant contact with anyone else almost anywhere in the world. That means that I could recommend life with a diplomat with a reasonably clear conscience."

"Thank you," Maya said, reaching across the desk to shake Eve's hand. "I've learned a lot, Madam Ambassadress."

Eve winced.

**As an example:**

*When I was the British ambassador to Ethiopia at the height of the disastrous famine in the mid-1980s, my wife, J, and I were heavily involved, like most of the other western ambassadors and their wives, in the huge international famine relief effort. Both of us spent long hours and days visiting and supporting British relief workers in Oxfam, Save the Children, Red Cross, and other feeding and medical centres in remote areas of that huge country. I had taken the initiative to encourage the senior EEC ambassador, at that time the Italian, to organise and chair a coordinating committee of all the ambassadors of the countries giving large-scale humanitarian aid to famine victims, to pool information about areas of need as they became known and to minimise the danger of donor governments duplicating each other's efforts. When the senior ambassador and chairman came to the end of his posting and left Ethiopia, I succeeded him as chair of the coordinating committee, which entailed a good deal of time-consuming work. At the same time, there was a never-ending stream of demands from the FCO at home for information about every aspect of the famine and the relief effort, to enable them to answer parliamentary questions, MPs' letters, and continuous media enquiries. We tried to have UK relief workers to a good square meal at the Residence when they came back to Addis Ababa for a week's rest before they returned to the camps out in the highlands; this involved a lot of extra work for J, although she never complained about this aspect of our activity. On top of all this, the intense publicity in Britain for the famine and its pitiful victims, watched every night on television, stimulated an extraordinary pilgrimage of celebrity visitors to Ethiopia, anxious to see the situation for themselves, sometimes to find out how they or their organisations could help, more often to have themselves filmed and photographed with photogenic starving Ethiopian babies, to reinforce their reputations at home as great humanitarians.*

*These included UK government ministers (some with responsibilities only tenuously connected with Ethiopia and the famine), members of parliament of all parties, actresses and film stars, bishops of various denominations and sects, and, above all, print and electronic media journalists—some* bona fide *reporters who sought detailed briefings to enable them to send or write accurate and responsible stories, others who arrived with fixed ideas about* "who was to blame" *for the tragedy, using their visits to collect supporting evidence for what they were going to write anyway. Then there were the press magnates and self-appointed heads of minuscule "relief agencies" who would arrive with consignments of food and other supplies intended for famine relief, seeking maximum publicity for their uninvited and often unusable contributions. All these visitors, virtually without exception, expected to be received at the Residence for a briefing by the ambassador (me) and often expecting to be entertained by J and myself to lunch or dinner as well. All this placed a considerable burden on J. We were more than happy to do everything we could for the genuine visitors who had something of value to contribute to the relief effort, either with physical donations in money or kind or by publicising Ethiopia's real needs to the outside world. But we had no option but to welcome, brief, and feed the grandstanders on their ego trips, too: had we snubbed them, their revenge could have done great harm to the willingness of the UK government and public to continue to provide generous support for the millions of famine victims.*

*At the height of all this frenetic activity, we had an alarming telephone call from the well-regarded boarding school in Kent where our son, O, was in his Oxbridge term preparing for his Oxford entrance exams and interviews. He had been staying for this final term with one of the school's housemasters and we had been persuaded to agree, reluctantly, that he should be allowed to use a motor scooter, or moped, to travel between the housemaster's house and the school. Coming out of a side turning on the scooter, he had been hit by a car and broken his leg in several places. We were assured that there was nothing to worry about: he was in a hospital in Kent where the leg was being set and he was in safe hands. J would be welcome to fly home to be with him but there was, the hospital said, really nothing that she could do for him. He would be in hospital for several weeks. His two older sisters would be visiting him regularly, making sure that he had everything that he needed, and keeping us informed of his progress.*

*J's immediate instinct was to get the next flight to London and go at once to the hospital in Kent to be with our son. We were five thousand miles from home with patchy and unreliable communications with O's hospital and our two daughters. On the other hand, it was probably true that there would be little J could do if she flew home at once, except to sit by his bed and hold his hand, which would do little to raise the morale of a 6'2" 17-year-old young man. There would be nowhere for her to stay in Kent: she would be commuting by unreliable car or train between the hospital in Kent and our home in London. Our daughters assured us in a series of telephone calls that they would do all that was required, keeping us informed as necessary. But they both had demanding jobs and there were obvious limits to what they could do.*

*Then there was the problem of the demands of our famine relief work in Addis Ababa. Our splendid hard-working Ethiopian Residence staff would continue to do everything we asked of them, and more, but without J's daily, often hourly, supervision and monitoring, there could be no certainty that the residence could continue to function efficiently and busily as a combined care home, relief workers' and celebrity visitors' restaurant, and hotel for visiting government big-wigs. I didn't need to tell her that there was no way that I could step into her shoes as hotel and restaurant manager and social worker for our Ethiopian staff, as well as gracious hostess for our never-ending flow of high-level visitors, politicians and officials, serious reporters and commentators, and the "famine tourists," as we used to call the rest. I knew J felt she should go home to support our son without delay and I couldn't in all conscience ask her not to go. At the same time, I couldn't imagine how I would be able to cope without her, perhaps for many weeks or even months. With a heavy heart, J decided to stay in Ethiopia, at any rate, while O was still in hospital. But it was a dilemma that caused her real anguish, and she has never managed to rid herself of a feeling of guilt that when the chips were down, she had in effect let down her own son, while I felt, and feel, only a little less guilty for having failed to press her to go, leaving me to cope as best I could.*

***Postscript:*** *Many weeks later, J had to fly home anyway. O was abruptly discharged from the hospital in Kent with almost no advance* *notice and with no one at home able to look after him. His school was neither able nor willing to put him up in what was by now the school holidays. His sisters managed to get him home to London and put him to bed. At this point it was clear that J had no alternative but to fly home. Back in London she nursed him, his shattered leg still in a very bad way. The hospital warned that he would probably have a perma-nent limp—lamed for life. After desperate appeals to varyingly helpful contacts, J got him a place at a government rehabilitation centre which put him through months of intensive, eye-watering physiothera-py, chivvying and bullying him mercilessly until he developed a deter-mination to recover. He emerged fitter than he had ever been before, with a new-found commitment to daily running, cycling, swimming, and every other kind of exercise: improbably, he became, and remains, a fitness freak.*

*While he was still in serious pain and dependent on crutches, J had taken him in foul weather and our wreck of a car, constantly breaking down, to his chosen university for his entrance exams and interviews. Most of these required him to drag himself on his backside up narrow spiral staircases to the interviewing dons in their college rooms on the top floor. Three often tempestuous years later, he got a first-class degree.*

Adam, as the ambassador's deputy at the embassy in "Boronia," devel-oped quite a close relationship with his head of mission, as often happens. (Later, when Adam became an ambassador himself, he found that being a head of mission is in some ways a lonely job, especially if you don't have the kind of relationship with your number two that enables you to discuss sensitive matters frankly with him.) Adam's ambassador in Boronia, Maurice Johnson, was a shy man behind a rather grand and imposing manner and it was some time before Adam felt he could talk to him in a relaxed and uninhibited way, especially if what he wanted to say to him was implicitly critical of the way Johnson was running the embassy.

Adam had been prevailed upon by his wife, Eve, to try to persuade the ambassador to come to the annual staff Christmas party which had always been given by the embassy Number Two since the arrival of Maurice Johnson as ambassador, and also to stay long enough to chat with mem-bers of his staff.

"Last year," Eve reminded Adam, "poor Maurice came to our Christ-mas party, stood looking miserable for about ten minutes with a drink in his hand, and then left. He was too shy to talk to any of the staff—

probably embarrassed at not recognising most of them and not knowing their names or what they did—and all the staff except you and me were uncertain about whether it was the done thing to go up to him and talk to him. Can't you persuade him to pluck up the courage to circulate a bit and talk to people even if he doesn't know who they are? I know you think he's shy and not naturally standoffish, but still."

A few days later, Adam was seeing Maurice Johnson in his office in the embassy about a telegram just in from the FCO. When they had agreed about the answer to be sent (which Adam was now to draft), Adam asked if the ambassador had a moment to talk about a purely social matter that he wanted to raise with him.

"Of course, Adam. Fire away."

"Sir, it's about our Christmas staff party the week after next. Everyone was so pleased that you were able to spare the time to look in on our Christmas party last year, and Eve and I were hoping that this year you might be able to stay a little longer and have a chat with some of the junior members of the staff who naturally don't have many opportunities to meet you."

"As you know, my dear Adam," said the ambassador cautiously, "small talk with people I don't really know is not exactly my forte. But I'll certainly perform an *acte de présence* at your and Eve's admirable party if you're good enough to invite me to it again."

"Well, we'll certainly be inviting you again, sir, that goes without saying. But Eve was wondering whether it would help if she took the responsibility for bringing one or two of the junior staff over to you, one at a time, to have a brief word with you. She would remind you of the name in each case, and which section of the embassy the person works in, just to jog your memory."

In fact, Maurice Johnson rarely had any contact with junior staff, relying on Adam to tell him of any personnel problems. The staff took this to be evidence that the ambassador was too lofty and grand to take an interest in them; in fact, as Adam had soon discovered, he was simply too shy.

"Well," said Johnson. "You know I can never say No to your charming and persuasive wife. I would appreciate it enormously if Eve were to be willing to perform such a service."

That evening, as Eve and Adam were changing to go out to dinner with Adam's opposite number in the German embassy, Adam told Eve how he had used her as bait to persuade the ambassador to stay longer and talk to some of the staff at the Christmas party.

"But I never suggested any such thing!" protested Eve. "How am I supposed to do my stuff as the hostess at the party if I'm to spend the whole evening introducing His Excellency to his own staff?"

"No, no," said Adam. "Other way round. You'll be introducing the members of his staff to His Excellency. Got to observe proper protocol. Anyway you've always been good at multitasking. It will work fine."

And so it did, Eve being Eve.

Early in the new year it was once again time for Adam's annual confidential report, prepared by his line manager, the ambassador, Maurice Johnson. Adam received the ambassador's summons via his PA to go and see Johnson to read and discuss the report. As usual the ambassador was deeply embarrassed. Adam thought for a moment that this must be because he had written a negative and critical report.

"Adam, my dear fellow," said the ambassador, "have a seat while we go through this *ghastly* annual ritual. I need hardly tell you that once again your report is one long paean of praise for your outstanding performance during the year. A positive paean."

Adam, relieved, reflected that even if Johnson had thought him a complete dud, he would have been far too embarrassed to say so in the report, with the prospect of having to show it to Adam, explain and justify it to him face to face, and then having to work with him and socialise with him and his family for another year.

"That's very generous of you, sir," Adam said. "May I read it, then?"

"Yes, yes, of course," Johnson said, hastily handing the thick folder over to him across the big solid ambassadorial desk. "Let me say that I have no doubt that you will continue to have a most successful career in the Service. I have recommended you for an early head of mission appointment and I am confident that you will have many such appointments before you retire. Moreover, you will be a first-rate ambassador or high commissioner. Can you guess my reason for such a confident prediction?"

Adam could easily think of any number of reasons for taking this view of himself, but he read the signal and gave the reply indicated.

"No, sir."

"It's as much as anything because you are fortunate enough to have the support of such a delightful and committed wife and family. It's an asset beyond price in our business, Adam. With all your own natural skills and virtues—I have tried to list them in the report, shan't embarrass you by reciting them now—and with Eve and your children at your side, there will be no limit to how far you will go."

Adam shifted uncomfortably in his chair. Johnson, however, had not finished.

"I congratulate you on another year's fine work," he continued, "and most of all I want you to promise that you will pass on to Eve this expression of my gratitude for all that she does for the embassy, acting as the embassy's unpaid social worker and universal aunt. Unpaid, to be sure, but not unappreciated, I assure you. I rely on you to tell her every-thing I have said."

"I will with pleasure," Adam said, touched. "Naturally I entirely agree with everything you've said about Eve."

"Excellent," Maurice Johnson said, evidently relieved to have got this off his chest. "Good man. Well, take the report away and let me have it back when you have filled in the bit saying whether you agree with it. (It will be rather odd if you don't!) Then, according to the ritual devised by our masters in their infinite wisdom, we're obliged to have another of these deeply embarrassing chats before I send it in. Thank the good Lord that that will be it for another year."

"Well, thank you very much, sir," Adam said, getting up ready to go. "Except that you're supposed to do a mid-year assessment of me in six months' time, of course, halfway between the full annual reports."

"Oh, good grief," groaned the ambassador. "I'd forgotten that! How excruciating. Well, let's not think about that until nearer the time. By the way, I should have asked: how *are* Eve and your charming children—Anna and Irvine, isn't it? Busy and thriving as ever, I hope?"

"Anne and Ian," Adam said. "Anne has had her leg in plaster for the last two weeks—she broke it when a big girl from somewhere in Latin America stamped on it at the International School—but apart from that they're fine. Anne will be going away to boarding school in England at the beginning of the next school year."

"Oh, dear," Johnson said. "How does she feel about that?"

"She's quite looking forward to it." Adam was lingering half in and half out of the ambassador's office, gripping his annual report. "She's fed up with having to remember to pronounce zed as zee with her American teacher at the school. It's Eve and I who are dreading her going home to boarding school."

Adam didn't wait to receive Johnson's commiserations, completing his exit and closing the door softly behind him. He went back early to his house in the embassy compound to tell Eve what a fantastic asset she was for his career.

Adam always remembered his first overseas posting in hot, dusty Côte Noire, as a lowly Second Secretary. He had been dismayed to find himself standing in for the First Secretary, Jake, when the latter, with his young French wife, went home on their annual leave only three weeks after Adam's arrival. In practice the extra workload and additional responsibilities had encouraged Adam to get to grips with his new job more quickly, helped him to make useful local contacts from Jake's contacts list, and gave him confidence that he could handle the job. Despite this, he had been relieved when Jake and Françoise returned to "Cameko." On their second evening back, Adam invited them both to supper in his tiny flat. Jake asked what had been happening during his and Françoise's absence, and Adam (with some discreet pride) outlined his various minor successes while trying to do Jake's job as well as his own.

"Have there been any family problems while we were in England?" Françoise asked. "Poor Vera was in quite serious difficulties before we left: I hope that's all been sorted out now."

Vera was the spectacularly young wife of Rob, the only slightly older registry clerk. Adam knew nothing about the difficulties referred to by Françoise.

"She and Rob were in a crisis over when to start a family," Françoise explained. "Vera's desperate to have a baby soon, and probably lots more later, but Rob reckons it's much too early. If Vera became pregnant while they're in Côte Noire, she'd have to go home to have the baby—there are no facilities here except in the French hospital and the Office wouldn't pay for her to have a baby there—and Rob is afraid he'd go to pieces if he had to live and work here without Vera. And of course he'd be desperate to be with Vera while she had her baby. Also Rob doesn't think he's old enough to be a father (and I think he may be right!). When we went home on leave, Vera was threatening to go home anyway to talk it over with her parents and her sister—she's apparently emotionally very close to her sister. She's been terribly homesick, and she misses the support and advice of her and Jake's families."

Adam felt guilty at his ignorance of this family problem on his doorstep. "I had no idea. Although I don't know what I could have done even if I had known about it."

"I was spending evening after evening with Vera in the months before Jake and I went on leave," Françoise said. "I didn't try to give her or Rob advice—how could I?—but I just used to let her talk and talk and often have a little cry. Having someone sympathetic and understanding to confide in seemed to help a little."

"I suppose it had to be a woman, really," Adam mused. "Vera must have missed you while you were away."

"Well, Beatrice knows all about it," Françoise said, referring to the friendly and capable wife of the embassy Counsellor. "I'm sure she's been keeping in touch with poor Vera, and with Rob, too, and providing a—how do you say in English?—a shoulder to cry into. I haven't had a chance to talk to Beatrice, or to Vera, in effect, since we got back. I'll talk to them both tomorrow and find out how everyone's been coping. Adam, may I have another glass of your very good Sancerre?"

It had struck Adam for the first time that young and junior diplomats, especially those on their first overseas postings, and even more so their wives if they were already married, keenly felt the loss of the support, comfort, and advice of their families far away at home, and that the natural surrogates could only be the older wives of their colleagues in the embassy. A woman diplomat in the embassy, if there was one, could not easily fit the role of unofficial social worker and carer: her diplomatic service grade and her embassy job would get in the way, perhaps making it difficult for a distressed young woman to confide in her.

"I've been thinking," Adam said, "that life here in Cameko must be very difficult for people like Rob and Vera. They don't speak any French, as far as I know. They don't have a lot of spare cash, and the Côte Noire government doesn't allow diplomatic wives to get jobs on the local economy. The only shops are completely unfamiliar, they can't watch the local television, and there aren't many people outside the embassy they can make friends with. It's no wonder that morale in a difficult small post like this is such a problem."

"On the contrary," Jake said. "You'll find that morale is generally much less of a problem in a small post in a difficult, stressful place than in a big embassy in somewhere like Washington or Paris. In a small embassy like this one, everyone knows everyone else, and the older and more senior wives are always ready to help the younger staff and their families with any problems. It's always the embassy wives in difficult posts who organise playgroups, and outings to local museums and beauty spots, and family barbecues, and musical evenings, and choirs, and book clubs, and all the other things that help to keep people from getting lonely and homesick—at least, we hope they do."

"None of that seems necessary in a post in a big sophisticated city like Paris, where Françoise and I met. Older and more senior staff don't see any need to organise the lives of younger staff and their families, any more than they do when on a home posting in London. The result is that morale is often a much bigger problem in a post like Paris or Washington than it is here in Cameko, where people feel as if they belong to a kind of family. Junior staff in big embassies in developed countries often feel neglected by more senior officers, including more senior wives."

Adam was startled by the concept of "senior wives." "Surely wives of diplomats aren't senior or junior: they aren't employed by the government! They're all equal, or should be, in my view."

"Technically that's right, of course," said Jake. "But in practice wives tend to take on the place in the hierarchy of their husbands. It's the same in the army, or the law, or in a big company. There was a time when some ambassadors' wives used to treat the other embassy wives as if they were schoolgirls, lining them up before a big embassy drinks party to have their white gloves inspected by the ambassadress to make sure they were pristine clean. Honestly! I've talked to colleagues who actually experienced that! It doesn't happen now, of course, but the ambassador's wife in a big post can seem very remote to wives who are not much involved in the diplomatic social scene. They don't realise how demanding her life can be, running the Residence, acting as the gracious hostess to all the hundreds and even thousands of visitors who pass through for a meal, or come to stay as house guests; arranging programmes for wives of visiting ministers and escorting them around; travelling with the ambassador and doing the rounds calling on district governors' wives; visiting local charities; being expected to act as patron or chair the boards of charities with a British connection. It's just as well that wives of deputy heads of mission, like Beatrice, have always traditionally shouldered the role of universal aunt to the embassy. Naturally she will alert the ambassador—or more likely his wife—to any major worries but she'll try to nip problems in the bud before they reach that point."

"Of course there are some ambassadors' wives who do their stuff, entertaining in the Residence and accompanying their husbands on their official calls, and so on, but who play no particular part in the embassy staff's social life—which is more or less true of our ambassador's wife here, thank goodness."

Adam, getting ready for bed after Jake and Françoise had drunk the last of the Sancerre and left to go to their rather bigger flat beneath his, had difficulty getting his mind round the concepts of an ambassador's wife as headmistress, of "senior wives" organising the social lives of "junior wives," of Vera and Rob homesick and agonised over when to have a baby with no families round the corner to help them through it, and of the paradox that the staff's morale could be less of a problem in a difficult, poor, backward place like Cameko in a west African backwater than in a glamorous culture centre like Paris or New York. Years later, he was to reflect that despite some improvements, such as the designation of a "welfare officer" at every post with responsibility for spotting people with personal and family problems and doing something to help them, nothing had really changed. Loneliness, homesickness, friction between individuals and families in the tight little community of a small diplomatic mission, shortcomings in the leadership style of an over-mighty head of mission or unthinking abuse of authority by his wife: all these were, or could be, part and parcel of diplomatic life away from home; always had been, always would be.

# 13

# CONSULAR AND COMMERCIAL ACTIVITIES

*Helping one's country's citizens in distress; helping compatriot companies to sell, invest, and attract investment; trade missions; what compatriot businessmen want and what they need.*

In some countries the political capital is not the same as the main business, financial, and commercial centre in the way that London is both the political and the financial and business capital of the United Kingdom. The political capital is the home of the government and parliament or Congress, and consequently where the embassies and high commissions are, too. The business and commercial centre may be far away from the politicians and diplomats in the capital; and there may be more than one of them. Washington, D.C. and New York/Los Angeles, or Canberra and Sydney/Melbourne are examples. Because diplomats need to maintain contact with their host country's businessmen and bankers almost as much as with its ministers and politicians, overseas governments often also maintain a consulate or consulate-general in each of the main business centres. The consul-general heading a big consulate-general in a major business centre like New York, Sydney, or Melbourne, although technically subordinate to the ambassador or high commissioner in the national capital (Washington, D.C. or Canberra), may well be almost as senior in grade and just as experienced as his notional "boss" to whom he reports. His main tasks are consular (looking after the interests of the nationals of his own country, either resident in or visiting his consular area) and commercial (promoting his home country's business interests and relations with businesses in his area). But he also keeps in close touch with the political and civic events in his area and with leading political and media figures in it, both to underpin his office's consular and commercial work and also to enable him to send to his ambassador or high commissioner in the capital periodic political reports and analyses of events in his parish.

The British consul or consul-general and his staff, many of them probably locally engaged nationals of the host country or members of the local British expatriate community, will normally handle routine consular cases without the need for any input from or supervision by the British embassy or high commission far away in the capital: distressed visiting Britons who have lost their money, return tickets, and passports, or who have been arrested and charged with an offence, often an attempt to smuggle drugs into or out of the country, that may involve incarceration in an unsavory local jail, or who have been involved in an accident and injured or whose travelling companion has died or been killed—all these he would normally handle on the spot, while reporting them routinely to the embassy in the capital and to the Consular Department in the Foreign & Commonwealth Office in London. More serious emergencies involving British citizens are likelier to require support on the spot from the host country's capital, especially if they are attracting attention in the UK media: a hurricane or tsunami, the kidnapping of Britons in the consul-general's area by terrorist groups, the possibility of the state execution of a British national, an earthquake—any of these might involve the dispatch of an information officer from the embassy in the capital to help deal with press enquiries from the UK, internationally, or locally; often the ambassador himself will fly to the scene of the emergency to take charge of the consular operation in collaboration with his consul-general and his staff, not usually sufficiently numerous to cope with the emergency on their own. In really difficult high-profile cases, a support team, trained to deal with emergencies overseas, may fly out from London to support the ambassador and his consular staff on the spot.

Each embassy or high commission in the capital will also have a consul on its staff, supported by both UK-based and locally engaged staff, to deal with consular work in the area of the capital, which may include running a large and busy section dealing with applications for visas to visit the UK. The consul in a small or medium-sized embassy may combine his consular work with being the post's administration officer, since in a consular emergency he will have the full personnel resources of the embassy to support him if necessary.

### As an example:

*In Australia, the federal political capital is Canberra, the site of the federal government and parliament and the embassies and high commissions. But the major business centres are far away in the state capitals, especially those of the most important states of New South Wales and Victoria. In these, the British consuls-general at, especially, Sydney and Melbourne, are senior members of the British diplomatic service in their own right, of considerable stature in their own parishes where they are much in demand for speeches and interviews and a presence at important city and state functions. They may indeed be treated, and function, very much as if they were ambassadors to the state where they exercise their consular functions, and will inevitably acquire much more visibility locally than the high commissioner, who will only rarely be on public view in Sydney or Melbourne, however frequently he may visit them from Canberra, compared with the Consuls-General who live there.*

*When I was British high commissioner in Canberra, the Consuls-General in both Sydney and Melbourne were very experienced and capable officers, both of whom had previously served as British ambassadors to countries of less importance to UK interests than either of the Australian states of New South Wales and its state capital, Sydney, or Victoria and its state capital Melbourne. Both had been posted to their new Australian jobs as consuls-general on promotion to a higher diplomatic service grade, after serving elsewhere as British ambassadors.*

*On one of my earliest official visits to Sydney from Canberra as high commissioner, the then consul-general, Ray (not his real name), gave a big buffet supper at his Sydney residence to enable my wife and me to meet some of the leading political, business, arts, and media figures of his parish, New South Wales. Over pre-dinner drinks before we all sat down at 10 or 11 buffet tables for six or eight guests each, I got into conversation with a member of the New South Wales State Parliament called (naturally) Bruce. I was asking him about the political situation in NSW and the fortunes of his own party, the Australian Labor Party (ALP), about which Bruce spoke enthusiastically and at length. Ray, the consul-general and our host, had introduced us to*

*each other but it was obvious that Bruce had not heard my name or*
*function. Eventually he asked casually how I had come to know Ray.*

*"Ray and I are colleagues in the British diplomatic service," I*
*said, perhaps disingenuously. "We've known each other for years,*
*ever since we served together at the British embassy in Moscow, many*
*years ago."*

*"So you're on Bruce's staff here in Sydney," Bruce said. "What's*
*your job in the consulate-general, if I might ask?"*

*"I'm not in the consulate-general," I explained. "I'm the British*
*high commissioner to Australia—I'm visiting from Canberra."*

*"Ah," said Bruce, not at all impressed. "So you're in Canberra*
*working for Ray."*

*"Not exactly," I said. "Ray's in Sydney working for me."*

*"Aw, OK. Got yer." Bruce pretended to have understood, but I'm*
*sure he didn't believe me. For him, Sydney and New South Wales were*
*the centre of the universe, and it was inconceivable that anyone else-*
*where in Australia could be senior to the British government's exalted*
*representative in Sydney, his good friend Ray, the congenial and ex-*
*tremely effective British consul-general.*

*"Good to meet you, mate. If you don't mind, I want to go and have*
*a word with Ray about something, before I forget."*

*And he moved away in search of Ray, to his own obvious relief.*

Adam's last appointment before he retired was as high commissioner
in 'Scotston,' the federal political capital of the Commonwealth oil-producing country 'Hibernia.' He was responsible not only for the political
work of the high commission but also for the commercial and consular
work carried out by the British consulates or consulates-general in 'Tarnbrea' and three other capitals of different Hibernian provinces. The officers in charge of the two smaller consulates were "honorary consuls,"
local residents who were generally UK citizens and did some occasional
consular work virtually unpaid. The two bigger posts were "consulates-
general," each headed by a British career diplomat. Adam, as the high
commissioner in Scotston, was ultimately responsible for the work of all
these posts.

The consul-general in charge of the consulate-general in Tarnbrea was
a diplomatic service colleague and near-contemporary of Adam's, Percy
Kerr, who before his Tarnbrea posting had spent three years as ambassador to a Latin American country in South America—an indication of the
importance the Foreign & Commonwealth Office attached in those near-

sighted days to trade with Hibernia as compared to relations with Latin America. Adam, as the senior British diplomat in Hibernia, aimed to visit each of the two consulates-general at least twice a year and the smaller consulates at least once. In addition the four consuls-general and consuls attended an annual consular conference with Adam and his senior staff at the high commission in Scotston.

In the spring of Adam's second year in Hibernia, he went to visit Percy Kerr at the consulate-general in Tarnbrea. He and Percy had served together briefly in Boronia, where Adam had been a Counsellor while Percy had still been a First Secretary, but they had never got to know each other well. Adam had harbored doubts about Percy's abilities and performance, doubts which he had been obliged to convey to Percy when conducting his annual report interview at the embassy in Boronia. This had inevitably resulted in a certain chill in their relations. Adam guessed that Percy would not have been best pleased to discover that Adam was to be his new boss in Hibernia, especially after Percy had enjoyed the relative freedom and prestige of being an ambassador running his own mission before being transferred to a senior and responsible but subordinate post in Tarnbrea.

Adam and Percy Kerr had a tête-à-tête in Percy's capacious Tarnbrea office before Percy was to take him to the consulate-general's conference room for a meeting with the staff, both UK-based and locally engaged (the latter comprising both UK citizens and Hibernians). Meanwhile Percy sat in a deep armchair at an angle to the sofa where Adam was sitting.

"So you've been kept pretty busy in the last few months, Percy," Adam said. "There's been the hostage drama which we managed together, and which had a happy ending, thank God, and then you've had a rather eventful time with the UK Midlands Chamber of Commerce Trade Mission. How do you feel now about those two—er—challenges that you've faced?"

"I reckon they both went pretty well, actually," Percy said defensively. "A few hiccups with the Midlands Chamber, but no permanent harm done, I think."

"Any lessons that we need to learn?" asked Adam. "Let's talk about the hostage crisis first. Would you do anything differently if it happened again, which God forbid?"

Soon after Adam's arrival in Hibernia, a group of Hibernian activists campaigning for independence for the oil-rich province of "Allinsonia," the (banned) Allinsonia Liberation Front (ALF), had broken in to the Tarnbrea headquarters of the Anglo-Hibernian Oil Company, AHOC, held up a meeting of AHOC directors in its board room at gunpoint, kidnapped them and held them hostage for eight tense days, threatening to kill one of them every day unless the Hibernian government agreed to recognise the ALF as the sole representative of the Allinsonian people and to begin talks with the ALF leadership about the modalities for Allinsonian independence from Hibernia. Those held hostage included the AHOC Chairman and the company secretary, both Britons, the finance director who was a U.S. citizen, the Chief Executive and three other directors, all Hibernian citizens.

"Well," Percy replied, "perhaps I should have alerted you at the high commission in Scotston and the Office in London more promptly to what had happened, given that there were two UK citizens involved. When I first heard about it in a rather uninformative telephone call from the Tarnbrea police, and then another call from the Tarnbrea Provincial Governor's office, I thought it would all be sorted out very quickly by the Hibernian authorities, and there seemed no point in bothering you or London about it until the situation was a bit clearer."

"Yes, indeed," Adam said. "The first I heard about it was when I had a call from the *Daily Mail* in London asking what I was doing to safeguard the lives of two prominent Brits being held hostage in Tarnbrea. Then I had a call from the FCO asking why I hadn't reported what had happened, with my recommendations on what should be done about it. It was not a happy position to find oneself in. The next thing was a telephone call from the head of the Consular Department in the Hibernian ministry of foreign affairs asking me to attend an emergency meeting here in Tarnbrea in three hours' time. It was only then that I heard from you and we were able to make some urgent judgements about how best to proceed. By then we had lost quite a lot of precious time."

Adam recognised that Percy and his consular staff were reasonably competent when it came to handling routine consular cases: British citizens who had lost their passports and all their money, or who had been badly injured in car accidents and had to be helped to go home to Britain, or—in one memorable case—had lost their four-year-old daughter in a crowded department store and were convinced that she had been kidnapped (the little girl turned up, unscathed, two panicky days later in a small town some sixty kilometers away and no one ever found out what had happened to her). All such DBS (Distressed British Subject) cases, however straightforward, required close relations with the local police force and other provincial authorities, as well as careful handling of the DBS concerned. People under severe, even unbearable stress frequently tended to be enraged by the discovery that there were strict limits to what the British consul could do for them, whether because of the financial constraints under the rules imposed by London (which required a DBS to try to get money sent to him by relatives or friends at home before the consulate could offer to make them a minimal loan against early and prompt repayment later), or because the consulate had no resources of its own for detective work or search-and-rescue operations, and had no alternative but to rely on the relevant arm of either the provincial or the federal Hibernian government. Adam was not entirely confident that Percy had sufficiently strongly instilled in his staff the need for emollient, sympathetic, and helpful responses even to the most unreasonable demands and complaints from angry, tearful, or aggressive Brits in trouble. Threats to complain to one's MP or to a friend in the FCO, or to the *Daily Mail*, were not uncommon, and were often carried out, leading in the worst cases to questions in parliament and a lasting suspicion that a British post overseas (for which Adam was personally responsible) had callously failed to pull out all the stops on behalf of a British citizen in distress.

Then there were sometimes problems with appeals for help to the British Consulate-General from citizens of other Commonwealth countries which had no high commission or consulate of their own in Hibernia, under the long established convention that Commonwealth consulates looked after the consular problems of other Commonwealth countries with no local representation (a similar convention has developed among consulates of the European Union). Often complaints about an unsympathetic or otherwise inadequate response by the UK consulate concerned turned out on investigation to be unfounded; Adam suspected that at other times and in other places they were probably justified. But there were limits to how much he could micro-manage the office in Tarnbrea from the high commission in Scotston.

Percy was apologising for not having put Adam in the picture as soon as he had heard about UK citizens being taken hostage. "I admitted at the time that I should have acted more quickly to alert you," he said. "I've learned that lesson, I assure you."

"I think perhaps you also regret now, with hindsight, having tried to convince me that there was no need for me to fly down to Tarnbrea on the first available flight to help coordinate the rescue operation with the Hibernians and the Americans. The UK media would have had a field day if they had caught me sitting complacently in the high commission in Scotston while here in Tarnbrea two British VIPs were in imminent danger of being murdered."

"I was confident that I could handle it on my own, Adam," Percy said. "The chief of police here is a good mate of mine—we're both members of the same golf club, in fact—and we understand each other well. I thought it might be better if you remained in Scotston and handled the UK and Hibernian media frenzy while I took part with the Hibernians here in planning the rescue."

"Well, we know now that that was a misjudgment. It was essential that I should be seen to be here, coordinating the liaison with the Hibernian authorities while you handled the media. It was a case of all hands to the pump."

"All right, Adam," Percy said. "Point taken. Just as well for me," he added wryly, "that all the hostages were eventually rescued alive and well. It was thanks to you that we got that team of advisers on dealing with hostage situations flown out from London to help the Hibernians: the Hibernian security people relied heavily on that team for advice and guidance when they embarked on their negotiations with the hostage-takers. Anyway, it had a happy ending."

Adam took another folder out of the briefcase beside him on the sofa and opened it. "Let's talk a bit about the Midlands Chamber of Commerce Mission visit. It was not a very pleasant ending to that particular event when they complained to the FCO and the Department of Trade in London as soon as they got home that they had not been satisfied with the support they had expected to get from you and your people in the consulate-general. I've seen the explanations that you submitted to London, and I'm sure you're right that some of the Chamber's complaints were unjustified, but some of their other worries seemed to have substance. For example, was it true that you weren't prepared to advise them on the best ways to attract Hibernian investment in British companies in the midlands?"

"Not exactly, no. I told them that in my view British companies would do better to go into partnership with Hibernian companies than to look for direct investment."

"But surely," Adam objected, "that's a judgement for them to make, not you? What they want from you is advice on the most promising contacts to make in Tarnbrea, what the financial climate is like here, the economic and financial prospects here over the next few years, the political situation in the province, and how to set about getting favourable local media coverage of their visit—all things that you and your staff ought to be extremely well placed to provide."

"Well, we organised a very good programme of visits for them, they saw all the key industrial and financial figures, and they got good coverage on Tarnbrea radio and television. The leader of the team, Sir Reg, did give a long interview to the *Tarnbrea Herald*, which as you know is our leading newspaper here, widely read all over Hibernia, but for some reason it never got published. I gave the editor a piece of my mind about that afterwards, I can tell you."

Adam wondered how helpful that would have been, but kept the thought to himself. Instead he asked about another of the Midland Chamber's complaints.

"One of the things that seems to have annoyed them was that you didn't accompany the Midlands Chamber team leader when he went with the team's secretary to call on the minister of commerce in the Tarnbrea provincial government. The team leader, Sir Reginald Duckworth, as you well know, was and is a very prominent British businessman with excellent connections with government ministers and officials at home. I wonder why you let him go on his own to see the minister?"

"That was rather unfortunate, I agree," said the consul-general. "The trouble was, I had a previous appointment to see another UK businessman who was in town on the same day, and the time of the Midlands Chamber appointment with the minister was only confirmed at the last minute, too late for me to change my meeting with the other fellow. The worst thing was that the chap I was supposed to see didn't show up, so I could have gone with Sir Reginald—actually he told me to call him Reg—after all."

"Couldn't you have asked Fred to field the other man so that you could go with Sir Reginald to see the minister?" Adam asked. Fred was Percy's UK-based deputy.

"That was another unfortunate thing," said Percy unhappily. "Fred was at home that day looking after his sick daughter. My only other UK-based officer was too new here, and probably too young, to take it on. I didn't think any of my locally engaged staff were really the right people to field the other businessman, assuming that he was going to turn up. I mean one of them could have done it perfectly well, but our businessmen expect to see a UK-based officer when they come all the way to Tarnbrea in search of business opportunities, and they tend to get distinctly shirty if they get palmed off, as they see it, with one of our local staff."

Adam sympathised with Percy over the unfortunate combination of events that had caused such a problem. He knew that in practice a senior and highly experienced, locally engaged, Hibernian member of the consulate-general staff, who had been working there for years and had excellent contacts with local business and political leaders, built up over many years, would have been able to give the visiting British businessman a far better picture of the local business and political scene than Percy or his UK-based deputy. But perception was what mattered.

The thought prompted another question. Adam asked how the LE (locally engaged) staff were doing after the radical shake-up following the last FCO inspection almost three years earlier.

"Well, Adam, as you know we lost our two most senior LE staff at the last inspection, not because they were under-performing, far from it, but because of an edict from London that wherever possible old LE hands earning salaries at the top of their scales should be replaced by new people on short-term contracts and at the bottom of their lower pay scales—to save money, of course, although it was dressed up as a campaign to get rid of dead wood and bring in fresh young blood instead. So we lost a lot of invaluable experience and many excellent contacts, and some of us felt very badly about having to pension off two very sound officers when they were both at the top of their game. Luckily one other was spared, and is still with us."

"That's Ted Onukwanu, is it?"

"That's right. First-class officer, Ted. I don't know how we'd manage without him. He's been around for donkey's years. Knows everyone. If a problem crops up, Ted always knows how it was solved the last time and who helped to solve it." Adam agreed that the local staff at diplomatic missions often provided essential continuity and possessed a fund of knowledge of the local scene that couldn't be matched by a UK-based career diplomat on a three or four year posting who would be due for a move at just about the time when he was beginning to settle in to the job. This applied especially to commercial work, and to a slightly lesser extent to consular work, where in both fields knowing the right people was so important. On the other hand, what visiting British businessmen often needed most from a consulate-general or an embassy or high commission commercial section and the head of mission was not so much advice on how to conduct their business: they mostly, but not always, knew more about that than the local British diplomats or consuls. What they wanted was a frank analysis of the political scene and how it was likely to develop; a guide to local attitudes to business generally, and to British business in particular; identification of the key local decision-makers and help in gaining access to them; and a list of relevant local firms with a potential interest in contracts to buy imported goods in the appropriate category from Britain.

UK commercial officers, whether career British diplomats or locally engaged staff, were also tasked to put British business visitors in touch with local companies whose products or services might prove to be complementary to theirs so that a partnership between them might be mutually beneficial. They would also be on the look-out for investment banks and other financial institutions that might be useful sources of inward investment in cash-strapped British enterprises. They would be constantly looking out for invitations to bid for lucrative contracts that might be won by a go-ahead UK firm: they would keep the Department of Trade in London regularly informed of such opportunities so that the Department could alert relevant British companies all over the UK to them. The very biggest and most prosperous British companies generally got their information about local business opportunities from their own local subsidiary companies or partners in the main markets, and rarely needed that kind of help from UK consular, commercial, or diplomatic posts; but even the biggest and most sophisticated of them would usually value a talk with the British ambassador or consul-general about the political scene and how it was likely to evolve. Sometimes even the most experienced and self-confident businessmen were surprisingly naive or blinkered when it came to politics, as Adam had observed on more than one occasion.

"Adam," Percy said, looking at his watch, "I think it's time I took you along the corridor for your meeting with the rest of the staff. I know that some of them have worries that they're anxious to discuss with you. They don't see that much of you face to face, and after all the buck stops with you, not me."

"OK, Percy. I've got my bullet-proof vest on. But I think we've had quite a useful talk. Let's go."

**As an example:**

*During my time in Ethiopia, I made a point of keeping in touch with the Delegate (roughly equivalent to ambassador) of the EEC, now the EU. He was a gruff but friendly German called Hans (not his real name) with an unexpectedly wicked sense of humour and sharp eyes behind heavy-framed spectacles with thick lenses. Like all the other western countries' ambassadors, I had to get permission from an al-ways suspicious and risk-averse Ethiopian government, including its security apparatus, to travel more than a few kilometres outside the capital, Addis Ababa, and I was always on the look-out for a good reason to visit places out in the countryside. One day I suggested to Hans that we might pay a joint visit to a distant region where there was a water project funded jointly by Britain and the EEC (now the EU). At this point Britain was giving no bilateral aid to Ethiopia, a country with a repressive, Soviet-backed, quasi-communist military government whose economic policies were the opposite of everything that Britain and the IMF believed in; but we supported sound multilat-eral aid projects undertaken by UN agencies or the EEC if they brought specific benefits directly to poor local people. That was the case with a project to bring clean, safe, drinkable water to a group of villages where for centuries the women and young girls had had to walk for several hours every day of their lives to get water from a distant river and bring it back in heavy earthenware urns precariously balanced on their heads or shoulders.*

*So Hans and I did a trip together to see the UK/EEC project out in the wilds. We were gone for ten days, travelling over bumpy tracks in Land Rovers with clapped out springing, and staying in primitive con-ditions at our overnight stops. Predictably, we got to know each other quite well. Hans said it was the first time he had done a joint trip like this with the ambassador of an EEC country to fly the flags of both the donor country and the EEC itself and to highlight their joint contribu-tions to the welfare of ordinary Ethiopians and development of their economy. He was keen to do it again, whether with me or with other*

*EEC colleagues. I said I didn't think all of our EEC ambassadorial colleagues were equally keen on experiencing the discomforts and occasional dangers of travel outside Addis Ababa. The dangers were very real, with civil wars and armed insurrections breaking out all around the periphery of the country, and sometimes closer to the centre I was provided by a solicitous British government with an armed bodyguard who accompanied me at all times when I was outside the British embassy compound.*

*One day, a few months after our expedition to the water project, I had a telephone call from Hans.*

*"Brian, I shouldn't be telling you this, but I'm very concerned about an EEC development project in Ethiopia involving a massive contract that's about to be signed between the EEC, the Ethiopian government, and a big "Paralonian"[1] construction firm. I can smell trickery in this. The Paralonians shouldn't have won this contract: their bid was badly flawed and there was a much better bid by a British company, costing a bit more, but technically far superior. The British company ought to have got it. I'm convinced that there's been some underhand activity behind the scenes. I thought you ought to know—but for God's sake don't tell anyone I told you."*

*I had been following this project and the competition from a safe distance. "Paralonia," the fifth or sixth biggest country in the EEC, was known for its big and flourishing construction and engineering sector. The British company, Mills & Co., were the clear front runners and were getting, I thought, all the support they needed from the UK delegation to the EEC in Brussels. The news that the contract had apparently been awarded to Alessandro, the Paralonian company that had put in a cheap but dodgy bid, was a considerable shock. Several millions of EEC development fund Euros were at stake. I sent a quick telegram to the FCO, the Department of Trade, and the UK Delegation at Brussels urging a last-minute intervention to get the signing of the contract postponed while the bids were re-assessed. Within minutes William, the commercial Counsellor in the UK delegation to the EEC in Brussels, contrived to get through to me on the telephone, no mean feat given the state of the telephone system in those days. We agreed that it was not too late to pull out all the stops for Mills, the UK company: the Paralonians should not be allowed to get away with their jiggery-pokery. William, later to play a prominent role in British diplomacy, promised to make urgent contact with the key figures in the EEC Commission, especially in the Development and Finance Directorates but also in the office of the Commission President. He would threaten to expose the corrupt dealings that had obviously taken place, if the contract was allowed to go to Alessandro. I undertook to do the same in Addis Ababa. We would keep each other (and London) informed. There was no time to wait for instructions from the FCO, which would come, if at all, only after probably protracted consultations with the Department of Trade. There was also a danger that fastidious concern in the FCO about the implications for our relations with Paralonia of a rough campaign against Alessandro might water down our instructions and hamper our efforts. This was naughty on our part—London was better placed than either of us to take wider considerations and risks into account—but time was short and William's and my blood was up. We would keep London fully informed of what we were up to, and if they didn't like it, it was up to them to tell us so and instruct us to act differently, or not at all.*

*Hans's crucial call to me had taken place on Tuesday. The contract was due to be signed in Addis Ababa on Thursday by the Chairman of the Paralonian company Alessandro, who I discovered had already arrived with a large team from his company and was staying with my colleague, the Paralonian ambassador, in the large and opulent Paralonian Residence. The EEC's Development Commissioner in Brussels was about to leave for Addis Ababa to sign the contract on the EEC's behalf, until a telephone call from William warned him that it would be prudent to put his departure on hold, since there was every possibility that the signing ceremony with Alessandro would not take place.*

*I spent the rest of Tuesday and the whole of Wednesday morning touring the offices of Ethiopian ministers—Trade, Development, Finance, Foreign Affairs—bluffing my way into the ministers' inner offices over the protests of their private secretaries and security guards, telling them that Alessandro would never be able to complete the project at the unreal price they had quoted in their bid: that the project would collapse, at immense cost to Ethiopia, with awkward questions inevitably asked about who had benefited from the perverse decision to award the contract to the Paralonians; that if the contract with Alessandro was signed, we would ensure that it would be challenged in the European courts, that we would get it overturned, and that it would cause great embarrassment to the Ethiopian ministers who had agreed to it; that expert opinion was unanimous in holding that the bid from Mills, the UK company, was technically more sound, its cost estimates more realistic, and the prospects for its successful execution of the project extremely good.*

*In the midst of all this hectic activity a cautious telegram arrived from London warning William in Brussels and myself in Addis Ababa to be careful not to make allegations against the Paralonians or those who had colluded with them in Brussels that might not stand up in court, in case our action to overturn the decision were to be legally challenged. Fortunately or otherwise, it was far too late: if there was any damage from the way William and I were campaigning, it had already been done.*

*Late on Wednesday evening the EEC Commission announced that the ceremony of the signature of the contract had been cancelled, "for technical reasons," and that the Commission had decided to conduct a re-assessment of the five bids, including those from Mills and Alessandro. The Alessandro Chairman and his team left the Paralonian ambassador's Residence unobtrusively and got the next flight back to their capital. The Paralonian ambassador and I avoided each other for two or three weeks; when, unavoidably, we next met, at the regular monthly meeting of EEC ambassadors to Ethiopia, he surreptitiously winked at me and we shook hands with special warmth.*

*In due course the contract was awarded to Mills, the British company. A few weeks later Sir Nigel Franks, the chairman of Mills, with his chief executive, the company's chief engineer, and two Mills directors, arrived in Addis Ababa for the contract signing ceremony. This time the EEC Commissioner took the diplomatic decision to stay in Brussels, leaving it to a happy Hans to sign on behalf of the Commission. Franks and the Chief Executive came to stay with J and me in our Residence. Over a glass of Scotch after dinner on the evening before the contract was to be signed, Franks and I reminisced about the excitements of the last-minute campaign to save the contract for his company. Franks said he had been told by the EEC Commissioner in Brussels that he had never before witnessed such tough and proactive diplomacy on behalf of a private company.*

*Before he finished his last Scotch and went to bed, Franks confided to me that his company was still in a state of shock. They had not expected their bid to succeed: in fact, they had only submitted it to demonstrate that Mills was still a big player in the international construction game. It had been generally understood in the industry that the Paralonians had the contract sewn up right from the start: the Ethiopians and the EEC Commission in Brussels had thought they were simply going through the motions when they carried out the procedures for assessing the bids. Franks and his colleagues were far from sure that they were capable of carrying out the construction work*

*within the terms of the contract, or indeed at all, in view of the formid-*
*able technical challenge that it represented. But they were stuck with it*
*now, and I could be sure that they would give it their best shot.*

*Privately I thought it might have saved everybody a lot of effort*
*and some badly bruised toes if Mills had tipped us off at the beginning*
*that they had never expected to get the contract and that they would be*
*pretty worried about their ability to do the job if by some miscalcula-*
*tion it were to be awarded to them. I refrained from sharing this*
*thought with Franks, merely wished him good night, and went to bed.*

*At the signing ceremony on the following day, Sir Nigel made a*
*graceful speech expressing his company's pride at its success in win-*
*ning the contract "against exceptionally tough competition," and his*
*confidence that in collaboration with their capable and experienced*
*Ethiopian partners, they would bring this important project to a suc-*
*cessful conclusion, giving a significant boost to Ethiopia's economic*
*development. Some time after I had left Ethiopia for a new posting as*
*ambassador to Poland, I heard that Mills, Franks's company, had*
*completed the project successfully, under budget and on time.*

*Throughout all this I had managed to avoid identifying the EEC*
*Delegate in Ethiopia, Hans, as my source for asserting that the deci-*
*sion to give the contract to the Paralonians was open to question and*
*that it should be reconsidered. I had never imagined that my sugges-*
*tion of a joint trip with him to visit the water project would pay such a*
*spectacular dividend.*

Adam's meeting with the staff of the consulate-general in Tarnbrea pro-
ceeded much as he had expected. He took careful notes of all the points
raised by those present, and when he couldn't give an immediate answer,
he promised to investigate when he got back to Scotston, try his best to
devise acceptable solutions to the problems that had been put to him, and
tell those concerned the outcome. It was an especially useful opportunity
for him to hear about some of the things that concerned the Hibernian
staff, many of them trivial in themselves but obviously important to those
affected. These were matters that would no doubt have been raised with
Percy Kerr as the consul-general and head of post, but hardly any of them
would have seemed to Kerr sufficiently important to warrant consultation
with Adam about them.

Ted Onukwanu, the highly capable Hibernian who had worked for the
consulate-general longer than anyone else in the room, was telling Adam
about a problem over the limitation of locally engaged officers' powers of

decision in certain categories of consular cases, when there was a discreet knock on the door of the conference room and the tall Hibernian receptionist who sat at the front desk by the main entrance to the building tiptoed in, high heels clacking on the polished wood floor, to whisper in Percy Kerr's ear. He nodded understandingly to her and indicated to Adam that he needed to say something.

"High Commissioner, I'm sorry to interrupt the proceedings, but I'm afraid we seem to have a problem, and I think Ted and I will need to go and attend to it. A very distressed British lady has just come in to the entrance lobby to say that her husband and two of their small children have been badly injured in a car accident—apparently the taxi they were in collided with a bus—and she's at her wits' end to know what to do. What more can you tell us, Alicia?"

The tall receptionist said the husband was apparently unconscious in the hospital, his wife had no money and didn't know the combination of the safe in the hotel containing their money, passports, return air tickets, and other things, they were due to fly home the following day for a family funeral but the husband and children obviously wouldn't be fit to travel, she had no money to make telephone calls to her husband's parents in Glamorgan—"

"Thank you, Alicia," Percy said. "I think we get the picture. I'm sure we can get the hotel to open the safe, so that won't be a problem, but there'll be a lot of other things to be done and the lady will need a lot of support. If you'll excuse us, High Commissioner, I think Ted and I should go down and see her."

It occurred to Adam that the day-to-day work of a busy consul's office would make a good television drama series.

## NOTE

1. I'm calling it Paralonian for the purposes of this chronicle. You may ask which country the company actually came from, but I couldn't possibly comment. The names of the companies and individuals concerned have also been changed to protect the guilty.

# 14

# LOOKING BACK: REFLECTIONS ON THE DIPLOMATIC CAREER

*"Which was your favourite post?"; passing on to the home government the lessons learned; life after diplomacy. Was it all worth it?*

**"H**ibernia," the Commonwealth country where Adam was British high commissioner, was his last post before he retired at age sixty, then (but no longer) the fixed retirement age for British diplomatic service officers, apart from those who were made to retire earlier because there was no prospect of another job for them, or because they volunteered to take early retirement. A few months before his sixtieth birthday, Adam was interviewed by a reporter, Larry Gardiner, from the country's principal newspaper, the *Scotston Observer*. Larry opened with the standard question put by every friend, relative, or newspaper interviewer to every diplomat who has been at more than one post in the course of his career.

"Which was your favourite posting, high commissioner?"

Adam gave his practised standard answer.

"It depends on what you mean by 'favourite.' If you mean where did I have the greatest professional job satisfaction, I would say the answer is probably Côte Noire in west Africa."

"Why was there special job satisfaction there?"

"Because it's a very poor, developing country which is trying hard to reduce the poverty of several millions of its people and where quite modest development projects can make a visible, tangible difference to hundreds of the local people's lives—maybe thousands. It was my first overseas post and I was very junior, but I was personally involved in helping to identify two specific projects, finding funding for them from the British government and UN agencies and others, getting the cooperation of local people and their leaders, keeping an eye on them as they were being implemented, helping to sort out a few problems as they arose, attending the opening ceremonies that launched them, and then visiting occasionally to see them in operation. I got to know a number of the local people well and it was really exciting to see how the lives of some of them were changed by what had been done, in both cases at very modest cost."

"What kind of projects were they?"

"One was a clean water project in a village where previously water for cooking and drinking had to be brought from a lake about 35 kilometres away, always by the women and quite young girls of the village. Having a well and pump for clean, safe water actually in the village was a revolutionary development for them, although the men of the village were not terribly happy about having the wives and daughters around the whole time when previously they had been away for most of every day, trudging 35 kilometres to the lake to get the water and another 35 kilometres back to the village. That of course used to take up most of the day."

"And the other project?"

"That was starting up a girls' school in an area of Côte Noire where previously girls had never been to school at all. We arranged a link with a new teachers' training college in the capital, Cameko, funded by the EEC (as it was then—now the EU, of course), which agreed to take young women and some men from the area and train them to be teachers. We got some very basic school equipment as a gift from UNESCO—desks and benches, blackboards, and so on—and the whole thing was in the open air under some acacia trees which gave reasonable shelter from the sun and from the rain during the rainy season. (I heard recently that the locals were building a proper school-house, using local materials and voluntary labour.) There were girls at the school from ages 8 to 18 and a few adult women, too. We knew that even the most basic education would help these women and girls to get control of their own lives—for example, they would be able to control the number of children they would have, which would transform their lives compared with their mothers' experiences. That was very exciting, too. You felt that you were genuinely helping to make a difference in real practical ways. You can imagine how cross I get when people at home tell me that all our development aid is squandered and siphoned off by corrupt dictators and corrupt officials, and that it all does more harm than good. I wish people like that could be sent out to see my water project and the girls' school and the hundreds of other similar projects that are changing lives all over Africa."

Larry frowned. "Surely what you have described isn't really diplomatic work—it's aid work, that an aid and development officer would do?"

"Often there's no clear distinction between diplomatic and aid work," Adam replied. "In some posts, development aid is the most important element in the relations between the diplomat's home country and the country where he's posted. If there's a completely separate aid and development ministry in the home country, like the Department for International Development (or DfID) in London, which is concerned with all aspects of development, not just aid, it may have its own officers on the staff of embassies and high commissions where development aid administration is a major activity, but in other, smaller posts the work will probably be done by an ordinary diplomatic service officer, probably taking his instructions mostly from DfID rather than the FCO. Indeed, in countries with a significant UK aid programme, DfID sometimes has its own separate office headed by a senior DfID officer who may not even be listed as a member of the embassy staff. Unfortunately this kind of rather blurred dividing line can lead to quite fierce turf wars, both in posts and at home. But by and large, it works."

"So the idea that diplomats sit in luxurious offices all day and at black tie dinners all night isn't the whole story?"

"Exactly. Diplomatic work often involves getting honest dirt under one's fingernails, and often that's the most rewarding part of the job."

"And other kinds of favourite postings?"

"Well, in terms of creature comforts and local amenities, obviously New York, where I was at the UK Mission to the United Nations, was a wonderful place for some of the world's best restaurants, opera, ballet, concert halls, art galleries, theatre—you name it. Almost as good as London! Also a city from which one could drive in just a few hours to magnificent beauty spots and resorts for fabulous holidays, if you could get away from work for long enough. Washington, DC was similar but a bit less so—much smaller, but of course politically fascinating."

"How about the places with the best climate?"

"Oh, Hibernia, any day!" Adam laughed.

Larry took care to write that down for his article. He thought he might get away with a headline: "Hibernia Is UK Envoy's Favourite Posting."

**As an example:**

*There was never any doubt about which of my postings had offered the greatest job satisfaction. During the prolonged famine emergency in Ethiopia in the mid-1980s, at whose peak some nine million Ethiopians were in immediate danger of death from starvation and hunger-related disease, all the western countries' diplomats and many others besides were heavily involved in the massive international relief effort which unquestionably saved many millions of lives. Britain was among the most prominent contributors to the international relief operation, partly because of its special relationship with Ethiopia—the UK had directly or indirectly administered the country for a period after British and Commonwealth forces had liberated it from Italian occupation in 1941, and had directly governed Eritrea for much longer—but more importantly because it had been British television reporters and others who had alerted first Britain and then the world to the realities and huge scale of the famine and the suffering it was causing. As the British ambassador, I played an active part in the relief work, along with my wife and many other members of the embassy staff and the small British community in Ethiopia, identifying sudden needs and devising ways to address them, investigating allegations of diversion of relief supplies, helping with the targeting of the RAF's airlift of grain and other supplies from the ports to the mountainous famine areas, travelling by air and road to visit relief centres in remote areas where British NGOs were doing fantastic work in harsh conditions, and providing what comforts and support we could—mostly in the form of square meals—for British and other relief workers when they came back to the capital, Addis Ababa, for the occasional week of rest and recreation before they returned to the clinics and feeding centres out in the remote wilds of the country. The Assistant Secretary-General of the United Nations sent to co-ordinate the famine relief work of the UN agencies in Ethiopia commented in his memoirs that almost all ordinary diplomatic work in Ethiopia was suspended for the duration of the emergency while all the diplomats became full-time relief workers. It was exhausting, often frustrating—there was always the feeling that one ought to be doing even more—and occasionally dangerous (my wife and I narrowly escaped being taken hostage by armed separatist guerrillas while on our way to visit the Save the Children feeding centre at Korem in the north of the country), but we were living and working in luxury compared with the young relief workers scattered all over the famine areas, tending to the sick and feeding the starving, day after day virtually without respite, with no creature comforts and often very little food or shelter.*

*Of course the contribution that my wife and I made to the common effort was barely a small drop in a very large ocean. But it was one of the rare occasions in a diplomatic career in peacetime when it was possible to feel that the situation was one involving life and death on a huge scale, and that whatever you did was helping to save the lives of real people who without our help would have starved to death. There is similar "job satisfaction" in a great deal of the aid and development and consular work that diplomats do, but it rarely dominates one's life as starkly and over such a long period of several years as it did in Ethiopia during my time as ambassador there.*

After a break for a cup of coffee, Larry Gardiner, the young newspaper reporter, turned on his little tape recorder again and resumed his interview with Adam.

"High commissioner, what has it been like being a diplomat for all these years? Has it been exciting or mostly just boring routine work like ordinary people do but with more, um, glamour?"

Adam bridled at the suggestion of glamour as a feature of his job.

"Ninety-nine per cent of the time there's nothing glamorous about it, Larry. You spend most of your time at a desk dealing with mostly uninteresting papers or at meetings discussing routine matters of administration or personnel matters, much the same as any other office worker does. The more experienced and senior you get, the more time you spend on management instead of negotiating with foreign governments which is probably what you thought you'd be doing as a diplomat. In that respect I suppose it's like being a teacher or a lawyer: you spend less and less time teaching in the classroom or addressing the jury in court, and more and more time running the school or the legal chambers.

"The big difference is that as a diplomat you'll probably spend a good half of your career in foreign countries, or Commonwealth ones which we don't regard as foreign, and that's what makes it one of the most fascinating careers in the world. Of course other people spend a lot of time working abroad—in the army, or as foreign correspondents for newspapers or television channels, or for an oil company, or just as businessmen or businesswomen with overseas interests. But as a diplomat you

usually have access to the most interesting, powerful, or influential people in the land. Some of them you'll get to know personally and spend
leisure time with them. You'll probably travel all over the countries that
you serve in, rather than being stuck in an office in the capital, and in
some places it will be real travel: you'll be more like an explorer than a
tourist. Your job is not to visit a couple of beauty spots and leave again
after a week, but to spend several years in the country, studying its history
and economy and politics, getting to understand what makes it tick, learning how to analyse all that information and melt it down into pithy illuminating assessments for your government at home."

"But diplomats aren't always posted in foreign countries, surely?"
Larry asked.

"No, that's true. You have your spells of duty at home in your country's foreign ministry. That's not usually so varied or exciting—unless
you're involved in some international crisis, which can be very exciting
and demanding, indeed. But building a close relationship with one's minister while working in the foreign ministry at home can be stimulating
and rewarding in a different way. One of the main things that diplomats
do is to persuade, and sometimes you need more persuasion skills when
you're dealing with your own ministers at home than you do with a
foreign government. Analysing the information that comes in to you in
your foreign ministry and turning it into coherent and persuasive policy
advice to ministers can be remarkably challenging. Then turning your
ministers' decisions into practical instructions to be sent to the relevant
embassies abroad can be quite a challenge, too. I can't say its 'never a
dull moment'—not many jobs never have a dull moment—but there's
plenty of fascinating and difficult activity in a diplomat's life, I can assure
you."

Scribbling on his note-pad, Larry quoted Adam's words: "'One of the
main things that diplomats do is to persuade,' you said, high commissioner. I must get that down. Very quotable."

"It's true," Adam said. "Of course, others have to be good persuaders,
too, not just diplomats. But it's really central to diplomacy."

Larry took a moment or two to ponder Adam's words.

"I suppose that nowadays, with such fast communications world-wide,
diplomats are hardly any more than messenger boys—or messenger
girls—for their ministers back home, relaying messages to the host
government on instructions from home, and then relaying the replies

when they get them. Or is there still a real job for a diplomat with initiative and judgement?"

"Oh," Adam said, smiling, "that's a very common misconception. Diplomats often have to react quickly to a fast-moving situation without time to get instructions from home. You often have to act first and seek instructions later. You report back to your foreign ministry as soon as possible what you have said or done and hope that your government will approve. The traditional form of retrospective endorsement is a telegram saying simply 'You spoke well,' signed by your foreign minister. Sometimes, of course, your masters at home will disagree with what you have said and instruct you to retract it or amend it accordingly. But that's very rare, I'm glad to say."

**As an example:**

*When I was in Ethiopia, several areas around the periphery of the country were in open revolt against the central government in Addis Ababa. One of these rebel movements, widely supported in Tigray, the Ethiopian province concerned, had succeeded in occupying an appreciable strip of Ethiopian territory along the north-western border with Sudan, whose government sympathised with the rebels and provided them with a safe rear area from which the fighters were supplied with essential food, arms, and ammunition, including extensive famine relief supplies for distribution in the rebel-occupied area since this was inaccessible from the rest of Ethiopia. A number of western governments, including the Americans, which had exceptionally bad relations with the military communist government in Addis Ababa, also discreetly supported the Tigrean rebels, while formally maintaining correct diplomatic relations with Addis. The international famine relief operation then in full swing in Ethiopia proper, i.e., the vast majority of the country under the control of the Addis government, was seriously complicated by the fighting between the Ethiopian government's forces and the various rebellions around its borders, especially in Eritrea— at that time part of Ethiopia—and Tigray. Neither the diplomats of countries that had diplomatic relations with the Addis government, nor relief organisations bringing aid to famine victims and operating with the necessary approval of the Addis government, could be seen to enter or operate in rebel-held areas of Tigray without fatally compromising their relations with Addis Ababa, thus putting at risk their relief activities throughout the rest of the country.*

Late on a Friday morning I received a summons to see the Ethiopian foreign minister, Goshu Wolde, in his office in Addis Ababa
later in the day. There was no indication of the reason for this. I
discovered after some telephone calls to other embassies that various
other western ambassadors had received similar summonses to see the
foreign minister at intervals throughout the afternoon. I arrived a little
early for my own appointment with the minister, in time to have a word
or two with the US Chargé d'Affaires as he emerged from Goshu
Wolde's office.

"What's this all about, Phil?" I asked.

"Goshu says they're going to bomb the columns of trucks entering
the rebel parts of Tigray from Sudan on the grounds that they are
taking arms and ammunition into Ethiopia for the rebels without the
permission of the Ethiopian government."

"What did you say?"

"I promised to report what he had said to Washington."

There was no time for any further discussion before it was my turn
to be ushered in to the minister's office. After the usual exchange of
courtesies, Goshu Wolde spoke in the same terms as those reported by
my American colleague.

"These vehicles and their crews are entering Ethiopia illegally,
with the purpose of supporting an armed rebellion against my government," the minister said. "We can no longer tolerate such intervention
from Sudan. We shall warn the Sudanese government that unless these
incursions cease by midnight tomorrow, we shall attack the intruders
from the air and destroy them without mercy. We have every right to
do so, in defence of our territorial integrity, under international law.
We wish your own government, Mr. Ambassador, to understand our
position and to give us your full support."

I said that I would report the minister's message at once to my
government, and that anything that I might say by way of comment was
of course without instructions from London and reflected only my own
personal view.

"But as you well know, Minister, it's very generally understood in
the international community in Ethiopia that these columns of vehicles
entering Tigray from Sudan are actually carrying food and medicines
for the relief of starvation in the areas under Tigrean rebel control.
Whether they are also bringing in arms for the rebels obviously I don't
know and couldn't say, but there seems little doubt that the bulk of the
cargoes are relief supplies provided by various governments and
NGOs in Sudan for purely humanitarian purposes."

*Goshu expressed scepticism. Even if the columns of trucks were bringing relief supplies as well as arms for the rebels, he said, it was totally illegal and the Ethiopian government had every right to take military action against them.*

*"Minister, I wouldn't argue that your government has every right under international law to attack these convoys," I said. "But I respectfully urge you to consider the political consequences of any such action, not just your legal rights. You will be portrayed throughout the world as an Ethiopian government bombing convoys bringing desperately needed food and medicines to your own fellow-Ethiopians, at the very time when people all over the world are contributing money and resources to the relief of famine in your country. Have you considered the effect that will have on the willingness of governments and private individuals everywhere to continue to support the international relief effort? Without that international support, the relief operation in the rest of Ethiopia will collapse and millions of your fellow-countrymen will die unnecessary and avoidable deaths. I believe that my government would wish you to have second thoughts before you embark on an attack that would be of very little military significance but which could have such disastrous political and humanitarian consequences for Ethiopia. However, as I say, I am speaking without instructions, and if my government disagrees with what I have said, I will of course inform you immediately."*

*There was a long pause while the minister stared at me without expression.*

*"Mr. Ambassador," he said eventually, "I appreciate your frankness. You have given us food for thought. But you will understand that I can give Your Excellency no undertaking that my government will deviate in any way from its chosen course."*

*On my return to the embassy I sent an urgent telegram to the FCO in London reporting my conversation with Goshu. A few hours later I was relieved to receive the reply I had hoped for: "You spoke well. You should immediately inform the Ethiopians that we strongly endorse the warning that you delivered. We are telling our western partner governments of Goshu's message and of your response, and urging them to speak urgently to the Ethiopians in similar terms."*

*I told Goshu's office that the British government had now endorsed what I had said to him. I heard later that several other embassies in Addis Ababa had had similar instructions from their capitals and had subsequently delivered the same warnings to the Ethiopians. I never*

*had any reply from Goshu, but no attacks on the convoys from Sudan
into Tigray took place at that time.*

*A year later, in December 1986, Colonel Goshu Wolde, Ethiopia's
foreign minister, defected from Addis Ababa and sought political asy-
lum in the United States, publicly denouncing the Ethiopian revolution, in which he had participated and which had taken the then Ethiopian government to power, for having deteriorated into "absolute
dictatorship and cruelty."*

*There was nothing special or exceptional about my exchange with
the Ethiopian foreign minister; diplomats the world over constantly
have to respond quickly to sudden events and warnings, without time
to get instructions. This example was interesting because of the mag-
nifier effect of my reply to Goshu produced by London's immediate
appeal to other like-minded governments to deliver the same warning
to the Ethiopian government. If I had waited for instructions from
London before warning the foreign minister of the likely political and
humanitarian consequences for Ethiopia of carrying out their threat to
bomb the food convoys in Tigray, it might well have been too late.*

Adam's interview with the reporter from the *Scotston Observer* continued.

"But when you're working in the foreign ministry at home, you aren't
really a diplomat anymore, are you?" Larry asked.

"Yes, of course you are. It's just a different form of diplomatic activity. You're still involved in foreign policy, both advising on it and carrying it out. You don't have diplomatic status in your own country, of
course, no diplomatic privileges and immunities, no duty-free liquor, but
you still probably have plenty of contacts with foreign diplomats in the
embassies in your capital as well as with your own country's embassies
and high commissions overseas. It's still quite different from the work of
a home-based civil servant in an ordinary home department."

"What are you going to do in your retirement, high commissioner?
Have you got some nice lucrative directorships lined up already?"

"No, I haven't," Adam said. "I'm really too steeped in the traditions
and ethos of the public service to transfer easily to a private sector job,
even if someone were to offer me one, which is not very likely. Others in
my service take a different view and some go on to make very distinguished careers for themselves in business or the City after they have
retired from the diplomatic service. A few of my more scholarly colleagues have gone on to become Masters (or Mistresses) of colleges of

our ancient and more prestigious universities or to take other academic posts, which I suspect often means in practice becoming full-time fundraisers—not my kind of job at all. But there are lots of jobs in NGOs and charities that would be very worthwhile. Personally I won't be looking for a full-time job. I know 60 is not old by today's standards, but several decades of work in different places around the world do involve some wear and tear and my wife and I are looking forward to a more restful and relaxing life at home."

"So if you had your time over again, would you still choose to be a diplomat?"

To the reporter's surprise, Adam pondered this question for several moments. Finally, he replied:

"Yes, on balance I think I would. There aren't many jobs available to ordinary people from ordinary backgrounds like me that let you see so much of the world, from such a privileged vantage point, or in which you work with such serious, interesting, able colleagues, or where you get to meet so many of your own country's movers and shakers, from government ministers to business tycoons and often famous actors and musicians and writers and religious leaders and academics, who visit the country you're serving in and automatically come to see you and probably have lunch with you or even stay with you for a few days. I've made some good friends as a result of visits like that, including some household names. After I have retired my wife and I will look back with real nostalgia on many of those visits to our lunch table and guest rooms, and our travels to faraway places with strange-sounding names, and some of the excitements and thrills that we've experienced. Do you feel like another coffee, Larry? Or something stronger, perhaps?"

**As an example:**

> *Looking back, I find it difficult to imagine a different career that would have afforded my wife and children and myself so many memorable experiences. Many of my diplomatic service colleagues and friends led far more adventurous and dangerous lives than I did, especially those serving in places riddled with violence and war. Others led peaceful, rather boring existences as they moved around the world. No one diplomat can be guaranteed as much excitement and fun as we were lucky enough to enjoy. But most practitioners of this strange profession (if an occupation requiring no formal training or qualifications and without an independent governing body can be called a*

*profession) may confidently expect a life filled with incident, constant-*
*ly enlivened by unpredictable and unexpected events, and supplying a*
*rich fund of anecdotes with which to regale their uncomprehending,*
*and probably not greatly interested, grandchildren.*

"So: no downside to this glittering career, high commissioner?" Larry
Gardiner of the *Scotston Observer* asked, swirling the Scotch around the
tinkling ice in his glass.

"Of course there's a downside," Adam said. "There's always a downside to all good things. The main thing is that you weaken your English
roots (or Scottish or whatever) by spending so much of your adult life
overseas. It's very difficult to play the kind of part in your local community that you would play if you were a home civil servant or indeed any
other kind of worker based in your own home town, just going abroad for
a few weeks a year on holiday. When I retire in a few months' time and
go home to London, I'll be a virtual foreigner in my own country and a
stranger in my own community. I'll have much more in common with
other former diplomats from other countries than with my own neighbours at home. I won't have been watching the same television series or
experiencing the same weather or noticing that some familiar shop in the
shopping centre has closed and been replaced by a charity shop. If I try to
talk about what I've been doing for the past 30 or 40 years, my neighbours will roll their eyes and look out of the window: it will all be so alien
to their own experience that they won't really want to know about it. My
friends will be some of the people I have worked with in the diplomatic
service over the years plus the people I got to know at school or university, many years and decades ago: I probably won't have spent enough
time at home since then to have made new friends."

"How do your children feel about being brought up in a diplomatic
family?" Larry asked.

"Mixed feelings, I suppose. They both chose to go to boarding school
in England when the time came, because they couldn't bear the upset of
having to adjust to a new school and new friends every two or three years
whenever I had a new posting, which would have happened if we had
kept them with us as we moved around the world. They were both reasonably happy at their boarding schools, I think, give or take occasional
bouts of home-sickness or bullying or problems with the work. But they
missed us, and my wife and I missed them probably even more. We
missed out on a sizeable part of their childhoods. I remember our son,

Ian, coming out for the school holidays to Boronia during our posting there: when he and the other boarding school children came streaming through into the arrivals hall at the airport, we literally didn't recognise him, he had changed so much during that term. He had been a child when we had seen him off at the beginning of that term, and he came back a young man at the end of it. He had even grown several inches taller in those three months away.

"On the other hand, they did have the excitement of spending their school holidays in all sorts of exotic places. Sometimes they were able to come on tour with us and that was always exciting for them. When I became an ambassador they enjoyed living in a Residence with a domestic staff to do the washing up and make their beds, but at the same time they were embarrassed by it. They thought it was hilarious when their Dad was called 'Your Excellency.' The first time that happened was when the embassy fixer, Tommy, went out to the aircraft to meet them as they came down the steps onto the tarmac, to shepherd them through local customs and immigration (which could be quite tricky without an experienced helper). Tommy told Anne, our daughter, that 'His Excellency' was waiting for them in the VIP lounge, and Anne had no idea who he was talking about. But they both caught the travel bug and both now spend a lot of their time overseas, sometimes in places that they first knew when I was posted there."

"And what now? Will you miss the diplomatic life when you retire in a few months' time? Will your wife miss it?"

"Absolutely not," Adam said with considerable emphasis. "We've both had quite enough of trailing round the world, constantly packing and unpacking our precious possessions (some things always get lost every time, however careful you are), getting to know new colleagues and finding out how to survive in a completely new unfamiliar environment. We'll never want to see a packing case or a suitcase again. We've mostly enjoyed it while it lasted, but enough is enough."

"And what," Larry asked, "will you tell your bosses in London about the lessons you have learned in your 30 years—"

"More like 40," Adam said.

"—your 40 years working as a diplomat?"

"Well," Adam said, "there used to be a tradition that just before you retired you sent what was called a 'valedictory despatch' to your minister, describing how you felt about your career and recommending changes in the things you had disliked over the years. People would sometimes be quite brutally frank in their criticisms—after all, at that stage there's nothing to lose! But a couple of times someone's very frank valedictory despatch, with a lot of searing criticisms of the way the FCO was managing the Service, was leaked to a UK newspaper, which naturally published it with great relish. This caused much embarrassment in Whitehall and in the end some genius hit on the perfect solution: ban valedictories! This has been a great loss: we all used to enjoy reading our copies of the valedictories sent like intercontinental ballistic missiles into the heart of the Foreign Office. And suddenly they dried up."

"So you won't be sending one yourself?" asked Larry.

"Oh yes, I will," Adam said. "It won't be a formal despatch—they are hardly ever used these days—but I'm certainly going to write to the head of the diplomatic service, with copies to the Secretary of State and every other British ambassador and high commissioner in the world, to say thank you for a wonderfully interesting life and for the comradeship of so many lovely colleagues, but also to give them a piece of my mind about the surrender of the diplomatic service to an army of private sector management consultants with their out-of-date nostrums for perpetually reforming everything in sight. I'm going to explain in simple language the inevitable consequences of constantly cutting the FCO's budget while increasing its work-load. Except for a small group of very senior diplomats who do an excellent job in helping to shape events overseas, for the rest of us there's virtually no time for diplomacy, these days: we spend the whole time trying to understand the stream of circulars telling us to do everything differently, and filling in questionnaires containing questions that don't quite apply to actual diplomats overseas. I can't wait to get it off my chest."

"Great!" exclaimed Larry. "Can I print all that?"

"Certainly not," Adam said hastily. "All that was purely background, not for use, unattributably or otherwise."

"'Off the record,' then," Larry said.

"No, we never use that formula," Adam explained. "It's either For Use and Attributable, meaning you can give the name of your source and publish whatever he says, or Unattributable, meaning you can use it but not name the source—you just say 'a reliable source close to the high commissioner' or something like that (everyone will know what you mean); or it's Not For Use, Background Only. 'Off the record' is too ambiguous. I rely on you to be sensible about what you quote me as having told you, even if I said it. If you don't, I'll make sure you never get access to anyone in this high commission ever again."

"Well, with respect, sir, you should have told me in advance when you wanted to change the terms of the interview," Larry said. "It's a bit late to tell me now that I can't use some of what you've said but I can use the rest. You'll just have to rely on my judgement of what you meant to be off the record and what you agreed I could use without restriction."

Adam was relieved when at this precise moment his wife Eve poked her head round the door of the study in the Residence where the interview was being conducted, to see if the man from the *Scotston Observer* was still there.

"Sorry to interrupt," Eve said. "I was just wondering when I could have my husband back, Mr—er—"

"My name's Larry," said Mr. Gardiner, getting up and extending his hand to shake Eve's.

"Well, Mr. Larry," said Eve, "I think it's time you were going, if you don't mind me saying so. I'm looking forward to reading the interview in your newspaper. I hope you got what you wanted."

"All that and more, thank you, Ma'am. I'll be off now, then. Thanks for the Scotch."

After Larry Gardiner had gone, Adam told Eve that he was kicking himself for his failure to observe rule number 1 in the interview handbook: make it clear at the start whether what you are going to say is for attributable, unrestricted use, or unattributable, or not for use at all, just background; and if in the course of the interview you want to change the ground rules, make that clear before you say anything that you don't want to see in print or hear on the radio.

"After all these years of cultivating the media wherever we have been serving, and after the one really useful training course that I ever attended—on how to handle the press—I go and blunder like that. It must be time I retired."

"Time we both retired," Eve agreed. "We've had a good inning, as your cricketing colleagues would say, but it's time we declared, and went back to the pavilion."

Adam nodded. "Enough of a good thing, I agree. But it *has* been a good thing, hasn't it?"

"Of course it has, darling," Eve said. "We've had the time of our lives. If we were starting all over again, I wouldn't do a single thing differently, even if I knew then what I know now. Let's go out and celebrate."

# INDEX

# ABOUT THE AUTHOR

**Sir Brian Barder**, KCMG, retired from the British Diplomatic Service after thirty years as a diplomat, including twelve years as an Ambassador (to Ethiopia, Poland, and Bénin) or High Commissioner (the title of an ambassador from one Commonwealth country to another, in his case to Nigeria and Australia). He had previously served in the UK Mission to the United Nations in New York for four years, dealing with decolonisation issues; in the British Embassy in Moscow as a political officer and press attaché; as head of the political section in the high commission in Canberra; and as Assistant Head of the West African Department and later as Head of the Southern African Department in the Foreign & Commonwealth Office in London. He also spent a year travelling the world as a course member of the Canadian National Defence College in Kingston, Ontario.

Brian Barder did his two years' National Service in the Army after leaving school (and was commanding a troop of tanks in Hong Kong when still aged seventeen). Armed with an honours degree in classics at Cambridge University, he joined the UK Home Civil Service and worked on decolonisation for the Colonial Office in London for seven years before (somewhat reluctantly) transferring to HM Diplomatic Service and (enthusiastically) going to the UN in New York. He was made a Knight Commander of the Order of St. Michael and St. George shortly before he retired from diplomacy at the then statutory retirement age of sixty.

Since then Sir Brian has served as a lay member (with judicial status) of the Special Immigration Appeals Commission, as a member of the Commonwealth Observer Mission at Namibia's first elections after independence, as a consultant in diplomatic training in east and central Europe for the UK's Knowhow Fund, as a member of the Committee for Speech and Debate of the English Speaking Union, as a Chair of the Civil and Diplomatic Services' Selection Boards, and as a member of the Board of Governors of the Royal Hospital for Neuro-disability in London. He is an honorary visiting fellow in the Department of Politics and International Relations at the University of Leicester.

CPSIA information can be obtained at www.ICGtesting.com
Printed in the USA
BVOW07*1702150714

359015BV00003B/3/P